EVERYTHING
BUT THE BURDEN

WHAT WHITE PEOPLE ARE

TAKING FROM BLACK CULTURE

Edited by
GREG TATE

HARLEM MOON
BROADWAY BOOKS
NEW YORK

A hardcover edition of this book was published in 2003 by Broadway Books. Published by Harlem Moon, an imprint of Broadway Books, a division of Random House, Inc.

PRINTED IN THE UNITED STATES OF AMERICA

HARLEM MOON, BROADWAY BOOKS, and the HARLEM MOON logo, depicting a moon and a woman, are trademarks of Random House, Inc. The figure in the Harlem Moon logo is inspired by a graphic design by Aaron Douglas (1899–1979).

Visit our website at www.harlemmoon.com

First trade paperback edition published 2003

Book design by Richard Oriolo

Permissions acknowledgments appear on p. 263.

The Library of Congress has cataloged the Broadway Books hardcover edition as follows:

Everything but the burden: what white people are taking from black culture / edited by Greg Tate.—1st ed.
p. cm.
Includes bibliographical references.
1. United States—Race relations. 2. African Americans—Social conditions—1975– 3. African Americans—Intellectual life. 4. Whites—United States—Attitudes. 5. Culture conflict—United States. 6. Racism—United States. 7. United States—Civilization—African American influences.
I. Tate, Greg.

E185.615 .E86 2003
305.896'073—dc21
2002026115

ISBN 0-7679-1497-X

10 9 8 7 6 5 4 3 2

In Dedication

Michael Richards

Joe Wood Jr.

Lester Bowie

Phillip Brown

Whose gifts and graces always made the burden
seem a blessing in disguise.

CONTENTS

Nigs R Us, or How Blackfolk Became Fetish Objects

BY GREG TATE

"*Ex Africa semper aliquid novi.*" (*Out of Africa, always something new.*) —PLINY THE ELDER

"*. . . in memory they are equal to white; in reason much inferior, as I think one could scarcely be found capable of tracing and comprehending the investigations of Euclid; and that in imagination they are dull, tasteless, anomalous . . . never yet could I find a black had uttered a thought above the level of plain abstraction.*" —THOMAS JEFFERSON, 1803

"*Have you forgotten that once we were brought here we were robbed of our name, robbed of our language. We lost our religion, our culture, our God. And many of us, by the way we act, even lost our minds.*" —MINISTER LOUIS FARRAKHAN

"*The history of the world, my sweet, is who gets eaten and who gets to eat.*" —STEPHEN SONDHEIM, *SWEENEY TODD*

"*After a dignified WASP medievalist from an Ivy League university confided in an airport bar that her eminent husband spoke 'black talk' to their dog, I began to expect white people to respond to a description of my project with some kind of confession about the prominence of racial parodies in their own lives. An Irish-Catholic college administrator exhibited his perfect Stepin Fetchit shuffle; an Italian physician whispered his secret black nickname, intoning it à la Kingfish; a Jewish friend from college expressed her delight that her complexion and kinky hair led Parisians to fete her (since her looks had only incited wary glances in the segregated neighborhood of her native Bronx) . . . After months spent writing about the centrality of cross-racial mimicry in twentieth-century culture, I found myself less shocked, more bemused, at a wedding reception when an ersatz 'Zulu Warrior Chant' presumably taught to the paterfamilias of a Southern family by General Patton during the Second World War, was performed, accompanied by rhythmic hand-clapping and foot-stomping, by all his sons, son-in-law, and grandsons."*—SUSAN GUBAR, RACE CHANGES: WHITE SKIN, BLACK FACE IN AMERICAN CULTURE

"It's not good to stay in a white man's country too long."
—MUTABARUKA

THE TITLE OF THIS BOOK IS a Florence Tate original. Mom once wrote a poem of the same name to decry the long-standing, ongoing, and unarrested theft of African-American cultural properties by thieving, flavorless whitefolk. A jeremiad against the ways Our music, Our fashion, Our hairstyles, Our dances, Our anatomical traits, Our bodies, Our Soul continue to be considered ever ripe for the plucking and the biting by the same crafty devils who brought you the African slave trade and the Middle Passage.

What has always struck Black observers of this phenomenon isn't just the irony of white America fiending for Blackness when it once debated whether Africans even had souls. It's also the way They have always tried to erase the

Black presence from whatever Black thing They took a shine to: jazz, blues, rock and roll, doo-wop, swingdancing, cornrowing, antidisimanation politics, attacking Dead Men, you name it.

Readers of Black music history are often struck by the egregious turns of public relations puffery that saw Paul Whiteman crowned the King of Swing in the 1920s, Benny Goodman anointed the King of Jazz in the 1930s, Elvis Presley propped up as the King of Rock and Roll in the 1950s, and Eric Clapton awarded the title of the world's greatest guitar player (ostensibly of the blues) in the 1960s. Whatever Count Basie, Duke Ellington, Chuck Berry, B. B. King, and other African-American pioneers thought about these coronations, they seem to have wisely kept between pursed lips—at least until Little Richard declared himself "the architect of rock and roll" rather than announce the winner at a late-eighties Grammy Awards ceremony. The same market forces that provided Caucasian imitators maximum access to American audiences through the most lucrative radio, concert, and recording contracts of the day also fed out whatever crumbs Black artists could hope for in the segregated American entertainment business.

For much of the last century the burden of being Black in America was the burden of a systemic denial of human and constitutional rights and equal economic opportunity. It was also a century in which much of what America sold to the world as uniquely American in character—music, dance, fashion, humor, spirituality, grassroots politics, slang, literature, and sports—was uniquely African-American in origin, conception, and inspiration. Only rarely could this imitation be enjoyed by African Americans as the sincerest form of flattery or as more than a Pyrrhic victory over racist devaluations of Black humanity. Yet today, counter to Thomas Jefferson's widely known notions of Black cognitive inferiority, the grandsons and daughters of antebellum America's slave commodities have become the masters of the nation's creative profile.

Legal and economic inequality between the races, though diminished to varying degrees by the advances of the civil rights and black power movements, still defines the quality of alienation which afflicts Black/white relations. The history of racism is more alive than dead for many African Americans—much of our public policy around crime, public housing, health care, and education continues to reflect a belief in second-class status for African Americans born in slavery.

The African-American presence in this country has produced a fearsome, seductive, and circumspect body of myths about Black intellectual capacity, athletic ability, sexual appetite, work ethic, family values, and propensity for violence and drug addiction. From these myths have evolved much of the paranoia, pathology, absurdity, awkwardness, alienation, and anomie which continue to define the American racial scene.

This book is an interrogation of those myths and the ways they have become intertwined with the popular culture of the country, and the world, since before the First World War. This is admittedly a peculiar book about a peculiar fascination: our peculiarly American notions of racial difference and the forms of pleasure, sometimes sadomasochistic in nature, that have sprung from the national id because of them. It features a peculiarly African-American twist on Marx's and Engels's observations about capitalism's commodity-fetish effect—the transformation of a marketable object into a magical thing of desire. It is my belief that capitalism's original commodity fetish was the Africans auctioned here as slaves, whose reduction from subjects to abstracted objects has made them seem larger than life and less than human at the same time. It is for this reason that the Black body, and subsequently Black culture, has become a hungered-after taboo item and a nightmarish bugbear in the badlands of the American racial imagination. Something to be possessed and something to be erased—an operation that explains not only the ceaseless parade of troublesome Black stereotypes still proffered and preferred by Hollywood (toms, coons, mammies, mulattoes, and bucks, in Donald Bogle's coinage), but the American music industry's never-ending quest for a white artist who can competently perform a Black musical impersonation: Paul Whiteman, Elvis Presley, the Rolling Stones, Sting, Britney Spears, 'N Sync, Pink, Eminem—all of those contrived and promoted to do away with bodily reminders of the Black origins of American pop pleasure.

It is with this history in mind that African-American performance artist

Roger Guenveur Smith once posed the question: Why does everyone love Black music but nobody loves Black people? Readers will find that politics (the power to address who gets eaten and who gets to eat) matters in this book's discussion of the Black American Burden, but so does Eminem. This latest pure product of white and crazy America, here to claim his fifteen minutes of MTV-generated fame as a Black male impersonator, and who has his gangsta-rap records routinely played by rock stations that consider Black rappers anathema.

This book, then, is about Black resentment and discontent to no small extent, but be reminded that Black irony and contrariness are never far away. Because while *Everything but the Burden* is largely devoted to scrutinizing the need by white Americans to acquire Blackness by any means necessary, it is also about the fascination that desire has provoked in a contemporary generation of African-American artists and intellectuals who hold complicated ideas about "Whose Black culture is it anyway?"

There is a panopticon effect being generated here. Just imagine a nest of Black scribes secretly, sometimes surgically, observing white people parading around as imitation Negroes. Now imagine those same scribes measuring the distance between the simplicity of white mimesis and the complexity of Black expression, and wondering where they fit into the equation. And the joke.

In this sense, *Everything but the Burden* is also about what white people can't see when they see Black—the sight of a Black imagination "playing in the dark," to use Toni Morrison's apt description, making hay out of what happens in the wily and wounded African-American psyche when it goes messing about, marketing, and sometimes making sense of race in these United States and abroad.

Given that most of these writers are, like the editor, civil rights– and black power–era babies, our take on the Burden differs from that of my very hip septuagenarian Southern-born mother. Our take on white appropriation has been colored, when not softened, by the socioeconomic gains, opportunities, and legal protections the struggles of earlier generations have provided for Black thinkers and cultural entrepreneurs today. Note that those two categories, thinker and huckster, are no longer, if they ever were, separate.

. . .

Nelson George once correctly identified the African-American equivalent of postmodernism as post-Soul culture. Soul music, widely understood as the classic sound Black gospel vocalists like Sam Cooke made as they turned away from praising Jesus and toward the more lucrative romantic pop market, subsequently produced a secular faith of sorts—one built around the verities of working-class African-American life. Soul culture succinctly describes the folkways African Americans concocted in the desegregating America of the fifties and sixties as the civil rights movement was on the ascendancy. Post-Soul is how George describes the African-American culture that emerged out of the novel social, economic, and political circumstances the sixties Black movements produced in their wake. Post-Soul would include the plays of Ntozake Shange, the novels of Gayl Jones, the films of Spike Lee, the music of Fishbone, Tracy Chapman, and Living Colour, the presidential campaigns of Jesse Jackson, the songs and the cosmetic surgery of Michael Jackson, the art of Jean-Michel Basquiat, and of course that postmodern expression par excellence, hip-hop. All this work managed the feat of being successful in the American mainstream in a language that was as easily referenced to white cultural models as to Africans-American ones. Its signature was not its smooth Blackness but its self-conscious hybridity of Black and white cultural signifiers. Hence, Basquiat referenced Rauschenberg and Dubuffet before Bearden, as the members of Living Colour and Fishbone found Led Zeppelin and the Sex Pistols as praiseworthy as James Brown and George Clinton. By the same token, all of these artists left an African-American critique of racism visible in the foreground—a recognition that Black discontent was as alive as white supremacy in the land of the hybridizing freakyfree.

Yet with post-Soul's new forms came new psychological relationships to older (and arguably, perhaps, even outdated) takes on such platitudinous topics as Black oppression, Black propriety, Black identity, Black community, Black family, Black femininity and feminism, and, most of all, Black marketability. For the first time in history, mainstream success became a defining factor in the cultural value of an African-American arts movement—primarily because it would be through the country's major channels of mass communication and mass marketing that debates about these figures moved from margin to center, from the hood to the floors of Congress.

The seventies, eighties, and nineties saw lively and sometimes bitter debate arising in Black America over whose idea of African-American culture would prevail in the public imagination. The Black feminist writers who emerged in the seventies—Alice Walker, Toni Morrison, Ntozake Shange, and Michelle Wallace—may be said to have kicked off the aspect of post-Soul that critiqued Black cultural nationalism, and particularly the patriarchal strain of the same. Camps and divisions within Black culture became more pronounced and hysterical as time went on: old-guard Afrocentrists versus freakydeke bohemians and newly minted Ivy League buppies, all of the above thrown in relief by those gauche ghettocentrics who would come to be known as the hip-hop nation.

The omnipresence and omnipotence of hip-hop, artistically, economically, and socially, have forced all within Black America and beyond to find a rapprochement with at least some aspect of its essence. Within hip-hop, however, as in American entrepreneurship generally, competing ideologies exist to be exploited rather than expunged and expelled—if only because hip-hop culture and the hip-hop marketplace, like a quantum paradox, provide space to all Black ideologies, from the most antiwhite to the most pro-capitalist, without ever having to account for the contradiction. The aura and global appeal of hip-hop lie in both its perceived Blackness (hip, stylish, youthful, alienated, rebellious, sensual) and its perceived fast access to global markets through digital technology. The way hip-hop collapsed art, commerce, and interactive technology into one mutant animal from its inception seems to have almost predicted the forms culture would have to take to prosper in the digital age.

By now the basic history of hip-hop will read as holy writ or apocryphal horror story, depending on where you're standing. From the predominantly African-American and Puerto Rican South Bronx (and Jamaican DJ Kool Herc's sound system), it came in the mid/late 1970s, a cultural revolution whose first shots were hardly intended to raze Babylon. Reflecting the age-old desire of underprivileged teenagers everywhere to invent their own entertainment, hip-hop expressed the zeitgeist of your average South Bronx youth of the day in music, dance, fashion, and visual art. That the music was made by turntables, the dance made by whirling the top of the head on the floor like a helicopter, and the visuals murals painted sometimes overnight on ten New York subway cars from "top to bottom," are what caught the rest of the planet's attention.

Twenty-five years on, this thing we call hip-hop is not only a billion-dollar subset of the music industry but one whose taste-making influence makes billions more for every other lifestyle-and-entertainment business under the sun: from soft drinks, liquor, leisure wear, haute couture, automobiles, to sports events, electronics, shoes, cigars, jewelry, homes. With this affluence and newly minted mass cultural clout have come debates that have divided the U.S. Senate, incited police organizations and political opportunists of every ideological stripe, cleaved generations, genders, and classes among every ethnicity in America.

One of the more peculiar outgrowths of hip-hop's popularity has been the birth of the "wigga"—the so-called white nigga who apes Blackness by "acting hip-hop" in dress, speech, body language, and, in some cases, even gang affiliation. Some in the African-American community see the appearance of the wigga mutant as a comical form of flattery, others as an up-to-date form of minstrelsy.

Minstrelsy, or "Blacking up"—the application of burnt cork grease to a white or Black performer's face—became a staple of American entertainment in the nineteenth century, when our homegrown vaudeville circuit turned this crude and mocking form of maskery into a means of making a living wage. Though the cork-grease appliqué has faded away, the sight of white performers attempting to replicate Black features still generates among African-American spectators a host of responses—from joy to horror to sarcasm to indifference. There seem, for example, to be as many African Americans of the hip-hop persuasion who embrace Eminem as reject him. For some a white rapper will always be an oxymoron; others, like retired basketball star Charles

Barkley, find great humor in the irony of living in a time when the best rapper (his words, not mine) is white and the best golfer is Black.

What has changed since the days of Elvis is the degree to which Black American hip-hop producers function as arbiters of who is and who is not a legitimate white purveyor of hip-hop. In part, this is because hip-hop remains as much defined by the representation of Black machismo as by Black aesthetics. The impact of African-American music and musical culture on white British and American notions of masculinity and style plays no small role in accounting for the largely white male and Japanese fandoms of jazz, blues, rock and roll, soul, funk, reggae, and now hip-hop. Once the music of marginalized minorities, they have become the theme musics of a young, white, middle-class male majority—due largely to that demographic's investment in the tragic-magical displays of virility exhibited by America's ultimate outsider, the Black male. This attraction became inevitable once popular notions of American manhood began to be defined less by the heroic individualism of a John Wayne and more by the ineffable hipness, coolness, antiheroic, antiauthoritarian stances of bona fide–genius Black musicians like Coleman Hawkins, Lester Young, Charlie Parker, Miles Davis, Charles Mingus, and Thelonious Monk—African-American rebel icons whose existential glare at white-bread America now seems to be what Marlon Brando, Paul Newman, Montgomery Clift, James Dean, Frank Sinatra, and Steve McQueen were trying to project in their influential film portrayals of American male discontent.

There is equally a case to be made for the deep impact of African sculpture and dance and jazz on what we call European modernism in art. For some, merely bearing witness to these forms of Black expressivity, or even learning to replicate them, would not adequately satisfy their desire to become intimate with Africa. The desire to vicariously rebel against European culture from within an imaginary Black body took on a philosophical dimension in this century as the conceit inspired the cosmopolitan inventors of Cubism and Dadaism to defy European conventions in the name of going native. To no small degree the African-American emphasis on improvisation, performance, and cast-off materials could be said to have influenced much of what has occurred in American poetry and fine arts since the Second World War. More on these subjects than I'm allowing for here is touched on in the *Burden* by Carl Hancock-Rux and Arthur Jafa in their scintillating deconstructions of modernism's hidden Black faces. (Interestingly, both writers, our opening and closing acts, as it were, also intimate that divestment in the performance of "Blackness" is where true Black liberation must begin.)

Though the much-maligned "wigga" figure mimics the surface forms of African-American culture (i.e., the songs, the speech, the dress codes, and the bad attitude of hip-hop), his more sophisticated brethren have spent most of the last century trying to translate their Black/white baggage into remedies for Western culture's spiritual malaise. In popular music since the sixties, complicated characters like Bob Dylan, Frank Zappa, Joni Mitchell, Steely Dan, Johnny Rotten, (and now Eminem) complicated the question of how race mythology can be creatively exploited. They have also made us understand how influence and appropriation can cut both ways across the racial divide. These are white artists who found ways to express the complexity of American whiteness inside Black musical forms. In turn, these artists came to appeal to many among the post-Soul-generation African Americans who have no problem, as their forebears Lester Young, Miles Davis, and Charlie Parker didn't, in claiming a white artistic ancestor. It is for this reason that Vernon Reid and I decided a dissection of Steely Dan's nappy roots was required for the *Burden*.

African-American admirers of white artists have historically transcended the picayune boundaries that define the world's race-obsessed ideas about skin and cultural identity, drawing freely from the world's storehouse of artists for models. Ellington loved Debussy and Stravinsky, Jimi Hendrix had a special thing for Bach, Bob Dylan, and Handel. Jean-Michel Basquiat held special fondness for Dubuffet, Twombly, Rauschenberg, Warhol, and *Gray's Anatomy*. Charlie Parker embraced country-and-western music, much to some of his idolaters' chagrin. Ralph Ellison credited T. S. Eliot with inspiring him to study the craft of writing as assiduously as he already had that of European concert music. Toni Morrison speaks of García Márquez, Fuentes, and Cortázar as if they were blood relations, and so on. There should be no revelation in this, but the sad truth about the dehumanization of Black people is that it can strap blinders on us all regarding the complexity of human desire within the divided racial camps. When reading Beth Coleman's marvelous exposé of pimp culture as a demoralized attempt to re-create the master-slave dynamic, we are reminded of how distorted one's self-image can become in a morally deformed culture.

During the high period of Black cultural nationalism, when Amiri Baraka was out to purge himself of all his past associations with white people and white art movements, a certain anxiety over influence, plus anti-intellectualism and countersupremacy, surged up in ways that made white influences nearly taboo. Those days are long behind us, but one effect of that movement has been the emergence of a separate-but-equal America where even middle-class Black people make literature, music, film, television, and theater for other Blacks' consumption and rarely socialize outside of a work context with their white counterparts. The increased opportunities for Black ownership and profiting from Black entertainment have largely made moot the once vociferous arguments against white profiting from Black culture. The doors to Black entrepreneurship within corporate America have been swung wide open.

To the degree that the sixties movements changed anything about race in America, they began to sweep away the denial of economic opportunity that had kept African-American entrepreneurs off the playing fields where the big bucks were being made from Black talent. The advent in hip-hop of multi-millionaire Black moguls like Russell Simmons, Andre Harrell, and Sean "P. Diddy" Combs has largely made the question of white co-optation of Black culture more a joke among younger African Americans than a gibe. They've seen hip-hop topple "white rock" as the most influential and lucrative form of pop music among middle-class youth in America. They've watched with amusement and admiration as Black star-grooming firms concoct the hip-hop Soul-flavored songs and dance moves of 'N Sync and the Backstreet Boys. Savored the victory in every other nu-metal band on MTV throwing up a rapping singer and a lead guitarist who's ceded his once-exalted sex-symbol position to the band's resident "turntableist."

If hip-hop had done nothing but put more money in the hands of Black artists and business managers than ever before, it would mark a milestone in American cultural history. What that wealth has not been able to transform, however, is the social reality of substandard housing, medical care, and education that afflicts over half of all African-American children and accounts for as many as one out of three (and in my hometown of Washington, D.C., our nation's capital, one out of two) African-American males being under the control of the criminal justice system. (Projections by African-American genocide theorist Jawanza Kunjufu indicate that the numbers may swell to two out of three by the year 2020.) Nor have the gains made in the corporate suite fully dismantled the prevalent, delimiting mythologies about Black intelligence, morality, and hierarchical place in America.

The instruction given to all the *Burden*'s writers was to tackle the all-American fascination with Blackness in the realms of music, literature, sports, fashion and beauty, comedy, political activism, modern art, science-fiction cinema, hero worship, machismo. Some approached the assignment through an iconic figure whose life and work seemed to embody the history of shame, blame, idolatry, denial, stalwart bravery, tomfoolishness, and misapprehension that marks the subject. It is a history that mocks us all as we attempt to reduce the world's possibilities to its racial inequities.

Warning: A specific emphasis has been placed on key figures and movements whose lives and work have inadvertently made race in America a subject as demanding of complex reasoning and ethical inquiry as genetically modified organisms. In "The New White Negro," Carl Hancock Rux takes on the Eminem phenomenon, hitting it right between the eyes and finding a self-made cipher wrapped in a hard nigga dreamcoat. In Melvin Gibbs's "Thug-Gods: Spiritual Darkness and Hip-Hop," the long history of criminalizing and mythifying Black culture is detailed from ancient India to the Wu-Tang Clan, finally resting on a powerful reading of white American Taliban follower John

Walker Lindh. Gibbs sympathetically reflects on Lindh's search for a way out of America's spiritual darkness through the dark spirituality of hip-hop and fundamentalist Islam.

Robin Kelley presents the bizarre world of white activists who seek to overcome the race problem by browbeating African-American militants about their fixation on race, and Black radicals who struggle to get white-run lefty organizations to understand that the race problem deserves more than a footnote in the war on capitalism. In my dialogue with Vernon Reid, we present the ways Steely Dan ran away with Black cool and disguised it in their own critique of the American dream. In Beth Coleman's "Pimp Notes on Autonomy," we are made to see the pimp figure as an appropriator of the master-slave dynamic that has programmed the psyches of Black and white American men for centuries. Novelist Jonathan Lethem provides a clue as to how a guilty liberal who's been mugged can find his muse riled to action by the event rather than by his kneejerk conservatism.

With Michael C. Ladd's poem "The New Mythology Began Without Me," we get the buying and selling of the Black American dream rendered as a cultural nightmare. The two scenes from Eisa Davis's play Umkovu use dark wit to make light of a white businessman and a Japanese deejay who live to reduce Black culture to its most marketable clichés. From Hilton Als comes a study of the career of Richard Pryor, who more than any other American performer of the past century exemplified the promise and the compromises expected of angry Black performers who long for white love and mainstream success. Further expanding our vista of Black America's impact on the world, we offer Manthia Diawara's account of how James Brown fomented a social and stylistic rebellion among young people in sixties and seventies Mali. Meri Danquah details how hair-straightening and skin-bleaching, à la Michael Jackson, has run amok in Ghana.

In Latasha Natasha Diggs's "The Black Asianphile in Me," we are given a near-parodic view of the fetishism that fetishism begat: Her exotification of Asian penises and fighting techniques offers an inverted Afrocentric image of white appropriation at its worst. In Tony Green's personal writing on larger-than-life subjects Muhammad Ali, Norman Mailer, and George Foreman, one is allowed to see how ineptly the Black Superman model favored by Black mythifiers like Mailer fit on an average Joe like Green's younger athletic self. Professional fashion and beauty stylist Michaela Angela Davis delves even deeper under the skin to point up how the country's obsession with Hollywood and Condé Nast's prescriptions of beauty has wounded young Black women unaware that their style innovations feed the beauty industry that denies them affirmation. Cassandra Lane's "Skinned" opens up more than skin-deep woundedness, depicting the whyfores of her anxieties about imaginary white women showing up as sexual threats in her marriage bed.

The essays of Danzy Senna, Renée Green, and Arthur Jafa form an Afro-futurist troika: Senna looks back on ghettocentricity from 2037 in her parody of Harvard-trained literary anthropology, Green delves into space, race, and injustice as they have been conjoined in Hollywood potboilers and the work of Octavia Butler, while Jafa provides a reading of Stanley Kubrick's *2001* that would startle even Sun Ra. Jafa also takes on Picasso, Duchamp, Pollock, and Kubrick, whose visual critiques of whiteness through Africanist myths he sees as having led them to formal breakthroughs and conceptual cul-de-sacs.

Taken in total, these essays present the myriad ways African Americans grapple with feelings of political inferiority, creative superiority, and ironic distance in a market-driven world where we continue to find ourselves being sold as hunted outsiders and privileged insiders in the same breath. In a world where we're seen as both the most loathed and the most alluring of creatures, we remain the most co-optable and erasable of cultures too. It is the singular, historic power of this chilling, maddening, schizophrenia-inducing paradox that it has always called some of the country's more exceptional, daring, and fecund literary minds to order—Twain, Douglass, Melville, Crane, Faulkner, Du Bois, Robeson, Hughes, Hurston, Baldwin, Morrison, West all come to mind. It is the deepest wish of this editor that the *Burden* honors and serves this quintessentially American theme as well as its predecessors have—complicating and elevating our "Cipher" in the process.

1. Eminem: The New White Negro

BY CARL HANCOCK RUX

*"From the Negro we take only the magical-liturgical
bits, and only the antithesis makes them
interesting to us."*
—HUGO BALL

*"There is a zone of non-being,
An extraordinary sterile and arid region,
An utterly naked declivity
Where an authentic upheaval can be born.
In most cases the Black man lacks the advantage
Of being able to accomplish this descent
Into a real hell."*
—FRANTZ FANON, FROM "BLACK SKIN, WHITE MASKS"

1. REVENGE OF PENTHEUS

Pentheus, the protagonist of Euripides' *The Bacchae*, was a young moralist and anarchical warrior who sought to abolish the worship of Dionysus (god of tradition, or perhaps better said, god of the re-cyclical, who causes the loss of individual identity in the uncontrollable, chaotic eruption of ritualistic possession). When Pentheus sets out to infiltrate the world of the Bacchae and explore the mysteries of savage lore, his intention is to save the possessed women of Thebes (from themselves), who engage in hedonistic practices somewhere high in the mountains. Dionysus derails the young warrior's lofty mission by titillating his sexual curiosity (inviting him to take a quick glimpse of the drunken women as they revel in their lesbian orgy). In order to witness firsthand the necromancy of the inhumane, Pentheus must disguise himself as *one of* the inhumane. Ultimately the young moralist's disguise mirrors the appearance of Dionysus, the very god he seeks to subjugate. The transformed soldier, now possessed by the spirit of his nemesis, is set on the highest branch of a fir tree, elevated above all and visible to none—or so he is led to believe. Pentheus' disguise is as transparent as his voyeuristic fetish, and it is because of this very visible elevated space he inhabits that he is brutally dismembered by the gang of possessed women on the mountain (led by his own mother), who see him for what he is.

Historically, academics have neatly interpreted the characters of *The Bacchae* as belonging to themes of good versus evil, rational versus reason, nobility versus paganism. In the casual study of classical realism, Pentheus is noble in his efforts to eradicate paganism, and Dionysus is an all-powerful demonic and *immoral* force. But in a more careful study (or at least, an alternate one), we may learn that Dionysus is a traditional Olympian god, neither good nor bad. His powers are *amoral;* they are powers informed only by the powers that control human existence. Real life—death, sex, grief, joy, etc.—in its entire splendor. Dionysus and his worshipers cannot be controlled or converted. Their humanity *has been perceived as* inhumane, and in defense of their right to preserve an identity and a culture for themselves, an extreme cruelty befitting of inhumanity is enacted. The mother's murder of her son is a necessary *evil;* we accept the death of Pentheus as the inevitable defeat of his judgmental and moral idealism, but because this act of brutality is performed by the mother of its victim, we also question the value of human existence above the existence of humanity (couldn't she have just given him a slap on the hand and a good talking-to and said, "Baby, some people live differently than others, but ain't nobody better than the rest . . ."?). Perhaps the moral of the story is: The identity of the individual is most often sacrificed for the identity of the collective, so we must now all live and speak in broad familiar terms and forsake our sons and daughters for the ultimate good of humanity as we see it. The evolution of human existence is propelled by a constant narcissism; a struggle to negotiate one's perception of self and one's perception of the other, and some of the most (historically) flawed (though pervasive) acts of negotiating a collective identity are politicized oppression and cultural mimicry of the other—both of which seek agreement. Inevitably, collective agreement regarding identity produces a common design for humanity, or a morality relative to the perceptions of a particular group. Hierarchical notions of humanity are formed, and, eventually, once the tracks are laid, people will have to pitch their tents on either side. Conflict. War. Somebody (or bodies) in opposition to the populace will have to be dismembered so that new orders of identity can be formed.

Fast-forward a few thousand years to a more contemporary but parallel heroic-antiheroic protagonist—Eminem, the platinum-domed, Caesar-haircut, pop-prince bad-boy superstar of late-twentieth/early-twenty-first-century postmodern hip-hop culture. Like Pentheus, Eminem may also be seen as a rebellious and beardless icon with disdain for the majority, and like Pentheus, he dresses himself in the garments of the outcasts, has learned their language, their songs and rituals. But unlike Pentheus, Eminem is no moralist martyr with a secret desire to objectify. The real Slim Shady does not make the mistake of re-creating the Theban soldier's vain attempt to destroy the god of mass appeal. He accepts the unholy ghost as his personal savior, and with a slight flip of the Greek tragedy script (with hip-hop flare), introduces to us his first sacrifice—his own mother, whom he publicly debases and strips of all garments of integrity, drags nude into the spotlight, and ritualistically murders hit single after hit single. Though savagery is expected to call for misogyny of magnanimous proportions, Eminem's humiliation of the maternal figure is not just limited to his *own* mother, but extends itself to she who is also the mother of his own child (or in ghetto fabulous vernacular, his *baby mama*). In one of his first award-winning acts of hit-single hedonism, the real Slim Shady murders his baby mama right in front of his baby (for our entertainment pleasure)—and later, in his sophomore phase, morphs into a fan of himself who is inspired to do the same. A continuum, thereby raising the inhumane status of outcast culture to new bacchanalian heights.

The postmodern pop-culture icon of the outlaw is complete and to be carried into the new millennium; Eminem does not *seek* to know pagan lore—he was *born* into it, has always spoken the language of it, has always danced to the music of it, has always dressed himself in the latest pagan wear, has never used this language, this music, or this apparel to *disguise* his true identity or to disguise his race, and he has never tried to dissociate himself from the source of his performance, the black male outlaw or outcast of hip-hop fame. Rappers Big Boi and Dre may go by the moniker Outkast, but Eminem proves that a *real* outcast has got to do more than make *Miss Jackson's* daughter cry—you got to fuck the bitch, kill the bitch, dump the bitch's dead body in the river, and not apologize for any of it.

Eminem's politically incorrect vaudeville routine (an oxymoron) is not to be attempted by everyone. Even his protégés, D-12, failed miserably as horror rappers on their debut album *Devil's Night* (if poor record sales and bad reviews are any indication). With boasts of slapping around handicapped women, gorging pills, and sodomizing their grandmothers, the effect is less tongue-in-cheek than tongue-in-toilet. And, when old-school mack daddy of hip-hop cool, Slick Rick, made a cameo appearance on the recently released Morcheeba album, *Charango*, derivatively flowing à la Eminem style ("Women Lose Weight") about murdering his overweight wife in order to hook up with his sexy blond secretary, MTV did not come-a-calling. The result is derivative at best. Incidentally, not long after the Morcheeba album release, Slick Rick found himself arrested by the INS and awaiting deportation from this country (because somebody *just* found out that he has been an illegal resident for over thirty years). Not to suggest that his penal consequences are the direct result of imitating Eminem, but so far, only Eminem gets away with *being* Eminem, perhaps because he uses his visors and disguises to disguise his split personality as undisguised—raising the questions, who is the real outcast, who is the real Slim Shady, what has he inherited from culture to achieve his bad-boy, outcast minstrel, rebel superstar status, and *exactly* what identity crisis is being performed?

2. FANON HAD A (SEMANTIC) DREAM

Frantz Fanon tells us that the oppressed must identify an oppressive archetype in order to overcome historical oppression. But before the oppressed can achieve acts of true upheaval, they must first realize that they have yet to achieve "non-being" status. The oppressed may have attempted prior acts of resistance, but have never actually "descended into a real hell" that will scorch into the very nature of seeing an *effective* upheaval that brings the non-being into being. For now, the oppressed continue to live in the dream of identity, the dream that (in reality) the oppressed are, in fact, Negro, Colored, Black, Minority, Afro or African American, Hispanic, Oriental, Dykes, Queers, Bitches, Hos, Niggaz. All accepted as real identities. The acceptance of these identities further compels a performance of these identities, whether compliant or rebellious.

The oppressed identity performance relies upon a collective agreement informed by a historical narrative that either supports the validity of, or opposes the construct of, these identities. Before a revisionist identity can be forged, there was an inheritance and an acceptance of a construct—thus, even when the oppressed think they are revising their identities, updating the language of their identities, or endeavoring to better the circumstances of their identities, they are not—not completely and not actually—because no language in the American polyglot has ever been subscribed to by the collective that points to the very nature of human identity beyond elementary categorizations, and no accurate language regarding race-identity exists in our collective agreement. We are comfortable with vague concepts of identity, and the ghettos and empires these concepts create.

What the oppressed figure in America has been working with as an identity is actually an archetypal construct born out of a dream (as in aspirations and imaginings) belonging to an oppressive figure who is not only the architect of the dream that oppresses us, but is also the Dionysian-like landlord of our realities—both good and bad—neither real nor unreal, and completely exempt from being vanquished from our realities. We inhabit an oppressive dream, and until that descent into Fanon's "real hell," the oppressed will continue to pay a high price to rent substandard space in the dream that we call *race* in America.

3. EMINEM, THE OTHER WHITE MEAT

". . . If all the Niggers
Started calling eachother Nigger,
Not only among themselves . . . but among Ofays . . .
Nigger wouldn't mean anymore than 'Good night,'
'God bless you,' or 'I promise to tell the whole truth
And nothing but the whole truth so help me God' . . .
When that beautiful day comes,
You'll never see another Nigger kid
Come home from school crying
Because some Ofay motherfucker called him Nigger."
—LENNY BRUCE

Eminem, a.k.a. Marshall Mathers, was born in St. Joseph, Missouri (near Kansas City), spending the better part of his impoverished childhood in Detroit, Michigan—which, by the way, is about 90 percent *ethnic minority* and has one of the highest concentrations of African Americans in the nation, at 83 percent, while non-Latino whites comprise only 12 percent of the city's population. Detroit's recent dip below one million is largely attributed to continuing *white flight,* and 10 percent of the state's population has lived in poverty for more than twenty years (a family of three with an income of a little more than $9,300 earns too much to qualify for welfare in Michigan— but is about $4,000 below the federal poverty guideline), according to the American Community Survey released by the U.S. Census Bureau. Translation: Eminem may have been born *white* but he was socialized as *black,* in the proverbial hood—and the music of the proverbial hood in America for the last twenty-five years has been hip-hop music. The same inner-city struggles and impoverished circumstances that brought us blues, jazz, rhythm and blues, doo-wop and soul, brought us hip-hop music—it began as a form of identity-boosting vocal scatting over pulsating beats and progressed to become a means of expressing the social realities of African-American urbanity. By the time it became a major moneymaker in the music industry, the genre of hip-hop transformed into a bodacious representation of gangsta life and gangsta obsessions replete with murder, money, sex, alcohol and drug consumption—and, when this got tired, narrowed itself down and preoccupied itself with the glam of capital gain.

The legend of Eminem, a.k.a. Slim Shady, a.k.a. Marshall Mathers (and his psychotic nasal slapstick trips of alienation) begins with his Detroit exposure to rap, performing it at the age of fourteen and later earning notoriety as a member of the Motor City duo Soul Intent. The legend is that he dropped out of high school, worked minimum-wage jobs, practiced beat boxing and freestyling his lyrics on home recordings, and worshiped rap groups like NWA—he admits he "wanted to be Dr. Dre and Ice Cube," wore big sunglasses while "lip-syncking to their records in the mirror." He also honed his style in the company of five black Detroit MC's (D12). Together, the racially integrated posse decided that each of them would invent an alter ego, thus the six MC's were to be thought of as twelve MC's—dubbing themselves, the Dirty Dozen. When Eminem emerged as a solo artist in 1996 with the independent release *Infinite,* he was accused of trying to sound "too much like Nas," so he perfected a nasal white-boy, horror-rap cadence, following *Infinite* with *The Slim Shady LP*, which led the hip-hop underground to dub him hip-hop's "great white hope."

The legend of his discovery varies. Allegedly, Dr. Dre discovered Eminem's demo tape on the floor of Interscope label chief Jimmy Iovine's garage. Another story goes that Dre first heard Eminem on the radio and said, "Find that kid whoever he is! I'm gonna make him a star!" or something like that. Either way, not until Eminem took second place (who won first?) in the freestyle category at 1997's Rap Olympics MC Battle in Los Angeles did Dre agree to sign him, producing the bestselling triple-platinum *Slim Shady LP* in early 1999. With controversial yet undeniable talent (the right mix for stardom of any kind), Eminem became the white-boy cartoon god of surreal white-trash humor and graphic violence, a stratum of Roseanne Barr–meets–Quentin Tarrentino–meets–Mickey Mouse Club–cum Snoop Dogg and beatnik Dobie Gillis. *The Marshall Mathers LP* followed and sold close to two million copies in its first week of release, making it one of the fastest-selling rap albums of all time, and his latest album, *The Eminem Show*, was the first album since 'N Sync's *Celebrity* and the September 11 terrorist attacks to sell over one million copies in its debut week. To top it all off, Eminem's roman à clef feature film debut, *8 Mile,* is described as a story about "the boundaries that define our lives and a young man's struggle to find the strength and courage to transcend them." In his great struggle to transcend boundaries, the surrealist rap icon has also managed two weapons charges, an assault charge, a lawsuit from his mother for humiliating her in his lyrics, and his baby mama's attempted suicide—all to keep it real, as they say.

But Eminem does not offer us the real, he offers the *surreal*—several alter egos further immersing our bacchanalian notions of race-inclusive hip-hop lore. We all want to be Bacchus or Dionysus. Especially black people, especially Niggaz, who have invented the alter ego of a New Savage God— a gun-toting nationalist radical with supreme sexual prowess and unsurpassable talent to counter Bill Cosby's 1980s middle-class Negrodum. We, who are members of the so-called ethnic minority and belong to a hip-hop generation, have inherited an imposition and elaborated on it until it has become an opportunity, borrowing our new black character from a relevant history of slavery, reconstruction, ghetto realism, black civil rights, arts and radical movements, and mythic Blaxploitation heroes like Shaft and Foxy Brown. But lest we get high-minded about it all, the badass thug and gangsta bitch are not purely the inventions of inner-city urban imagination. They are also products of Hollywood's imaginary American heroes: second-generation immigrants turned Depression-era gangster moguls, as portrayed by Edward G. Robinson, James Cagney, Humphrey Bogart; John Wayne's cocky cowboy; Sean Connery's hyper-heterosexual sci-fi upper-class guy, "James Bond."

Hip-hop inventors have grown up with these archetypes on their television screens, and incorporated them into a contemporary gothic myth set in the housing projects they know America to be. In order for this merger of white and black icons to evolve, there had to be in place a basic understanding of race among a contemporary generation. The new power brokers of culture had to inherit an inherited concept of race and form vaguely similar ways of seeing the construct of race. If it appears that the history of race in America means less to the new generation of pop-music icons and their fans—socially, politically, and psychologically—than the performance of class and outlaw status, it is because a race-inclusive product for the American cultural marketplace demands short-term memory.

What has emerged from an old system of cultural supremacy and inferiority is a new superpower contingent upon our informed (and uninformed) race perception. The final incarnations of the black male figure in a century that began with sharecroppers and first-generation free peoples trying to avoid the hanging tree are their gun-toting, dick-slinging capitalist descendants. The black male outlaw identity is a commodifiable character open to all who would like to perform it. In order for the oppressed figure's dream of attaining ostentatious wealth and fame while defying conventional structures of morality to come into fruition, the dream *had to* be race-inclusive, race-accessible, and dangerous enough to pose an idealistic threat to a conservative society—translation: like jazz, white people had to like it, buy it, invest in it, and benefit from it, and above all, identify with it too. And the seduction had to appeal to a fascination with and fear of a complex figure they'd been taught to disdain. Not unlike Pentheus's objectifying curiosity, white culture watched the evolution of the hip-hop character from afar before the hip-hop character knew they were watching at all. Thus, hip-hop culture has evolved into another classic ready-to-wear American original, like rock 'n' roll—except this time, the black hip-hop artist participates in the profit and control of the industry (to some extent) more so than ever before. But it is still an outsider culture, perpetuating its own outsider mythology, and if there are non-black, economically privileged teenagers who wear their oversized jeans pulled down around their knees and sleep beneath posters of self-proclaimed rapists, gang members, and murderers with record deals, it is because every generation of youth culture since Socrates has identified with outsider/outcast/radicalism, and typically pursued some kind of participation in it. Because radicalism, whether political or not, is a multicultural and universal sentiment.

Some may contend that white artists who pioneer their way into so-called black music forms take the privilege of being allowed to do so seriously and pursue lofty goals of destroying race barriers, thereby bridging gaps of new race perception in America. But others may contend that race *inclusivity* (*sic*) diminishes the organic intention of race music (*sic*) until it simplifies into yet another popular entertainment form in the marketplace, where its inventor will compete for a right to exist (i.e., if Eric Clapton, Bonnie Raitt, or Lyle Lovett stopped playing the blues, what would it mean to B.B. King or Keb' Mo's pop chart eligibility?).

Race performance in America—however guilty we all are of it (and we *all* are guilty of it)—has suffered an uneven exchange. There are allowances made for some to a greater degree than others. From jazz to rock 'n' roll, white representation in black music forms is completely acceptable and rarely questioned (even if contemporary black representation in rock, alternative rock, or any kind of rock warrants front page *New York Times* explanations), but some have questioned whether or not white representation in black music ultimately diminishes the sentiment of black music, or distracts a critical audience from narrowly perceiving black music innovations *as* black music. Whom does music or race belong to? Whether or not race is to stake its claim in music, race performance prevails as much now as it did in the good ol' Al Jolson days. One can easily see a careful study in the color-line cross-over iconography of artists like Vanilla Ice, the first popular hip-hop "wigger" to top the charts, who cooked his character with the main ingredients of authentic angry black male aggression, by promising dope hits and throats slit (from *"Livin'"*), further validating himself with essential sociopolitical blues lamentations of existential thug life, screaming his hatred at society (from *A.D.D.*), and offering us some insight to the familial dysfunction of ghetto life that produced his incredulity, blaming an abusive father and excusing his mother from all responsibility for his compulsive and unexplainable brain-blasting (from *Scars*)

But Vanilla Ice's middle-class white-childhood reality emerged and ruined the authenticity of his performance—though his hip-hop icon still left an indelible mark on hip-hop culture. As with all great rock stars or rock-star hopefuls, it is the image of these icons and their proclamations of themselves that reach beyond them, creating a mass of followers who are inspired by their belief in the performance, not the person. In this way, those few artists fortunate enough to achieve superstar status become ancient, distant archetypes that appeal to our psychic dispositions, like Jesus or Gatsby—the icon we believe in helps us validate what we believe about ourselves and the world as we see it, whether it's real or not.

4. THE GOOD, THE BAD, AND THE NIGGA

"It's not right to start penalizing good people . . .
We need a humane monitoring system to
search out the good and bad."
—SLICK RICK, WHILE AWAITING DEPORTATION IN A FLORIDA
DETENTION FACILITY

Both Eminem and Vanilla Ice take their cues from a savage model, and it is this savage model that has informed everyone from the Surrealists to the

Bohemians. If there is an eternal plan, it is a primitive one with no bearing on virtue. Their performances are rooted in a supposed realism. Realism places God in heaven, makes distinct social classes where moral law distinguishes between good and evil—an orderly world with gradual changes: wars, revolutions, inventions, etc. One can belong to the outcasts of this world and still be a realist. It's all in the style of your performance. Style becomes the only authentic instrument of classic realism, and an important elemental style of hip-hop realism involves daily mortal danger. However, within one's own existence, one is influenced not only by the current circumstances of life but by the style of life where we are experiencing it. Style both replicates reality and takes us away from our reality. Style also heightens and produces a counterbalance to the realism of life (i.e., your hip-hop icon du jour may live with a sense of daily mortal danger—like you do—but unlike you, he drives a Mercedes jeep, wears diamonds and furs, and maintains a harem of scantily clad women with bodies endowed according to his fickle fetish fantasies).

Those of us who choose to deny that we now live in a society psychically impacted by hip-hop realism may still embrace the changing styles of hip-hop realism because it removes us from our actual reality (as all good forms of entertainment should). If the edict of early hip-hop lore shifted its weight from the innocence of Sugarhill Gang's party babble to Public Enemy's urban radicalism and political consciousness, it seemed to be a call to arms—an insistence that the oppressed figure recognize something about his status-elevation potential. If hip-hop again shifted its weight from Suge Knight's heyday of East Coast/West Coast rivalry and gangbanging to Puffy's epoch of Versace gear, Cristal champagne, and Harry Winston diamond–encrusted platinum jewelry, it read as an attempt to break from the tradition that celebrated the kind of violence that produced the sudden and actual deaths of Biggie Smalls and Tupac Shakur—an attempt to make a gradual transference from ghetto realism toward escaping conventions of death. An oppressed capitalist's bargaining with life.

The antisymbolic nature of the savage archetype from which Eminem creates his character is different from Vanilla Ice's invention. Vanilla's performance was classic in nature—a form of modern realism where human truth was more important than the poetry of words. Eminem's eminence rarely attempts to address serious social or political ills, nor is it obsessed with hypercapitalism. Eminem does not attempt to perform the authentic Nigga as much as he performs a New White Nigga. He maintains his whiteness with quirky vocal Jerry Lewis–like phrasing and a bright Greek-god bleached-blond buzz cut; and the classic hip-hop realism he was initially influenced by when he first studied the style of Naughty by Nature and Nas has been replaced by his own brand of contemporary Surrealism that abstracts and exaggerates hip-hop lore more so than any of his authentic heroes or contemporaries dare try.

Eminem's lyrics speak to the wayward descendants of Fanon's Negroes: Niggaz. Niggaz hear him and Niggaz understand him; still, he comes as a representative of what Niggaz have produced in their dreams—someone who is not them but worships them and belongs to them and, by virtue of socialization, is one of them. He confounds Niggaz and white people alike in the multicultural schoolyard with his mastering of Nigga language and assumption of Nigga style. His presentation is not overtly authentic, but infused with authenticity because he has lived in Nigga neighborhoods and listened to Nigga music and learned Nigga culture—and the integrity of his performance does not overtly attempt mimicry, like those culture bandits who came before him, after him, or share pop-chart status with him. He frowns at white people like Moby, Christina Aguilera, Fred Durst, and Everlast, who poorly adapt yet successfully co-opt the aesthetics, ideologies, and style of Niggaz. He comes already revered by a relevant society of new and old royalty—Dr. Dre who discovered him, Busta Rymes who once dubbed him "the baddest rapper out here," Madonna and Elton John who have knighted him their heir apparent. But before we give him the NAACP Image Award, it should remain clear that Eminem's race performance is not (solely) intended to impress the oppressed. He's already done that and moved on.

Eminem takes the mythology of the oppressed—identifying himself as impervious, armed and dangerous, sexually superior, economically privileged, radical—and turns this dream on its head. Makes it a macabre comedy of internal warfare. We must laugh at our anger and still be angry, he says. We must be offensive and still be funny, he says. Our enemy is not race . . . our enemy is everybody and anybody who is not "us," and "us" is defined as outsiders who have grown up disenfranchised with strange, irreverent dreams—the problem with "us" Niggaz is we don't take our irreverence far enough, lyrically speaking. We talk about killing each other and celebrate our daily drug and alcohol consumption, but we still get up at the MTV awards and *thank and praise my Lord and Savior Jesus Christ* for small favors like best rap video. We aspire to make millions of dollars any way we can, to get rich quick and stay rich forever, but as soon as we sign our souls to a record contract, we take our advance to the nearest check-cashing place, lay away sneakers with diamond soles, slam a deposit down on any house Cher once owned, (equipped with gold-leaf toilet paper) and wait for MTV Cribs to drop by. (At least Eve promises to buy herself a Warhol every year for her birthday.)

Niggaz may talk bad about bitches and they baby's mama—Eminem brutally murders his. Niggaz may have issues regarding absent fathers or dysfunctional mothers—Eminem comically exposes their dysfunctions, and hangs his mother's pussy high up on a wall for all the world to see. Niggaz may be misogynist, may boast of sexual superiority and sexual indiscretions with a multitude of women, may commonly relegate women to *just another piece of ass prime for the taking status*—but Eminem drugs the bitch, fucks the bitch, moves on to the next bitch. This horror-rapping member of the oppressed nation has won. He has proven to the oppressed that he is not one of us, but he is down for us—and he has proven to the oppressor that he is not one of them, but he is the product of their extreme idea of "us"—and, by virtue of neutralizing the nebulous medium, Eminem *becomes* us with supernatural powers beyond us. Ultimately, he *replaces* us, paying homage to an old abstract idea.

5. THE NEW SURREALIST MANIFESTO

The early-twentieth-century European movement of white male artists who attempted to perform a poetic, political, revolt by way of anti-cortical [sic] understanding, insisted that there was to be no distinction made between what they considered to be abstract and what they considered to be real. In "Surrealist and Existentialist Humanism," Ferdinand Alquie wrote, "To claim that reason is man's essence is already to cut man in two, and the classical tradition has never failed to do so. It has drawn a distinction between what is rational in man (which by that sole fact is considered truly human); and what is not rational (instincts and feelings) which consequently appears unworthy of man." Freud also spoke of the mortal danger incurred for man by this split, this schism between the forces of reason and deep-seated passions—which seem destined to remain unaware of each other. Surrealism wanted to save impulses and desires from repression.

Like Eminem, the Surrealists borrowed the sinister dreams of the oppressed—aspirations for economic success outside of traditional structures; achieved narcissism born to overwhelm self-loathing and inherent existentialism; illusions of grandeur used to counter inescapable depressed circumstances; dismissal of history in order to fashion a new reality in a present tense.

The Surrealist as well as the early Modernist movements fashioned themselves after their associations with the outcasts of society—in most cases, the outcasts were either of Spanish or African descent, and in all cases, the outcasts (or savages) were economically and socially disenfranchised. Gautier and Alexander Dumas traveled through Spain and wore gypsy costumes as if to make their willed identification more real, and this escape into the exotic became the trend of many pre– and post–World War II European writers, artists, and autodidacts, or White Negroes.

It was Verlaine who first coined the phrase "White Negro" when describing Rimbaud, calling him "the splendidly civilized, carelessly civilizing savage," though the origin of the phrase is usually ascribed to the title of a Norman Mailer essay, in which he attempts to explain the impulse of the white man who dares to live with danger by attempting the art of the primitive.

"The White Negro," written in 1959, was Mailer's response to William Faulkner on the topic of school segregation, and the relationship between blacks and whites. He insists, "Whites resist integration and the prospect of equality" because whites secretly know "the Negro already enjoys sensual superiority . . . The Negro has had his sexual supremacy and the White had his white supremacy." Mailer further identified himself as a "near-Beat adventurer" who identified with Negroes and "urban adventurers," those who "drifted out at night looking for action with a Black man's code to fit their facts." "The hipster," he said, "had absorbed the existentialist synopsis of the Negro and could be considered a White Negro" because "any Negro who wishes to live must live with danger from his first day . . . the Negro knew life was war . . . The Negro could rarely afford the sophisticated inhibitions of civilization, and so he kept for survival the art of the primitive. The Black man lived in the enormous present, he subsisted for his Saturday night kicks, relinquishing the pleasures of the mind for the more obligatory pleasures of the body, and in his music he gave voice to the character and quality of his existence, to his rage and the infinite variations of joy, lust . . . and despair of his orgasm . . ."

Mailer's pronouncement of Beat culture (a mid-century replication of radical Bohemian culture) as "the essence of hip" further emphasized that "the source of hip is the Negro, for he "has been living on the margin between totalitarianism and democracy for two centuries . . . the Bohemian and the juvenile delinquent came face to face with the Negro . . . the child was the language of hip, for its argot gave expression to abstract states of feeling." James Baldwin countered Mailer's racist and myopic views in his essay "The Black Boy Looks at the White Boy," calling Mailer's sentiments "so antique a vision of the Blacks at this late hour." But countering Baldwin, Eldridge Cleaver called Mailer's view "prophetic and penetrating in its understanding of the psychology involved in the accelerating confrontation of Black and White in America."

Fifty years before Mailer's ethnographic fantasy, Flaubert traveled to

Egypt out of a desire for a "visionary alternative," for something "in contrast to the grayish tonality of the French provincial landscape"—resulting in his "labored reconstruction of the other." Baudelaire said true civilization was comprised of ". . . hunters, farmers, and even cannibals—all these . . . superior by reasons of their energy and their personal dignity to our western races." Gautier (whose best friend was a Negro from Guadalupe, Alexandre Privat d'Anglemont) when commenting on the Algerian influence on turn-of-the-century French fashion, said, "Our women already wear scarves which have served the harem slaves . . . hashish is taking the place of champagne . . . so superior is primitive life to our so-called civilization." Before Josephine Baker reared her beautiful black ass in Paris in the 1920s, European Bohemia was already fascinated with their perceptions of Negroes, and as explained by Firmin Maillard, Bohemians were "philosophers who couldn't have cared less what their philosophy was based on . . . [they were] brave searchers for infinity, impudent peddlers of dreams . . ." And Erich Muhasm admitted, "It emerged that all of us without single exception were apostates, had rejected our origins, were wayward sons." Maurice de Vlaminck was already collecting African art as early as 1904, and Picasso ennobled the command of African sculpture on his own work by stating, "I understood what the Negroes used their sculpture for . . . to help people avoid coming under the influence of spirits again."

In 1916, Hugo Ball, founder of the Dada movement, opened a cabaret in the red-light district of Zurich, called the Café Voltaire, where prostitutes and Africans commingled freely with starving European artists, like Jean Arp, Tristan Tzara, and Walter Serner, who became infamous for their illogical simultaneous poems—explained by them to be "elegiac, humorous, bizarre." They wore black cowls and played a variety of exotic drums, titling their performance the "Chant Nègres." Ten years later, in Paris, Surrealist artists Robert Desnos and André de la Rivière moved into studio apartments next door to the Bal Nègre, a bar frequented by Negroes who lived in hostels on the same street. Hugo Ball explained, "We drape ourselves like medicine men in their insignia and their essences but we want to ignore the path whereby they reached these bits of cult and parade."

These "bits of cult and parade," co-opted by European Bohemians, leaked into the mass culture of modernity, much in the same way hip-hop and R&B have produced Eminem, Britney Spears, and 'N Sync. The result is not associated with race as much as it is associated with an abstraction of culture. Alfred Jarry (author of the infamous nineteenth-century French play *Ubu*) also re-created himself as an avant, but the invention was so abstract that it could not directly be linked to the Negro—Jarry lived in a room with nothing except a bed and a plaster cast of a huge penis (his ode to both poverty and the wealth of hypersexuality). He perfected a staccato speech for himself, a Negro slang of sorts, without directly impersonating the Negro. He publicly performed the fictional character he'd invented for himself by walking up and down the boulevards or attending the opera in white clown masks, cycling clothes, or dirty white suits and shirts made of paper on which he had drawn a tie—demanding outcast inclusion in a formal world. Heseltine, a writer who possessed a sweet, boyish face and closely cropped blond hair, was described by D. H. Lawrence (in *Women in Love*) as "degenerate," "corrupt," married the beautiful Puma (who eventually committed suicide—much like Em's baby mama tried to do—an ode perhaps to the tragic *grisette*, or working girl, of Paris who loved the self-indulgent Bohemian savage artist), and composed music under the nom de plume Peter Warlock. Heseltine was also known to smoke a lot of weed, and delve into the occult. Eventually, he gassed himself to death—death by suicide translated into immortality for most existentialist Bohemians, much like death by driveby once meant the same for hip-hop dons.

Fifty years or so after the European Bohemian era, the Beat generation invented itself with Jack Kerouac, Allen Ginsberg, Neal Cassidy, and William Burroughs at its forefront (LeRoi Jones is often omitted from the history of insurgent Beat culture—most likely because any true Beat poet is to be remembered as a *performer* of savagery, not an *actual* savage). When a young Allen Ginsberg admitted in an interview that while growing up he "developed a tremendous tolerance for chaos," and described the world as "absolutely real and final and ultimate and at the same time, absolutely unreal and transitory and of the nature of dreams . . . without contradiction," he easily validated Verlaine and Norman Mailer's theoretical view of the Negro and their psychological profile of the White Negro.

Like hip-hop culture, Beat culture emerged in an era of economic prosperity and political paranoia. If the mid-twentieth-century American White Negro emerged in a postwar era of convention, in which hip and cool Negro icons created a counterculture of style, immorality, and self-destruction, the latter twentieth-century American New White Negro patterned himself after hip-hop culture's era of rebellion, taking him on an uncharted journey prone to danger. Ronald Reagan and Rodney King were good reasons to re-create a new generation of Charlie Parkers and Billie Hollidays—undeniably gifted icons of artistic genius, personal style, and self-destruction. If the Negro hipster lived without a definable past or future, the hip-hopster never let you forget his past and elaborately decorated his present with excess in anticipation of a life without a future—which elevated him to the status of potential martyr. He (or she) emulated Robert De Niro (in *Taxi Driver*) or, the hip-hop favorite, Al Pacino (in *Scarface*)—an outlaw feared for his enormous ferocity, and survivor skills, or revered for his unsurpassable stolen wealth, and for living daily with the threat of assassination or mutiny. Beat culture produced popular icons that offered a more abstract version of the White Negro. Its superstar, Jack Kerouac, was a Dionysian figure whose impulses toward the primitive conflicted with his tendency toward culture, education, and ego.

Ultimately, Jack was not as interested in being an outlaw as he was interested in being a star—the celebrity that white status could afford him. And as Baldwin pointed out, the Beat hipster could, at the end of the day, "return to being white." The threat of daily living could never mean as much to him as it did the Negro because the hipster's was an avant-garde performance of cool. Vanilla Ice has returned to the beach, has formed a heavy-metal band, and reflects on the days when Suge Knight hung him by his ankles over a balcony railing—Ice has escaped the danger of hip-hop lore by returning to the comfort of fundamental whiteness. Eminem escapes the actual danger of hip-hop lore by maintaining fundamental whiteness in the context of comical blackness. As Sir Elton John assuaged us all, we mustn't "take him seriously."

6. LIVING IN THE DREAM
(Types & Tropes, Symbols & Signs)

In the reality that is our daily human existence, Eminem does not exist. He never did. But he is a real product of the American dream—a character born out of our nation's collective unconscious, our inborn predilection to produce parallel images or identical psychic shapes common to all men. He is conjured from what we think of ourselves and what we think of others. He is born out of *The Jerry Springer Show*, *South Park*, Jack Kerouac, Carl Van Vechten—all part of a dream, and within this dream there is a dream. Singling out Eminem as an archetype of race perception and performance in America is a shallow undertaking—the composition of his character has its history within the context of the American dream, which is now a conundrum of dreams within dreams. Dreams may be difficult to interpret—because they are, after all, indistinct metaphors and allegories of fantasy—but the dream of race and its performance in American culture is not difficult to track. It has a history, and that history comes with presupposed rules and presupposed character traits that are familiar to us all.

In the dream that is identity, there are archetypal conflicts between the free will of the human maker (his savage creative impulses—an unconscious state of being) and what is the human thinker's intellect (culture, and historical perspective—a conscious state of being). The landscape of democracy and freedom for all men is also the invention of a dream—a utopian impulse, a way of perceiving an eternal plan in the contingencies of time; a creation of the human will born out of fiction where there is no transcendental dimension or registration of the infinite "I am."

Race is a recent historical invention used to make a distinction between people for purposes of colonization. C. Loring Brace, professor of anthropology at the University of Michigan, explains that the concept of race "does not appear until the Trans-Atlantic voyages of the Renaissance." But the prevalence of race as a concept—and its relationship to appearance, human status, and identity formation—is actually more significant today than it ever was. Our obsession with race is surpassed only by our seemingly polite and progressive neutrality regarding race. The Racial Privacy Initiative, a ballot promoted by black businessman Ward Connelly (who also successfully ended affirmative action in the state of California), is designed to obliterate the "race box" on school and government forms because it forces us to "pay attention to immutable and meaningless characteristics like skin color and ancestry" ("When Color Should Count," Glenn C. Loury, *New York Times*). But even if race does not accurately identify a people, the concept is firmly in place and forces a social dynamic as well as pinpoints a social perception of a people. We don't see each other as one in the same. Never did. Never will. The perceived image of race is based on individual (or collective) sight, which has been re-created and reproduced. It is an appearance, or a set of appearances, which has been detached from the place and time in which it first made its appearance and preserved (in language and colloquialism) for a few moments or a few centuries. Once we are aware that we can see, we are aware that we can be seen, and "the eye of the other combines with our own eye," . . . we are always looking at the relation between things and ourselves . . . our perception of what we see depends on our way of seeing. Images, for instance, were first made to conjure up the appearance of something that was absent. Gradually, it becomes evident that an image can outlast what it once represented, but the verbalized perception of image arrests the object in a perceived context for as long as the perception and the original language for the perception are upheld (*Ways of Seeing* by John Berger). In the case of race in America, it is physiology and the historical perceptions of and common terminology used to describe physiology that most often informs the individual's sense of defining race.

The dream of race as identity is born only in a perceived land of diversity (or difference). Race is a regenerated fantasy owing its genesis to neurosis (or as Freud said, "some early trauma repressed") and our need to achieve psychic balance. What is actual is what we produce from our dreams—

symbols and signs of our expressions and intuitive perceptions. Our response to what we *think* we see. Identity. Race. Identity is an invented thing. Race is an invented thing. They are not real, but they are *actual*. Race and identity are based on perception and performance and are relative only to the perceptions and performances of the individual and the collective understanding of existence and the activity of being within the context of the dream. These symbols and signs cannot be expressed differently by us or better said by us. Language fails us—and the individual or collective mind is forced into overdrive in order to invent language and behaviors for archetypes of identity. Apertures into nonordinary reality.

It is therefore less significant that Eminem, easily identified as "white" (a nonspecific race term for people of European descent), identifies himself with "black" culture (a nonspecific race term for people of African descent, "black culture" being that which is socially produced by the collective of people of African descent). That is not what makes his archetype of nonordinary reality a significant landmark in the landscape of the American dream. Rather, it is how he has refashioned an old symbol that appeals to popular culture and its boilerplate concepts of race, class, and identity, to fit a new generation in a new yet strangely redundant way—and how that old symbol has transmogrified in the last one hundred years, owing its present-day existence not to the historical performance of *blackness* but to the historical performance of *whiteness* and the ingenuity of human dreams.

There is something called *black* in America and there is something called *white* in America and I know them when I see them, but I will forever be unable to explain the meaning of them, because they are not real even though they have a very real place in my daily way of seeing, a fundamental relationship to my ever-evolving understanding of history, and a critical place in my interactive relationship to humanity. If one believes in the existence of race, it is because one needs to believe in the existence of self (within a culture that relies on race as an important variable of human existence). One needs to believe in culture, and the products of culture that define identity and inform history. The concept of race has long been one of the most vital sources of cultural product (as well as cultural conflict) because race has as its square root a hierarchical structure of being expressed in symbolism. A semiotics of identity that has yet to be solved. These tropes and signs are produced from the unconscious as revelation. The collective unconscious creates them in order to survive (by confrontation) the present archetypal structure. Conveniently forgotten in our race sentimentality are the ever-changing faces of race. Whiteness *became* something one had to attain in America. Being of Nordic or European ancestry did not automatically translate into whiteness. Whiteness had more to do with class privilege than some notion of nationality or physiology (and class is a better definition). Whiteness was purchased and fought for by Jews, Catholics, the Irish, Italians, Polish, indentured servants . . . all considered to be, at one time or another in America, non-white (and even today, depending on whose definition of whiteness you subscribe to). Blackness was never something one had to attain, at least not outside of Bohemian circles. Today, it seems . . . it is.

If we look to Eminem's archetype to appeal to what we know about ourselves now, we do it without referring to what we know about the identity of the other. The Eminem show is supposed to make us forget about race and think about how rigid this society is. How we have never really loosened up, and just had barnyard fun with our sacred cows. He uses the vernacular of black hip-hop culture, as well as the psychoanalytical vernacular of the white intellectual—and this invention of character is transferable to any race. The old White Negro may have worn cork and Afro wigs, soaked up Harlem culture and delivered the talented tenth to the mainstream, given race music a haircut, tuxedo jacket, and orchestration, may have learned to shake his narrow white hips in the snakelike manner of the Negro, thereby creating just enough soul to gain Hollywood movie-star musical status, and may have heroicized Negro jazz musicians in his literature, proudly proclaiming to have actually shared a joint or some smack with one or two at the height of Bohemian subculture's race mixing—but the new White Negro—like Eminem—has not *arrived* at black culture . . . He has *arrived* at white culture with an authentic performance of whiteness, influenced by a historical concept of blackness.

And there is a difference . . . ?

SELECTED   BIBLIOGRAPHY

Arrowsmith, William. "Introduction to *The Bacchae*." In *Euripides V: Three Tragedies*, edited by David Grene and Richard Lattimore. Chicago: University of Chicago Press, 1969.

Berger, John. *Ways of Seeing*. New York: Viking Press, 1995.

Wilson, Elizabeth. *Bohemians: The Glamorous Outcasts*. New Brunswick, N.J.: Rutgers University Press, 2001.

2. *Scenes from* Umkovu, a play

BY EISA DAVIS

BLACKNESS IS CONSTANTLY REPRODUCING itself, like a mint releasing new currency as old bills age. When the blues got locked up in real estate, jazz kept its assets liquid; if rock and roll floated a bond, it had to mature into hip hop. New editions of the same funky beat printed to stave off inevitable mergers and acquisitions. But this drum won't stop, even when whiteness is defined as the performance of an ignorance of blackness, or when blackness refuses to teach whiteness its kitchen secrets—and sometimes no words come when these two forces meet. By representing these irreducible moments—one in which a black woman in a relationship with a white man may have less money but perhaps more power because she is ultimately *not* consumable, and another in which the white/black deadlock is exploded by an Asian voice—can we begin to develop a new language beyond economics or identity politics that reflects the contradictions we live?

SCENE TWO

JEFF, executive VP, Pacific Entertainment Group. 30s. He is white, short.

MAYA, A&R, Represent Records. A black woman in her 20s.

Pink's Hot Dogs, Melrose and La Brea. 2 a.m. Los Angeles.

JEFF: You know it's just terrible, terrible. Not O.J., no, I'm glad he got off. It's not O.J., it's not Osama bin Laden or Saddam or whoever, it's not about enemies, it's about whom you choose to love. That's why we get in all our troubles. We're in love with Israel, we're in love with—well, I guess that's it—besides black people, and the British, and Japanese—I mean, we don't create enemies from some plutonium uranium spark and poof diaphragm in the sky, no. We make our hate from our love. And this hot dog is absolutely delicious, absolutely no contest yes yummy do it to me. Hot dog at 2 a.m. Do you mind my philosophizing at such a late hour? I am an alien. I live in this acidic town damned by every Native American deity we know and I try to protect myself with turquoise amulets and pork between two pieces of bread. Why don't they serve drinks here?

MAYA: Because we've already had so many.

JEFF: I know I'm really chewin' your earlobe here, but earlobes, your earlobes, oh, they are meant for chewing, and earrings, and keloids. Now why can't I develop a keloid. I'm white, that's why. I'm not guilty, I'm just white, and it's sickening. Here I am, a mutant. I have mutated from the original Asiatic Black Man into this alien! Now you, you may have some slave master in there, but you are so very lucky to have been born at the source.

MAYA: Baldwin Hills?

JEFF: You think I'm garrulous. I am. I love my mouth. Only thing about me that gives me any pleasure. The rest is a big recycling bin of terror and reason. So blackness. Where can I get some. I want to ingest it. I want to exchange my transparent papery luftwaffe body for purification. It's not a secret. I have no wife. Just divorce, just kids. I'm not talking lust here. I don't wanna screw you, I mean I love screwing you, but—I wanna *be* you, a black woman, sitting there, quiet, munching on your hot dog, eyes gently patronizing, laughing at the appropriate moments. I want to wear your lovely face when I look into the mirror. Not minstrelsy, just getting rid of the enemy in my body that feeds on love.

MAYA: Jeff, we are too fucking drunk. I can't get offended when I'm like this.

JEFF: But can you help me out. Because I don't want any charity Salvation

Army bell blackness in tiny portions at holidays. I want something I can drown in.

MAYA: You too? You are pure arrogance. You're disgusting.

JEFF: Thank you. Beautiful.

MAYA: I know what you need. I know. This artist I've been working on—

JEFF: Violator. Rule number one is we don't talk shop. Wrecked my marriage.

MAYA: Your total inability to listen wrecked your marriage. You erase everything you touch.

JEFF: Not you. You are my inflatable emergency ramp. Plane went down—

MAYA: No more metaphors, okay?

JEFF: You got me drunk. You take me to Pink's, I spill my racial transvestitism on you and now you want me to—

MAYA: Buy Swive out of his contract at Represent.

JEFF: You want me to lay down, what, a mil to move someone named Swive over to us? We're not just a treehouse, Maya, we do have shareholders. So (A), no, and (B), who is he?

MAYA: I can't even pitch him to you. He's just one of those MCs that converts you. He's some kind of portal. I'm serious!

JEFF: In love with him?

MAYA: His music.

JEFF: Just checking. Black guy, huh?

MAYA: Yeah.

JEFF: Why aren't you with a black guy?

MAYA: Magic Shave powder. Swive's not the best in the world or anything, I just feel like he gives a real purpose to my life. That I'm giving myself to something bigger.

JEFF: Hm. And why buy now?

MAYA: Darryl doesn't know how to handle him. I thought working at a black label would give me room to grow the artists, but Darryl's a coward. Swive has like four albums' worth of material none of which is "radio" enough for Darryl—I've got the singles, videos, magazines all prepped to sear Swive's face on every state in the union and what. Darryl's pulling out the cookie-cutter. He also said he was gonna kill Swive, but that was a joke.

JEFF: Murder. That's a good way to make money. So naturally you wanna come over to Pacific with Swive.

MAYA: As long as you and I never work together. Your executive-VP day look is really ugly.

JEFF: Oh I know. Is Swive a Scientologist?

MAYA: No.

JEFF: I'm still not black.

MAYA: Isolate some DNA. Maybe you had black folk in your family passing long enough to make you.

JEFF: When am I gonna hear this artist of yours.

MAYA: Wrap party after the video shoot. You'll want him.

JEFF: No guarantees. I hate being The Man. So lonely. You give eloquence, they give mustard. I had so many words to caress you with tonight and I spouted them and now I have no more ballast to hold me down. I'm actually feeling nauseous from the height. Guess we're not having sex tonight.

MAYA: You'd be impotent anyway. The drinks.

JEFF: Or the Pink's. Why do I have to be so pink? What'd I do to be so pink and blue?

from SCENE FIVE

SHMOOVE, veejay and host of *Dead Homiez,* a biography show about deceased hip-hop icons. 20s, Asian, and a ladies' man.

DARRYL, president, Represent Records. 30s. He is tall, impeccably dressed.

Shmoove enters the lobby of Represent, doing a live video shot.

SHMOOVE: We're here at Represent Records, this once sleepy R&B label that has the music industry's attention in its grip. Ouch. Represent artist

Swive Jabal, whose video "Huh?" is in heavy rotation, is ready to giz-o. After busting an unorthodox freestyle and Darryl Jackson's face at his own wrap party, Swive may break completely from his label and move to Pacific Entertainment. [to Darryl] Now Darryl, president of Represent, your man is bizarre. I heard he just gave his Lexus to a homeless man on an offramp. What the dealy, yo?

DARRYL: Well, first of all, that Lexus is not his to give away. But besides the criminal charges and my civil suit, Swive will not be released from his contract with us. He is our investment, however risky, and we are going to profit from his success period point blank end of story.

SHMOOVE: When's the album gonna drop? Advance orders say it'll go double platinum. At least.

DARRYL: The album will be released once we handle the poachers over at Pacific. Swive may have assaulted my person, ruptured my septum, but this has not at all changed his status as an artist here.

SHMOOVE: Well good luck on that face, man. Swive, also known as the silent monk of hip hop, had no comment. I'm Shmoovy Shmoove with the news that shows and proves. Let's pay those bills, BAYbay. [Live shot ends.] And we out.

DARRYL: Get everything you need?

SHMOOVE: Always. Wish I could stay and parlay but I'm goin' east side for a little sushi with this new group. Rock band. Bunjee jump while they play guitar. They're each like seven years old. Hot. Ah-ight, nigga, check you later.

DARRYL: I don't think I heard you correctly.

SHMOOVE: Nigga, please.

DARRYL: That word is not yours.

SHMOOVE: Nigga, I'm the only Asian man on TV! So forget you. You burned down my parents' store in '92 so I'm a loot all your language and all your gear and your hair and I'm a work it. Who the hell is buying your daddy's jazz record anyway? Better recognize. Coltrane? Wu-Tang? Y'all as bad as white folks.

3. Reds, Whites, and Blues People

BY ROBIN D. G. KELLEY

WE CAN SPOT 'EM A MILE away. They're at every political forum, demonstration, panel discussion, cultural event, hawking their papers bearing names with "Socialist" or "Workers" or "International" in the title, shouting people down, hogging the microphone. They sometimes come with black, Asian, and Latino comrades, but their whiteness and often their arrogance underscore their visibility in a room full of angry black folk. They come hard, ready to throw down the gauntlet to the bourgeois nationalists, inviting everyone to join the class struggle, all the while saving their worst invective for their adversaries on the Left. Once at the mic, they don't usually identify themselves until two-thirds into their speech and the requests to "sit yo' ass down" begin to escalate. But we always know who they are, we tolerate their presence for the most part, and some of us even buy their papers and pamphlets. I know I did and still do. My library is overflowing with texts published by International Publishers, Pathfinder Press, and assorted lesser-known revolutionary basement presses. Sometimes you can find as much about black struggles in the Left sectarian newspapers and broadsides as in *The Final Call*—certainly much more than in *Ebony, Jet,* or *Essence.* Police killings of unarmed African Americans, conflicts in housing projects, Klan activity in North Carolina, you name it, you can find it in the *Revolutionary Worker* or the *Worker's Vanguard.* They even put out the writings of great black intellectuals in the form of cheap pamphlets. Why go to Barnes & Noble when you could get nicely stapled Xeroxes of Fanon and Malcolm X and Sojourner Truth for a buck?

Even if one knows absolutely nothing of the American Left and its history, anyone with a political bone in her body recognizes its unwavering interest in the plight of black people. We have a century of black opinion as to why. They're just using black people to promote their agenda or they're agent provocateurs sent in by the FBI. The less conspiracy-prone chalk it up to alienated white youths rebelling against their parental culture. Then there were those who regarded some on the Left as genuine revolutionaries willing to grapple with issues established black leaders tend to ignore. Committed black support for left-wing movements is hard to fathom after a half-century of Cold War in which the anti-Communist confessionals of Richard Wright, Ralph Ellison, George Padmore, Margaret Walker, and a host of others stand in for black opinion. Although some of these texts chastise the Communists for *not being radical enough,* they are usually read through an interpretive frame that can only see black people as passive victims of Communist conspiracy.

Of course, it is impossible to generalize about the American Left and its intentions since it has never been a singular, unified movement. Hundreds of sectarian parties have fought each other over the correct line on China or Albania, the "Woman Question," skilled versus unskilled workers, united front versus proletarian revolt, *ad infinitum.* Toward the top of the pyramid of political issues has been the ever-present "Negro Question." If there is one thing the twentieth-century American Left shares in common it is the political idea that black people reside in the eye of the hurricane of class struggle. The American Left, after all, was born in a society where slavery and free labor coexisted, and only skin color and heritage determined who lived in bondage and who did not. This is why the nascent Left in the U.S. understood the problem posed by racial divisions as the Negro Question, for even a German like Karl Marx recognized that African descendants stood at the fulcrum of the nation's racial identity and political economy. The old man said as much himself in 1867: "Labor cannot emancipate itself in the white skin where in the black it is branded." Put simply, the Negro Question was the Left's rubric for several related questions arising from their efforts to build a Socialist movement: how can we unite workers of different colors in a racist society? How do we convince whites to fight racism? How do we win the black working class to the cause of Socialism? What are the unique features of black life and culture that resist American capitalism and racism?

For our purposes, the last question is fundamental and partly explains why the American Left keeps coming back to black gatherings, why black people are so important to their overall vision of revolution. Beginning at least with the Communist party, African Americans were not only regarded as uniquely oppressed by both race and class, but their struggles were thought to have produced a deeply revolutionary culture. Black people's songs, their literature (especially their folklore), the way they moved, even their religion, embodied what Communist theoreticians regarded as a culture of resistance. One can certainly argue that the Communists fetishized black culture, but their reasons differed from those of the corporate entities who had taken poet Langston Hughes's "blues and gone." Black radicals, with a little help from their Soviet friends, forced the white U.S. Left to see and hear differently, and they heard in the sounds and movements and writings the birth of a utopian future rising out of the abyss of racism and oppression. In other words, I argue that the American Left's embrace of black culture cannot be reduced to a simple equation of white fascination with black bodies, black artifacts, or black experience, but is instead a product of the theoretical insights of African Americans inside the movement.

The dream of international working-class solidarity crumbled on the battlefield, where the proletarians of Europe and America traded in their red flags for the flags of their respective nations. Except for some of the peasants and workers in Russia, who were simply too poor and frustrated to fight for their ruling classes. Instead, they launched a revolution and backed Lenin and the Bolshevik party, who eventually seized power in 1917 and pulled out of the "war to end all wars." The Bolsheviks established a Third International and gave birth to the worldwide Communist movement. For black folk looking for radical alternatives to American Socialism, Lenin turned out to be somewhat of a friend. Despite his distance from American soil, he took a special interest in black people, in part because most Russian workers and peasants were also divided and oppressed by nationality and ethnicity.[1]

If the Third International, or the "Comintern," proved more sympathetic and sensitive to the racial nature of American class struggle, it is largely because black folk made it so. The momentary crisis of "Western civilization" caused by the chaos of war, worker rebellions, anticolonial uprisings, postwar racial violence, and talk of "self-determination for oppressed nations" contributed to the dramatic explosion of the Garvey movement and a new generation of "New Negroes" advocating a radical fusion of Socialism and "race politics." In 1917, Socialists A. Philip Randolph and Chandler Owen launched *The Messenger,* a new magazine dedicated to radical Socialism and black freedom. They published essays and poetry graphically depicting racist violence and editorials supporting Irish nationalism, women's suffrage, and the Russian Revolution, which they initially called "the greatest achievement of the twentieth century."[2] A year later, a group called the African Blood Brotherhood (ABB) was founded by the Caribbean-born editor Cyril Briggs, who published *The Crusader*—originally the organ of the nationalistic Hamitic League of the World. Its leaders might be best described as militant black nationalist Marxists; they advocated Socialism but the heart of their agenda was armed self-defense against lynching, universal suffrage, equal rights for blacks, and the immediate end to segregation. *The*

---

[1] In 1913, Lenin wrote a short article entitled "Russians and Negroes" comparing the plight of African Americans to that of emancipated Russian serfs. He went on to conduct a major study of the U.S. agricultural economy, paying particular attention to the conditions of Southern black folk. And in his "Notebooks on Imperialism" (1916) he sharply criticized the SPA's position on the "Negro Question" and expressed shock that the Mississippi Socialist Party would support segregation. (*Collected Works,* vol. 18, pp. 543–44; vol. 39, pp. 590–91.) (V. I. Lenin, "New Data on the Laws Governing the Development of Capitalism in Agriculture," in *Collected Works,* vol. 22, pp. 13–102; "On Statistics and Sociology," in *Collected Works,* vol. 23, p. 276.)

[2] Rod Bush, *We Are Not What We Seem: Black Nationalism and Class Struggle in the American Century* (New York: New York University Press, 1998), 83–112; Theodore Kornweibel, *No Crystal Stair: Black Life and the Messenger, 1917–1928* (Westport, 1975); Winston James, *Holding Aloft the Banner of Ethiopia: Caribbean Radicalism in Early Twentieth-Century America* (London: Verso, 1998); Philip Foner, *American Socialism and Black Americans: From the Age of Jackson to World War II* (Westport, 1977); Jervis Anderson, *A. Phillip Randolph: A Biographical Portrait* (New York, 1973), 85–137.

Crusader was imbued with a martial spirit, thus echoing the Garveyite *Negro World* and its constant appeals to militarism and manhood redemption. Moreover, they criticized President Woodrow Wilson for not applying the concept of self-determination to Africa, and during the "Red Summer" of 1919, when angry white mobs attacked black communities in several cities, Briggs demanded "government of the Negro, by the Negro and for the Negro." A unique experiment in black Marxist organization, ABB leaders had secretly joined the Workers (Communist) party very soon after the Brotherhood was founded.[3]

These "New Negro" radicals challenged traditional Socialist logic by insisting that struggles for black rights were inherently revolutionary. But the newly formed (and sharply divided) American Communist movement initially wasn't down with the program. Like the Socialists before them, the Workers (Communist) party believed that "the interests of the Negro worker are identical with those of the white" and that black nationalism was "a weapon of reaction for the defeat and further enslavement of both [blacks] and their white

---

[3] *Amsterdam News*, September 5, 1917; *The Crusader* 1, no. 8 (April 1919), 8–9; ibid., 1, no. 12 (August 1919), 4; Robert A. Hill, "Cyril V. Briggs, *The Crusader*, and the African Blood Brotherhood, 1918–1922," Introduction, *The Crusader*, ed. Robert A. Hill (New York: Garland, 1987), v–lxvi; Mark Solomon, *The Cry Was Unity: Communists and African Americans, 1917–1936* (Jackson: University Press of Mississippi, 1998), 3–21. Anselmo R. Jackson, associate editor of *The Crusader*, wrote that the paper was dedicated "to the doctrine of self-government for the Negro and Africa for the Africans." *Crusader* 1, no. 3 (November 1918). For more on the ABB, see "Cyril Briggs and the African Blood Brotherhood," WPA Writers' Project, No. 1, Reporter: Carl Offord, Schomburg Collection; *Crusader* 2, no. 2 (October 1919), 27; "Program of the African Blood Brotherhood," *Communist Review* (London) (April 1922), 449–54. See also Harry Haywood, *Black Bolshevik: Autobiography of an Afro-American Communist* (Chicago, 1978), 122–130; Mark Naison, *Communists in Harlem During the Depression* (Urbana, 1983), 3, 5–8, 17–18; Theodore Vincent, *Black Power and the Garvey Movement* (Berkeley, 1971), 74–85 and passim; Tony Martin, *Race First* (Westport, 1976), 237–46; Draper, *American Communism and Soviet Russia*, 322–32; Cedric J. Robinson, *Black Marxism: The Making of the Black Radical Tradition* (London, 1983), 296–301; David Samuels, "Five Afro-Caribbean Voices in American Culture, 1917–1929: Hubert H. Harrison, Wilfred A. Domingo, Richard B. Moore, Cyril Briggs and Claude McKay" (Ph.D. diss., University of Iowa, 1977); Theman Taylor, "Cyril Briggs and the African Blood Brotherhood: Effects of Communism on Black Nationalism, 1919–1935" (Ph.D. diss., University of California, Santa Barbara, 1981).

brother workers."[4] But across the ocean in Moscow, Comintern officials sided with the other "brothers." Even before the Bolshevik victory, Lenin had begun to think of a strategy for dealing with "national minorities" in the event of a successful Socialist revolution in Russia—a multinational creation of Tsarist imperialism. He proposed a union of Socialist republics that gave nations within this union the right to secede. No matter how this might have worked in practice, in theory Lenin was saying that all nations have a right to self-determination, and that the working class is not just a conglomeration of atomized proletarians but possess national identities. After the war, Lenin expanded his theses to include the colonies, which he regarded as oppressed nations. In 1920, with the assistance of Indian Communist M. N. Roy, Lenin drafted his famous "Theses on the National and Colonial Questions," insisting that the "communist parties give direct support to the revolutionary movements among the dependent nations and those without equal rights (e.g., Ireland, and among American Negroes), and in the colonies."[5]

Lenin's injunction shocked the U.S. Communist movement and invited America's black Bolsheviks to speak with authority. One of the most important figures to take advantage of the Soviet bully pulpit was Claude McKay, the Jamaican-born writer of the Harlem Renaissance whose poem "If We Must Die" became the unofficial anthem of the New Negro Movement. He

---

[4] Workers (Communist) Party of America, *Program and Constitution: Workers Party of America* (New York, 1921), 14; Workers (Communist) Party of America, *The Second Year of the Workers Party of America: Theses, Programs, Resolutions* (Chicago, 1924), 125.

[5] "Theses on the National and Colonial Question Adopted by the Second Congress of the Comintern Congress," in *The Communist International, 1919–1943, Documents,* edited by Jane Degras (London, 1956), vol. 1, 142. Roy's contribution to the theses, as well as to the general direction of the Commission, was quite substantial. Among other things, he recognized the existence of class distinctions in the colonies and he placed the peasantry in a pivotal position for waging the anticolonial movement. See, Manabendra Nath Roy, *M. N. Roy's Memoirs* (Bombay, 1964), 378; see also John Haithcox, *Communism and Nationalism in India: M. N. Roy and Comintern Policy, 1920–1939* (Princeton, 1971), 14–15; D.C. Grover, *M. N. Roy: A Study of Revolution and Reason in Indian Politics* (Calcutta, 1973), 2–13. A copy of Roy's theses are available in V. B. Karnik, *M. N. Roy: A Political Biography* (Bombay, 1978), 107–110. For Lenin's views on Roy's supplementary theses, see "The Report of the Commission on the National and Colonial Questions, July 26, 1920," in *Lenin on the National and Colonial Questions,* 30–37. For an excellent overview of the Comintern negotiations and debates on the Negro Question, see Solomon, *The Cry Was Unity,* 38–51.

made his way to the Soviet Union in 1922, just in time to be an unofficial delegate to the Fourth World Congress of the Comintern. The Soviets were so fascinated with Negroes that he and the Communists' official black delegate, Otto Huiswoud, were treated like celebrities. When McKay addressed the Congress, he put the question of race front and center, criticizing the American Communist party and the labor movement for their racism and warning that unless the Left challenges white supremacy the ruling classes will continue to use disaffected black workers as a foil against the revolutionary movement. In the end, McKay's point was clear: the Negro stood at the fulcrum of the class struggle; there could be no successful working-class movement without black workers at the center. Otto Huiswoud also addressed the Congress, emphasizing the incredible racism black workers confronted back home in the South and the role that Garveyism played as a force against imperialism worldwide. The Comintern responded immediately, forming a Negro Commission and committing resources to recruiting black cadre and supporting black liberation on a global scale.[6]

Comintern officials were so impressed with McKay's speech that they asked him to expand it into a small book, which was published in Russia under the title *Negry v Amerike* (1923) and eventually translated as *The Negroes in America*. This little book profoundly shaped Comintern policy on the Negro Question, offering a revisionist approach to Marxism, the implications of which we have yet to fully comprehend. Drawing on his observations as well as the writings of other Harlem radicals, such as Hubert Harrison and W. A. Domingo, McKay argued that race and slavery were the heart and soul of the

---

[6] Roger E. Kanet, "The Comintern and the 'Negro Question': Communist Policy in the United States and Africa, 1921–1941," *Survey* 19, no. 4 (Autumn 1973), 89–90; Haywood, *Black Bolshevik*, 225; Claude McKay, *A Long Way from Home* (New York, 1937), 177–80; William J. Maxwell, *New Negro, Old Left: African American Writing and Communism Between the Wars* (New York: Columbia University Press, 1999), 74–7; Solomon, *The Cry Was Unity*, 40–42; Billings [Otto Huiswoud], "Report on the Negro Question," *International Press Correspondence* 3, no. 2 (1923), 14–16. The full text of the "Theses on the Negro Question" is available in *Bulletin of the IV Congress of the Communist International* no. 27 (December 7, 1922), 8–10; Workers (Communist) Party of America, *Fourth National Convention of the Workers (Communist) Party of America* (Chicago, 1925), 121 and 122.

nation, repeating his point that only a commitment to black freedom can ensure socialism's success in the U.S. For McKay, a commitment to black freedom also meant support for self-organization and self-determination. Rather than attack black nationalist movements for not being "class conscious," McKay called on the Left to support them. Why? Because the overwhelming racism made it difficult for black folk to think like a "class"; instead, they saw the world through colored glasses. He wryly observed, "the Negro in America is not permitted for one minute to forget his color, his skin, his race."[7]

McKay turned out to be much too critical for the American Communists and they soon parted company. And no matter how many resolutions were passed in Moscow in 1922, American Communist leaders were reluctant to go along with the program and generally distrusted Marcus Garvey and his appeals to race pride.[8] In 1928, once again as a result of black initiatives, the Comintern adopted its most radical position on the Negro Question to date. Promoted by Harry Haywood (né Haywood Hall), the Nebraska-born black Communist who had come through the ranks of the ABB, and South African Communist James LaGuma, the Comintern passed a resolution recognizing Negroes in the "black belt" counties of the American South as an oppressed nation. As a nation, like the Lithuanians or Georgians of the old Russian empire, they had a right to self-determination. They could secede if they wanted, perhaps even form a Negro Soviet Socialist Republic, but they were not encouraged to do so.[9] The resolution, not surprisingly, met fierce oppo-

[7] Claude McKay, *The Negroes in America*, trans. Robert J. Winter, ed. Alan L. McLeod (Port Washington, N.Y.: Kennikat, 1979 [orig. 1923]); The best discussion of McKay's book can be found in Maxwell, *New Negro, Old Left*, 76–93. See also Winston James's forthcoming definitive biography of McKay.

[8] On the CP and Garveyism, see Vincent, *Black Power and the Garvey Movement*, 211; Robert Hill, ed., *The Marcus Garvey and Universal Negro Improvement Association Papers* (Berkeley and Los Angeles, 1984), vol. III, pp. 675–81; (quotation) Workers (Communist) Party of America, *Fourth National Convention of the Workers (Communist) Party of America* (Chicago, 1925), 122; James Jackson [Lovett Fort-Whiteman], "The Negro in America," *Communist International* (February 1925), 52; Robert Minor, "After Garvey—What?" *Workers Monthly* 5 (June 1926), 362–65.

[9] The best discussion of the history of the Black Belt thesis can be found in Mark Solomon, *The Cry Was Unity: African Americans and the Communist Party* (Jackson: University Press of Mississippi, 1999). For a copy of the original text of 1928 see, CPUSA, *Communist Position on the Negro Question* (n.d., n.p.), 41–56. See also, Roger E. Kanet,

sition from white, and some black, party leaders, but for several black Communists it confirmed what they had long believed: African Americans had their own unique revolutionary tradition and their interests were not "identical" to white workers'.[10]

The new slogan did not persuade black Communists to attempt to seize Mississippi and secede from the U.S., nor did it bring black folk to the party in droves. Those who did join were attracted to the CP's fight for the concrete economic needs of the unemployed and working poor, its militant opposition to racism, and its vigorous courtroom battles on behalf of the Scottsboro Boys (nine young black men falsely accused of raping two white women in Alabama). Nevertheless, "self-determination" did create an opening for African Americans to promote a cultural politics of race in spite of the party's formal opposition to "Negro nationalism." In 1929 the party launched *The Liberator* under the editorship of Cyril Briggs. Like *The Crusader* before it, *The Liberator* nurtured somewhat of a black nationalist literary movement. Ironically, Stalin's mechanical definition of a nation, which embraced a "community of culture" as a central concept, reinforced the modern nationalist idea that the basis of nationhood was a coherent culture. Stalin certainly did not invent this idea. Indeed, the proponents of "Negritude" in the Francophone world were also searching for that essential "Negro" or African culture that could lay the basis for Pan-African identity. Stalin's notion of a "community of culture" merely provided a Marxist justification for black Communists to join the search for the roots of a national Negro culture. As William L. Patterson, the outstanding attorney and Harlem Renaissance-supporter-turned-Communist,

---

"The Comintern and the 'Negro Question': Communist Policy in the United States and Africa, 1921–1941," *Survey* 19/4 (Autumn 1973), 101–4; Haywood, *Black Bolshevik*, 226 passim; R.D.G. Kelley, "The Third International and the Struggle for National Liberation in South Africa, 1921–1928," *Ufahamu* 15/1 (1986), 109–113; John W. VanZanten, "Communist Theory and the American Negro Question," *Review of Politics* 29 (1967): 435–56.

[10] Naison, *Communists in Harlem,* 18; (quotation) Gilbert Lewis, "Revolutionary Negro Tradition," *Negro Worker*, March 15, 1930, 8. Cyril Briggs published a whole series of essays on this score, such as "Negro Revolutionary Hero—Toussaint L'Overture," *Communist* 8, no. 5 (May 1929), 250–54; "The Negro Press as a Class Weapon," *Communist* 8, no. 8 (August 1929), 453–460; and "May First and the Revolutionary Traditions of Negro Masses," *Daily Worker,* April 28, 1930.

wrote in 1933, the African-American nation was bound by a common culture: "The 'spirituals,' the jazz, their religious practices, a growing literature, descriptive of their environment, all of these are forms of cultural expression . . . Are these not the prerequisites for nationhood?"[11]

Although few of Patterson's white comrades placed as much emphasis on black culture as an expression of nationhood, they did come around to the idea that there was something inherently rebellious in black folk culture. This is why, in 1932, a Communist critic as antireligious as Mike Gold could praise the spiritual expressiveness of black working people. Describing the black cadre in the Southside of Chicago, Gold wrote: "At mass meetings their religious past becomes transmuted into a Communist present. They follow every word of the speaker with real emotion; they encourage him, as at a prayer meeting, with cries of 'Yes, yes, comrade' and often there is an involuntary and heartfelt 'Amen!' "[12] Likewise, for white Communists such as Harold Preece, "the throbbing note of protest . . . is even in the spirituals. The Negroes were denied the most elementary civil rights. But they could sing and those songs were living prophesies of deliverance."[13] On the other hand, some white CP cultural critics found revolutionary content in black secular song, but were skeptical when it came to black sacred music. Lawrence Gellert, probably the party's most enthusiastic champion of black music, thought the content of black religious music from the institutional church was essentially reactionary, but the form of the spiritual provided a foundation for revolutionary music. He explained secular songs with anticlerical undertones as a reaction to the black preacher, "a pompous, fat-

---

[11] William L. Patterson, "The Negro Question" (tsc., unpublished ms., April 1933), 1, microfilm, reel 2, International Labor Defense Papers (Schomburg Collection). Black Party leader Harry Haywood traced the roots of a "national Negro culture" in "ancient African civilization [and] Negro art and literature reflecting the environment of oppression of the Negroes in the United States." See Harry Haywood, "Against Bourgeois-Liberal Distortions of Leninism on the Negro Question in the United States," Communist 8, no. 9 (August 1930), 700; also Haywood, "The Theoretical Defenders of White Chauvinism in the Labor Movement," in The Communist Position on the Negro Question (New York, n.d.), 31.

[12] Michael Gold, "The Negro Reds of Chicago," Daily Worker, September 30, 1932.

[13] Harold Preece, "Folk Music of the South," New South 1, no. 2 (March 1938), 13.

headed, blow-hard parasite, prating meaningless platitudes about 'de Lawd and his By an' By Kingdom.'"[14] Gellert and others were far more interested in the way black party members transformed old spirituals into Communist anthems or secular protest songs. African-American Communists gave classics like "We Shall Not Be Moved" and "Give Me That Old Time Religion" new lyrics and completely new messages. In the latter, the verse was changed to "Give Me That Old Communist Spirit," and party members closed out each stanza with "It was good enough for Lenin, and it's good enough for me."[15] No matter what they thought of secular versus sacred music, all of these writers agreed that there was a common, identifiable, "pure Negro culture," and that culture was a genuine expression of the most submerged segment of the American proletariat.

By 1935, the Communists abandoned their self-determination slogan in order to build a "popular front" against fascism. Even the Comintern bracketed the Negro Question and pushed its American cadre to build alliances with liberals and mainstream labor leaders. Yet the idea that black folk culture was inherently rebellious never lost its power. In 1937, Richard Wright, then the Communist party's black literary giant, published his infamous "Blueprint for Negro Writing" in which he observed that "the Negro has a folklore which embodies the memories and hopes of his struggle for freedom."[16] But the party's quest to build alliances with the black intelligentsia added a new dimension to its appropriation and promotion of black culture. Suddenly, the "folk" were no longer the sole progenitor of rebellious black culture. The work of black artists across class lines had come to embody not only a people's desire for freedom but the best American democracy had to offer. During the Popular Front, the Communist party attempted to remake

---

[14] Philip Schatz, "Songs of the Negro Worker," *New Masses* 5, no. 12 (May 1930), 6–8; Lawrence Gellert, "Negro Songs of Protest," *New Masses* 6, no. 11 (April 1931), 6–8.

[15] *Daily Worker,* April 7, 1934; *Southern Worker,* July 1936. For examples of adaptations of "We Shall Not Be Moved," see *Labor Defender* 9, no. 11 (December 1933), 80; Robin D. G. Kelley, *Hammer and Hoe: Alabama Communists During the Great Depression* (Chapel Hill: University of North Carolina Press, 1990), 105.

[16] Richard Wright, "Blueprint for Negro Writing," *New Challenge* 1 (Fall 1937), 53–61.

itself as the genuine voice of America, Left New Deal Democrats, whose vision of a "Soviet America" emphasized interracialism. Black nationhood was dead. Communist critics, for example, promoted jazz as the most profoundly democratizing culture the nation possessed—an argument we now associate with ex-Communist Ralph Ellison. Jazz permeated Communist party events during the 1930s, and some of the first serious jazz critics got their start writing for *The Daily Worker* and other Communist publications. The Harlem CP formed an interracial "swing club," the Young Communist League (YCL) in New York sponsored a "Swing America" pageant at its 1939 convention, and an article in the *YCL Review* published the same year claimed that "Swing is as American as baseball and hot dogs. . . . There is a good deal of audience participation in swing, a kind of give and take and mutual inspiration for the musician and the crowd, a rough democratic air invading the sacred halls of music." Nine years later, Communist critic Sidney Finkelstein would take these ideas further, constructing a theory of jazz as deeply democratic, American, *and* an expression of black identity.[17]

The Communist press became one of the biggest advocates of black theater, music, dance, and the plastic arts during the late 1930s. As black artists began working for the federally funded Works Progress Administration, a dynamic black woman named Louise Thompson became the party's critical liaison linking black popular culture and Harlem's literati with Communist Popular Front politics. In 1938, for example, she and Langston Hughes organized the "Harlem Suitcase Theatre," sponsored by the International Workers Order, which produced works by black playwrights. The party's high visibility in antiracist causes attracted more than a few bigwigs in the black entertainment world. Count Basie, W. C. Handy, Lena Horne, Andy Razaf, and Canada Lee performed at Communist-organized benefits, and the circle of black writers orbiting the Communist left included Ralph Ellison, Sterling Brown, Chester Himes, Countee Cullen, Margaret Walker, Owen Dodson, Arna Bontemps, Frank Marshall Davis, Robert

---

[17] David Stowe, *Swing Changes: Big Band Jazz and New Deal America* (Cambridge, Mass.: Harvard University Press, 1994), 65; Sidney Finkelstein, *Jazz: A People's Music* (New York: International Publishers, 1988 [orig. 1948]).

Hayden, Melvin Tolson, Dorothy West, the pioneering cartoonist Ollie Har-rington, as well as the usual suspects, Hughes, McKay, and Wright.

No one connected to Communist circles played a more pivotal role in demonstrating the revolutionary potential of African-American expressive culture than Paul Robeson. Son of a prominent minister, all-American ath-lete, honors graduate of Rutgers University, star of stage and screen, Paul Robeson was on the road to being the richest, most famous Negro of the century. But in 1927, he and his wife, Eslanda Goode, moved to London, and during their twelve-year sojourn were radicalized by their face-to-face confrontation with European fascism as well as their meetings with British Socialists and future leaders of the African, Caribbean, and Asian anti-colonial movements. He and Eslanda also toured the Soviet Union, whose people and history he came to admire even if he harbored private doubts about Stalin and his policies. The fact that the Soviet Union offered ma-terial support to anticolonial movements and backed democratically elected Republican Spain against General Franco's Fascist-backed armies further endeared Robeson to Russia and the Left more broadly.[18]

This is only part of the story. As historian Sterling Stuckey convincingly argues, Robeson was drawn simultaneously toward a radical black cultural nationalism.[19] A product of the American racial order, Robeson needed no political lessons about racism or the plight of his people back home. Nor did he need to be lectured on the resilient spirit of black people and the culture they created to survive slavery and Jim Crow. What he did come to terms with in Europe was the deep cultural bond between Africa and its Diaspora. Robeson studied several African languages and planned to un-dertake a thorough study of West African "folk song and folklore.[20] He even understood himself to be "African," both culturally and spiritually, and he saw in black cultural values the foundation for a new vision of a

---

[18] Martin Bauml Duberman, *Paul Robeson* (New York: Knopf, 1989), 3–232.

[19] See Sterling Stuckey, *Slave Culture: Nationalist Theory and the Foundations of Black America* (New York: Oxford University Press, 1987), 303–58. To really understand Robe-son's radical politics, this is essential reading.

[20] The editors of Freedomways, *Paul Robeson: The Great Forerunner* (New York: In-ternational Publishers, 1998), 66.

new society, one that could emancipate not only black people but the entire West.

Indeed, Robeson's cultural analysis could have become the basis for a radical revision of the Communist party's idea of self-determination.[21] Even as he became more deeply attached to the Communist Party USA, he supported an independent black radical movement grounded in cultures and beliefs of the folk. As he wrote in his classic book *Here I Stand* (1958), "The power of spirit that our people have is intangible, but it is a great force that must be unleashed in the struggles of today. A spirit of steadfast determination, exaltation in the face of trials—it is the very soul of our people that has been formed through all the long and weary years of our march toward freedom. . . . That spirit lives in our people's songs—in the sublime grandeur of 'Deep River,' in the driving power of 'Jacob's Ladder,' in the militancy of 'Joshua Fit the Battle of Jericho,' and in the poignant beauty of all our spirituals."[22] That spirit, he insisted, was the key to the freedom of all of humanity, particularly in the United States. Historically, black people had expanded democracy and rescued the United States from undemocratic forces, and had served as something of the moral conscience of the nation. During the 1940s and 1950s, as the FBI, Senator Joe McCarthy, and various anti-Communist "witch hunters" dogged Robeson's every step, he reminded his audiences of "the important role which my people can and must play in helping to save America and the peoples of the world from annihilation and enslavement." He told black labor leaders in Chicago: "In the Civil War, hundreds of thousands of Negro soldiers who took up arms in the Union cause won, not only their own freedom—the freedom of the Negro people—but, by smashing the institution of slave

---

[21] The story of the party's shifting positions is too complicated to go into here. Suffice it to say that in 1946–47, when the party experienced its own internal crisis with the expulsion of General Secretary Earl Browder and his replacement with William Z. Foster, the "black belt" slogan was resurrected as a reassertion of the extreme left-wing, but it was hardly promoted and dropped out as quickly as it was readopted. See Harry Haywood, *Black Bolshevik: Autobiography of an Afro-American Communist* (Chicago: Liberation Press, 1978).

[22] Paul Robeson, *Here I Stand* (Boston: Beacon Press, 1988 [orig. 1958]), 100.

labor, provided the basis for the development of trade unions of free working men in America."[23]

In other words, black self-determination was not simply a matter of guar-
anteeing democratic rights or removing the barriers to black political and
economic power, nor was it a matter of creating a nation wherever black people found themselves to be an oppressed majority. It was about promoting
and supporting an independent black radical movement that could lead the
way for a revitalized international working-class assault on racial capitalism.
Once again, black people and their rich culture were in a position to become
a revolutionary vanguard for all American workers. Of course, Robeson was
simply refining a version of an ongoing idea promoted by the African Blood
Brotherhood, Claude McKay, Richard Wright, and others we've met along
the way. They all believed that it was their culture that gave the black movement its special insight and character. In many ways, Robeson drew on an
old, biblical tradition of "choseness" that stretched from nineteenth-century
black nationalists such as David Walker to W. E. B. DuBois to his later contemporaries such as Dr. Martin Luther King, Jr. Black folk were the "chosen
people," the soul of the nation, whose redemptive suffering would bring salvation. But Robeson's talk of black spirit or even Negro spirituals was not
necessarily rooted in the Bible. Rather, it came from his understanding of
African culture, the peculiar history of enslavement in the modern world,
and, most important, a critique of Western civilization.

It is this last point where much of the white Left parts company. White
Communists could embrace black folk and their culture as inherently revolutionary, and they could critique bourgeois culture for being reactionary in the
twentieth century (though they understood it as revolutionary in the eighteenth
century, the age of democratic revolutions). But to suggest that Europe suffered
a civilizational and spiritual crisis whose roots could be traced to the Enlightenment was a bit much. In a 1936 article titled "Primitives," Robeson took the
Enlightenment tradition to task in an implicit attempt to explain the rise of Fas-

---

[23] John Henrik Clarke, "Paul Robeson: The Artist as Activist and Social Thinker," in
Paul Robeson: The Great Forerunner, p. 198; Robeson, "Negro-Labor Unity for Peace,"
reprinted in *Paul Robeson: The Great Forerunner*, p. 216.

cism, which he saw as proof of "civilization's" utter failure. "A blind groping after Rationality," he mused, "resulted in an incalculable loss in pure Spirituality.
Mankind placed a sudden dependence on the part of his mind that was brain,
intellect, to the discountenance of that part that was sheer evolved instinct and
intuition; we grasped at the shadow and lost the substance . . . and now we are
not altogether clear what the substance was." The answer, he believed, was to
make art and spirituality primary to social life, as it had been in the ancient
world and as it continued to be in the folk cultures of Africa. He was convinced
that American Negroes were in a unique position to make this happen, not only
because they embodied many of the core cultural values from their ancestral
homeland but because they represented the most self-conscious force living in
the belly of the beast. They know the West and its culture; they know modernity and its limitations; their dreams of freedom could overturn a market-
driven, war-mongering rationality and give birth to a new humanity.[24]

Robeson's vision of what black culture looked and sounded like tended
to be open and elastic. He recognized that the core values transmitted from
the "folk" continued to reappear in various forms of music, dance, and plastic
arts critics might have called "modern" during the post–World War II generation. Not all of Robeson's comrades shared his flexibility of vision. A few writ-
ers/critics in party circles sought to amplify Robeson's ideas, but ended up
depicting the "folk" and their culture as a kind of artifact: they were the down-

---

[24] Stuckey, *Slave Culture*, 338–39. Robeson was not alone in his critical assessment
of Western civilization, especially in the aftermath of World War II. The horrors of Nazi
genocide forced all thinking people to take stock, including black intellectuals all over the
African Diaspora. A group of radical black intellectuals including W. E. B. DuBois, Aimé
Césaire, C. L. R. James, George Padmore, Ralph Bunche, Oliver Cox, and others, understood fascism not as some aberration from the march of progress, an unexpected right-
wing turn, but a logical development of Western civilization itself. They viewed Fascism
as a blood relative of slavery and imperialism, global systems rooted not only in capitalist
political economy but racist ideologies that were already in place at the dawn of modernity. DuBois made some of the clearest statements to this effect. In *The World and Africa*
(1947), he writes: "There was no Nazi atrocity—concentration camps, wholesale maim-
ing and murder, defilement of women or ghastly blasphemy of childhood—which Christian civilization or Europe had not long been practicing against colored folk in all parts of
the world in the name of and for the defense of a Superior Race born to rule the world."
W. E. B. DuBois, *The World and Africa* (New York: International Publishers, 1947), 23;
see also, Robin D. G. Kelley, "Foreword" to *Aimé Césaire, Discourse on Colonialism*, trans.
by Joan Pinkham (New York: Monthly Review Press, 2000), 19–21.

trodden rural masses with one foot out of slavery whose art consisted almost entirely of spirituals and workaday songs. Although the party consistently attacked film and theater productions known for stereotyping African Americans (e.g., *Song of the South, Gone With the Wind*, and *Porgy and Bess*), many Communist critics continued to hold on to the idea that a key source of black resistance lay in a pristine, unpolluted rural folk culture. One of the most interesting essays that, on the surface at least, seemed to support this view of the folk was written by Abner W. Berry, a Harlem-based black Communist leader who joined the party in 1929. Published in the CP's arts journal, *Masses and Mainstream,* in 1953, Berry's essay "The Future of Negro Music" was a scathing attack on bebop—the latest development in modern jazz. He argued that the music of Charlie Parker, Dizzy Gillespie, and Thelonious Monk constituted a "dead end" for black music because these artists simply engaged in mindless improvisation that placed more emphasis on individual expression than the conditions of black life. Bebop, in his view, was divorced from "the people," more at home in white middle-class circles than among the black working class. As an alternative, he called on readers to listen to spirituals, gospel music, even the blues—in other words, pure expressions of the black working class. And, of course, he praised Robeson as one of the few musicians still committed to the authentic music of the black masses. While it is true that Robeson dismissed jazz as "decadent" during the 1930s, by the 1940s and 1950s he had had a change of heart. Indeed, he had come to admire Parker, Gillespie, and Monk, and he even said, "For my money, modern jazz is one of the most important musical things there is in the world."[25]

It may seem ironic that a Jewish Communist critic, Sidney Finkelstein, came much closer to Robeson's position than did Abner Berry. He defended bebop as part of black music's long revolutionary tradition in his *Jazz: A People's Music* (1948). Black music, he argued, "expresses hope and struggle for freedom, the vitality which enables a people to wrest joy out of misery and to assert the triumph of human beings over the obstacles which would

---

[25] Abner W. Berry, "The Future of Negro Music," *Masses and Mainstream* 6, no. 2 (February 1953): 15–22; Duberman, *Paul Robeson,* 177.

grind them down." In other words, bebop, like the spirituals, was not mind-less improvisation but had a story to tell. "In the spirituals," Finkelstein continued, "it was the love of freedom and the struggle against slavery. In the young musician's music of bebop, it is not hard to find the bitter experiences of the American Negro soldier in the past war, Jim-Crowed and treated as a second-class citizen, while he was told that the war was one for democ-racy. . . ." Like Robeson, Finkelstein regarded jazz as an expression of free-dom and humanity for *all* people, which is precisely the power of black culture: "[B]ecause the Negro people speak so powerfully in jazz, it has be-come loved and admired by all peoples. It discloses the qualities, universal to all people, of anger at oppression and triumph over misery."[26]

Here is appropriation in the grandest sense: the employment of black cul-ture in the service of emancipating the world. Perhaps Abner Berry's real cri-tique, disguised as an attack on bebop, was about his sense of discomfort over who identifies with and "owns" the music? After all, his point was that bebop was disconnected from the black masses and more or less the property of alienated white middle-class youth. The alienation of "White Negroes," as writer Norman Mailer called them in his infamous 1957 *Dissent* article, was the real dead end; the bop-identified Beat generation were not going to make a revolution. So for Berry, perhaps his critique was not a simple matter of fetishizing the folk. He was concerned about the *erasure* of the folk and de-politicizing black culture at the expense of black struggle. Interestingly, he would eventually leave the party in 1957 and, influenced largely by Malcolm X, become a leading black revolutionary nationalist. (He joined the African Peoples Party, changed his name to Baba Sufu, and went on to work with the African Liberation Support Committee and the Black Workers for Justice.)[27]

Berry's position shared much in common with that of another one of his black comrades, poet Ramon Durem. A veteran of the Spanish Civil War, Durem also left the Communist party in the 1950s, deeply disappointed over its

---

[26] Finkelstein, *Jazz: A People's Music,* 19.

[27] James Wrenn, "Abner Winston Berry," in *Encyclopedia of the American Left,* 2nd ed., edited by Mari Jo Buhle, Paul Buhle, and Dan Georgakas (New York: Oxford University Press, 1998), 85.

failure to back fully an independent black movement. "At the end of World War Two," he wrote, "I discovered that even the white radicals were not interested in a radical solution to the Negro Question."[28] Like Berry, he was not impressed with the generation of "White Negroes" who consumed black culture as an act of rebellion. His poem "Hipping the hip," a critique of the Beat generation and its false claim to radicalism, called on the "real" revolutionaries to look elsewhere for models: namely, the world where real revolutions were erupting:

Juice
is no use
and H [heroin]
don't pay

I guess revolution
is the only way

Blues—is a tear
bop—a fear
of reality.
There's no place to hide
in a horn
Chinese may be lame
but they ain't tame

Mau Mau only got a five-tone scale
but when it comes to Freedom, Jim—
they wail!

dig?[29]

---

[28] Ray Durem, *Take No Prisoners* (London: P. Bremean, 1971), 3.
[29] Ibid., 8.

Durem wasn't the only one to look to the Third World for models of revolution. In fact, the CPUSA's decline—the result of Cold War repression, internecine fighting, and unpopular Soviet policies—coincided with the African independence movement, the Chinese Revolution, the Cuban Revolution, and the hope of a real Third World liberation movement beholden to neither the U.S. nor the Soviet Union.[30] Inspired by these global developments, black radicals began to draw from the deep well of Third World cultures in order to fashion a new style politics, even as white radicals appropriated African-American culture. Dashikis as well as Chinese peasant outfits began to appear on the urban landscape, especially in places like Harlem. As early as 1962, critic-activist-ex-Communist Harold Cruse predicted that in the coming years "Afro-Americans . . . will undoubtedly make a lot of noise in militant demonstrations, cultivate beards and sport their hair in various degrees of la mode au naturel, and tend to be cultish with African- and Arab-style dress."[31] But the change was not simply a matter of style. Cruse seemed to have his finger on the pulse when he suggested that the Cuban, Chinese, and African revolutions influenced radical thought among black Americans. In the same 1962 essay, Cruse wrote that the new generation looked to the former colonial world for leadership: Already they had a pantheon of modern heroes—Lumumba, Kwame Nkrumah, Sékou Touré in Africa; Fidel Castro in Latin America; Malcolm X, the Muslim leader, in New York; Robert Williams in the South; and Mao Tse-tung in China. These

---

[30] The impact of these events on African-American politics is well documented. For a discussion of how these developments in Africa reshaped postwar black politics in the U.S., see especially von Eschen, *Race Against Empire;* Plummer, *Rising Wind;* Bernard M. Magubane, *The Ties That Bind: African-American Consciousness of Africa* (Trenton, N.J.: Africa World Press, 1987); Joseph E. Harris, ed., *Global Dimensions of the African Diaspora* (Washington, D.C.: Howard University Press, 1982); Immanuel Geiss, *The Pan-African Movement* (London: Methuen and Co., 1974); Robert Weisbord, *Ebony Kinship: Africa, Africans, and the Afro-American* (Westport, Conn.: Greenwood Press, 1973); P. Olisanwuch Esedebe, *Pan-Africanism: The Idea and Movement, 1776–1963* (Washington, D.C.: Howard University Press, 1982); Van Gosse, *Where the Boys Are: Cuba, Cold War America and the Making of a New Left* (London: Verso, 1993), 147–48; Komozi Woodard, A *Nation within a Nation: Amiri Baraka (LeRoi Jones) and Black Power Politics* (Chapel Hill: University of North Carolina Press, 1998), 52–63.

[31] Harold Cruse, *Rebellion or Revolution?* (New York: Morrow, 1968), 73.

men seemed heroic to the Afro-Americans not because of their political philosophy, but because they were either former colonials who achieved complete independence, or because, like Malcolm X, they dared to look the white community in the face and say: "We don't think your civilization is worth the effort of any black man to try to integrate into." This, to many Afro-Americans, was an act of defiance that was truly revolutionary.[32]

Sometimes style and substance came together. Quotations from Chairman Mao Tse-tung, better known as the "Little Red Book," made a tremendous impact in black radical circles. The idea that a pocket-sized book of pithy quotes and aphorisms could address a range of subjects from ethical behavior, revolutionary thought and practice, economic development, philosophy, etc., appealed to many black activists, irrespective of political allegiance. The "Little Red Book" prompted a cottage industry of miniature books of quotations compiled expressly for black militants. *The Black Book,* edited by Earl Ofari Hutchinson (with assistance from Judy Davis) was a case in point. Published by the Radical Education Project (circa 1970), *The Black Book* was a compilation of brief quotes from W. E. B. DuBois, Malcolm X, and Frantz Fanon that addressed a range of issues related to domestic and world revolution. The resemblance to quotations from Chairman Mao was striking: chapters titles included "Black Culture and Art," "Politics," "Imperialism," "Socialism," "Capitalism," "Youth," "The Third World," "Africa," "On America," and "Black Unity." Ofari's introduction placed black struggle in a global context and called for revolutionary ethics and "spiritual as well as physical unification of the Third World."

As we all know by now, new generations of white New Left radicals often found their inspiration in the black freedom movement, especially in the South. They were moved by the freedom songs and the power of black worship, they emulated the styles and speech of black youth, and they turned to groups such as the Black Panther Party as the new vanguard (and, not to

---

[32] Ibid., 73.

mention, a model of masculinity—however dysfunctional—for white men). There were young white radical women in head wraps and African prints talking about revolution, or young white men sporting chemically induced Afros, but for the most part white New Leftists simply expressed, as historian/participant Mark Naison recalled, an "emotional identification with African-American culture."[33]

Yet while many white New Leftists also read Mao, Malcolm X, and Frantz Fanon, and praised black activists for their militancy and courage, the growth of cultural nationalism remained a source of tension between blacks and whites on the Left. The Progressive Labor Party, a Marxist-Leninist party with roots in Maoism, attacked the entire Black Arts Movement and its theoreticians, calling them "bourgeois" and reactionary. " 'Cultural nationalism,' " the PLP argued in its newspaper, "is not only worshipping the most reactionary aspects of African history. It even goes so far as measuring one's revolutionary commitment by the clothes that are being worn! This is part of the 'Black awareness.' " The PLP dismissed black cultural nationalists as petty bourgeois businessmen who sold the most retrograde aspects of African culture to the masses and "exploit Black women—all in the name of 'African culture' and in the name of 'revolution.' " The same PLP editorial castigated the Black Arts Movement for "teaching about African Kings and Queens, African 'empires.' There is no class approach—no notice that these Kings, etc., were oppressing the mass of African people." Likewise, in 1973 the Communist Party (Marxist-Leninist) (not to be confused with the Communist Party USA) sharply criticized the Black Arts Movement for "delegitimizing the genuine national aspirations of Black people in the U.S. and to substituting African counter-culture for anti-imperialist struggle."

Certainly, white people were not the sole source of these critiques; the PLP, CP(ML), and other new-wave, "anti-revisionist" Marxist-Leninist organizations had their share of black members who attacked all manifestations of cultural nationalism. And they were not always off in their assessments re-

---

[33] Mark D. Naison, *White Boy: A Memoir* (Philadelphia: Temple University Press, 2002), 112.

garding the class politics of the movements they disparaged. But such criticisms did set a dangerous precedent. Predominantly white Left movements went from accepting African-American culture as inherently revolutionary to becoming a kind of cultural gatekeeper. They felt emboldened to decide what aspects of black culture were authentically black and therefore revolutionary. If anything, they violated the very principles of "self-determination" for black people, even as they promoted the slogan in their rhetoric. It is quite possible that their harsh criticisms and deep discomfort with African Americans claiming to be "Afrikans" revealed a long-standing and continuing love affair with the "folk." The idealized folk, after all, were familiar, naturally wise as opposed to well-read, spontaneous rather than calculating. Their melodies were familiar, deeply American even in their vernacular blackness, and they sang of justice and freedom and forgiveness by and by. The folk didn't speak Swahili or Yoruba, they didn't talk about reparations or leaving this place for the Motherland, they didn't call themselves New Afrikans, they didn't read poetry chanting "death to whitey," and, most important, they didn't close the door on their good white friends.

If this long-standing love affair with the "folk" even partly explains the growing tension between the Marxist-Leninist Left and black radicals, I can't prove it. Besides, the predominantly white Left has always been deeply divided on the Negro Question, and they continue to be to this very day. The problem is, of course, that most Leftists think of the race problem as a *Negro* Question rather than a *White* Question. Black intellectuals within Communist and other Left circles tried to make this point by convincing their comrades to pay attention to black culture, not for special insight into racial oppression but for a vision of human emancipation. While these same black intellectuals were not immune to making essentialist claims about African-American culture, as we have seen, they had no intention of becoming a fetish of the Left. On the contrary, they saw and heard in black culture utopian and visionary elements that could lay the basis for a new revolutionary movement. Perhaps one might characterize this as a form of "appropriation," but I think "embrace" is a better word. To these black radical theorists, to embrace black culture meant to embrace the people who created that culture and to fully embrace their liberation; it was never simply a matter of consumption.

And so we come full circle, back to the mic-hogging, holier-than-thou Leftists who believe they know "us" better than we know ourselves. I don't doubt their sincerity or their commitment to the liberation of black people and all oppressed people. But they continue to view us as objects rather than subjects. What they need to do is to pay more attention to the people whose culture they are so quick to praise for its unwavering resistance to capitalism and imperialism. Perhaps then they might be more willing to give up the mic for a moment, listen to the victims of democracy sing their dreams of a new world, and take notes on how to fight for their own freedom.

4. Pimp Notes on Autonomy

BY BETH COLEMAN

For R. D. G. Kelley, pimpologist and friend, and Joe Wood, Jr.

IF ONE HAD TO SAY IT FAST, the slave economy in America produced the American pimp. Pimping may be the second-oldest profession in the world, but it was in America first that the pimp became a black pop star. It is the particular undying racial swagger of the pimp as he has become famous in America that I pursue here.

Proposition one: What if a fetish is not a thing or a person, but a job?

Proposition two: You are free.

PIMPOLOGY

"At one time we lived on the coast of Africa that was called Mauritania. We were a proud family. We were people of dignity, people of structure. The Canary Islands is where they actually was making them slaves. By the time they got over to America the Europeans was so impressed with the beautiful black sister that he would often rape her. What happened was the male African got wise, 'What does he do to you when you are with him?' 'He makes me have sex and offers gifts like pork chops.' Being that we was in a precarious situation, being that we were in a negative disposition the African at that time who was a slave, he said, 'Alright, what you do is ask him for two pork chops,' you know what I'm saying, and the system of manipulation began for survival. The European, the slave master, knew that this was transpiring but he did not want to do anything about this because he was so into her he would get her at any cost, but his wife did not condone it and his children did not condone it, so it was a secretive movement. We being an intelligent people, we knew that it was happing any way so we had to benefit from it. At that time the white men called us wimps. In 1865 Lincoln freed the slaves, the African kings and queens. And once he freed them what happened was we remembered the things that had transpired during the plantation system so we began to execute certain elements. We would tell the European that I would connect you. They wanted to continue their barter system, the female for the money. People would see these brothers back in the day driving these horse and carriages. They thought they were driving these carriages for the master, but they realized these are not wimps, these are pimps. We went from wimps to pimps. From horsy backs to now modern day Cadillacs."[1]

I quote Pimping Ken from the video documentary *Pimpology*, of which he is executive producer. Pimping Ken breaks down the classic components of pimping like a banker with lyrical flow. He reduces the economy to two pre-conditions of capital: property and autonomy. In *Pimpology*, Pimping Ken draws a portrait of himself as a self-made man in the tradition of Benjamin Franklin and Iceberg Slim. In this case, he substitutes the printing press for the video camera. The "written" form for pimping in a postmedia landscape is video, website, DVD, and modeling agencies, forms which have become as indelible as ink. Like the rest of the culture, pimp culture dubs itself via virtual portals. What used to be an informal economy now has shelf space at Tower Vidco. To state the obvious, the pimp video exist because there is a market for them.

Post-gangster rap, the call for verisimilitude in black thug life is clearly demonstrated. When the pop star R. Kelly graced the cover of *Vibe* in

---

[1] *Pimpology*, a Ken Ivory film, executive producers Ken Ivory, Father Devine, Jarrod Cook, 2001.

November 2000, a story on pimp life also received a cover line. Magazines such as *F. E. D. S.* and *Murder Dog* publish monthly escapades into the real criminal-minded, creating a new order of penitentiary pinups: the mythic stories of "street life" told in the first person by the pimp stars themselves. The Hughes brothers' 1999 indie documentary *American Pimp* debuted at the Sundance Film Festival to controversy. The same year, "This American Life," the acclaimed National Public Radio show, ran a piece called "Pimp Anthropology" devoted to the nuances of the pimping game. Pimps, with the help of popular culture, have made a fetish of their business. A business which is, of course, based upon the appropriation of a person for commodity.

Pimping in the twenty-first century reflects a porous relationship between an illegal or at least illicit commodity and the hot glow of publicity. The media intersection expands the game in manners ingenious and diabolical. The video camera takes a profession with territory but no boundaries (sometimes a pimp has got to take his bitches on the road) into a space of accelerated circulation. The prostitutes don't know when they are on camera, thus video creates a tool for extended surveillance.[2] For the pimp, media extends control. In turn, covert operations extend his domain. The clandestine footage used to keep order functions equally well in the form of a calling card ("If you want an intro or outro, talk to Pimping Ken, I'll put you in the game"). *Pimpology* is unmediated (raw) but self-edited. It is a moving image ad for a culture of incarceration. The thing being advertised is not the women but the pimp himself.

Pimp theory lies at the intersection of fetish and pathology. The first really is external, such as a shoe, a show, or an exhibition, while the latter

---

[2] The home movies are a form of entertainment and punishment, as described by Pimping Ken: " 'Bitch, I don't want you to do nothing I don't tell you to do.' But that bitch is on tape recorder. Scoop her like ice cream. Once you play that tape for that ho I guarantee you, you won't have no more problems with that ho. These are some mutherfuker rules that I really should not be telling. I'm giving you mutherfukers some raw ass game" (*Pimpology*). Pedagogy has always been a critical issue in black communities and the pimps "give back" in these videos by providing instructional material for the aspiring young player.

is externalized, like pimping. And that is why pimps must wear good shoes, handmade genuine leather from Italy. Because the pimp is both. He is a parody of propriety, a levered mechanism, an electronic Negro. The essential overvaluation of the object, the black fetish, is his trump card. "Daddy, we sure been humping for you" is the siren's call in this the recapitulation of mastery. To play the black fetish one has to make one's peace with our man Osiris, he who rocks the double affirmation, who is kissing cousins with the dog-headed god—the dead dog is transformed into the top dog.

It is worth noting that the women who appear in *Pimpology* are silent, with the exception of an entrepreneurial "model" who gives the viewer a sample of a girl-on-girl moment that seems like a parody of sexual pleasure, low production values not excepting. The women are shiny, frosted, boosted, and bleached. They walk, they dance, they sex, but nobody home. In a sense, this is progress, as the industry organizes itself, proliferates, and celebrates itself. You can see the pimp balls and pimp award ceremonies much in the same style as the Oscars or music awards, just more razzle-dazzle (*bling bling*) to the participants.

You're a star, baby.

The fame of black people possesses the retro glamour of a Marlene Dietrich. It is a fame based on the foresight that race does not exist anymore, which does not necessarily make a body right. The definition of a fetish is an essential overvaluation of the object. It is a thing, often an inappropriate thing, like a shoe or hair, substituted for the person. In a tradition with Scheherazade or Salome, in her films Dietrich mastered her own representation. She did that iconic thing so well that Dietrich became a fetish of a fetish, a sign of a sign. *M* is for machine, the thing that turns you on. The "essential overvaluation" of the object is the basis of such performances as *Blue Angel, Thriller, Pimpin Ain't Easy,* and *Elephant Shit*. With Dietrich it was a performance about total control. For the black superstar, on the flip side, you are that famously abject thing. Whether old or young, rich or poor, you are famous for being invisible, and already misappropriated. (Criminality and black identity get linked from the getty up.) The pimp is the boss because he masters the art of black representation. He's a veritable signpost for black fame in his shiny shoes.

When Iceberg Slim wrote famously of pimp theory in 1969, what Slim made clear is that the sexy part of pimping is not the sex, but the control. He writes, "A pimp is happy when his whores giggle. He knows they are still asleep."[3] In the incredible opening paragraphs of the memoir, Slim describes the perils of leaving oneself wide open to interpretation. His nose inflamed from the "gangster" he just snorted, tired, and psychically leaky, he needs to stop up the holes in his persona. (The pimp is anal if nothing else.) To get himself together, Slim performs a ritual transformation that is repeated throughout the book. He disciples his whores by, uh, metaphorically speaking, tearing them a new asshole. The right of mastery is dedicated in the most mundane of manners: a car full of dirty, tired people, creeping through the early morning. But what is played out for the pimp, at the expense of the women, is the reassertion of right. He lays down the law.

Big Daddy Kane, the ur-pimp hip-hopper, rhymed, "I'll tax that ass like the government." The point is, you are the boss. Like the government, like inevitability, that ass will be taxed. The unchallenged patron rapper of pimping is the California wordsmith Too $hort. A featured interviewee in *Pimpology*, Too $hort tells the boys that he himself was turned out by a grade-school pimp when he was just a little Short: "[The guy] was nine years old and he said he was a pimp. I said, 'You nine, how you a pimp?' He said, 'People pay me to talk.'" You have to be a bad ass to get paid just for your breath. The magic trick of pimping is to make something from nothing. He is a student of power, a classic trickster. The pimp sees an impossible situation, then finds a way to maximize it. Eldridge Cleaver, Black Panther, author, and politician, wed sexual violence to black liberation. In doing so, he played a trump card that electrified the nation.[4] Get that second pork chop, brother.

---

[3] Iceberg Slim, *Pimp: The Story of My Life* (Los Angeles: Holloway House Publishing Co., 1996), pp.11–12.

[4] No doubt, the Black Panthers were (a) supersexy and (b) had some pretty Stone Age

America did not invent pimping, but it did invent the famous black pimp. He has run rampant through Europe as the devil or another figure of temptation for ages. In the Americas, due to the devilry of slave culture, he was made manifest. The black pimp produces such glee in his audience precisely because he cross-wires the machine. For him to be the master is a local revolution unto itself; for him to trade in a localized zone of human labor is the twist of the screw to the point of giddiness. The irony is that if he does his job well, in order to become a free agent, he must reproduce a peculiarly limited mode of bondage. For, of course, the commodity of pimping is sex. It is a commodity rendered *lifestyle* by the pimp, formatted across much the same blueprint as the plantation system. One might say pimps are simply repeating a scene of mastery dear to the history of Western culture. Fast-food slavery for a commodities market. Instead of selling the whole person, it sells but a part. It is the business of dealing with people reduced to parts at which the pimp excels. The pimp is the one who shines up some dark thing and takes her to the market. He maintains control of his stable by circumscribing all behavior, shuttering her down to size.

---

thoughts on the position of women in the revolution (prone). Nonetheless, the Panthers, and Black Nationalism in general, made the dangerous move in America of public black self-determination. Fundamentally, nationalism calls for the self-recognition of a people. Leather jackets and machismo aside, this is revolution. The pimp evacuates politics for style, which is a maneuver far more conducive to longevity. Leather jackets and machismo are the only things left. The glossy image of pimps that suffuse magazines, music, and Hollywood makes unintelligible the aspects of enforcement, terrorism, and violence that go with the business. A whore is broken. Pimp economy reaffirms the historically established Western mode of mastery: in mastering oneself, there is an indivisible urge to master others. In fact, the pimp is celebrated for doing it so well, reducing the figure of mastery to the crucial bits. The question is not so much, How does a punisher get to be king (that seems like standard inherited behavior)? No, the question is, Are there other role models that actually work in the representation of mastery *without* pimping?

CODE NOIR: THE HISTORICAL FETISH
OF SLAVE PROPERTY

Even from the point of view of early colonial travelogues, sexual repression was not an aspect of West African culture, but self-discipline was. Europeans mistook for lasciviousness in Africans the same qualities of self-determination hailed in liberal theory in the models of Greek and Roman republicanism. Sex and choice had not yet been invented in European culture. The European creation of primitivism in the literature and philosophy of the eighteenth century one might understand as a strategy to contextualize difference by making it ahistorical, thus nonthreatening. When we get to a formal theory of the fetish in the late nineteenth century it is not a coincidence that this same difference is ascribed to the dark continents and primitive peoples to provide an analogy for sexual perversion. In the fantasy of the Industrial Revolution and the destiny of the twentieth century all are subjected to mechanization (rendered object or fetish). Slavery had been a preview to what it's like to be a machine. And that subjection to the inhuman became a national obsession.

The *Code Noir,* a conglomeration of loosely assembled laws from early Spanish and French colonial endeavors, as well as strands retained from Roman slave law, established in the late seventeenth century the basic outlines that would govern black slavery in America through the nineteenth century. The *Code* attempted to address, as all slave law does, the classical anxiety of holding a person property. It is also, I would argue, a legal history that tells the story of how black became a fetish. I quote historian David Brion Davis in his description of the *Code*:

The capacity to marry was closely related to the capacity to make
contracts, own property, and hold offices or commissions, all of which
were specifically denied by the *Code Noir.* As early as 1623 Bermuda
prohibited Negroes from exchanging goods for tobacco without the

consent of their owners; and within a century British colonies from
Connecticut to Barbados had evolved an elaborate system of police
regulations which required Negroes to have a pass or ticket, signed by
their masters, for buying or selling goods. These measures, which were
designed to curtail theft, were a tacit admission that a slave might act
as his master's agent.[5]

As Davis points out, it is the possibility that the slave can *stand in* for
the master, i.e., be his agent or accurate representative, that reminds the
lawmakers why there is need for the law in the first place. One rarely fears
that one's cat or horse will pay for the groceries or sleep with one's wife. It
is the slave's ability to mimic the gestures of agency that make him the most
helpful of tools and the most dangerous. ("People pay me to talk.") The pro-
hibition against slave marriage is a critical point in dehumanization and the
"ruin" of slave mores. To allow a slave to marry recognizes agency and right
to contract—it would make the slave too close to the citizen. Of course,
slaves did marry and some masters blessed the unions, but the *law* went
unaltered. The fundamental shift between American slavery and the history
of world slavery is that in the New World, slavery was not a caste but a
race. All of the weight of the *Code Noir* would come to be justified not
upon "rightful" conquest but a racially organized holy mandate, and, by the
late eighteenth century, science. The basis of slavery shifts from social condition to genetic precondition. In the growing black population of the
colonies, and the growing imbalance of power between slave and master
class, the legal system and social custom moved further away from the slave
as subject by reinforcing the slave as property. That the use of black slaves
as sexual slaves became part of a black-market economy was an event
preestablished by laws such as the *Code Noir*. Slavery in the United States
created an economic and social order. What it also reflected was a cathec-
tic relationship to blackness.

---

[5] David Brion Davis, *The Problem of Slavery in Western Culture* (Ithaca, N.Y.: Cornell
University Press, 1966), p. 253.

Skin can't really be a fetish because it is a whole, not a piece. But color, like class, can be. "I go for maids." "I dig black girls." They are equivalent statements regarding desire for a type, not a one. In 1909, sitting in Vienna, Freud wrote that everyone is subject to perversion. "A certain degree of fetishism is thus habitually present in normal love," he wrote in *Three Essays on the Theory of Sexuality*. The distinction he draws between normal and broken is expressed as a difference of scale. You have tipped the scales once a lady's garter can actually replace the lady herself. This kind of mistake is characterized as a sexual perversion. What the *Code Noir* and other such documents institute is the serial repetition of taking the lady for a garter: slave law validates the condensation of a person into an intimate object quickened only by the desire of the master. This, one might say, is a social perversion. Fundamentally, a person is an unsuitable fetish. A fetish, by definition, has to be a thing. The specific and finite (personal perversion) is directed toward the public and general (a cultural mandate). One can say then that the overcompensation and overinvestment that historically characterize slavery can be considered a kind of fetishist behavior.[6] For black people to be treated that way was not just wrong, it was pathological.

Examples of race as a national pathology pervade the legal and political history of the country. A 1790 slave law stated that not only must slaves submit themselves to the usage of their masters, but slaves were also compelled to submit to the will of any white person encountered. That's anybody who counted (universal suffrage based on universal suffering). No one would allow a law that said not only you but also your neighbors had a right to treat your horse in a niggardly manner, yet that applied to bondsmen. Blacks had to be indentured in duplicate. There was a demand for a public, universal interpretation of blackness in order to mandate slavery. Subjugation was rendered racial terrorism. After emancipation the

---

[6] In psychoanalysis's history of sexuality, the urge toward mastery is the same as the urge toward pleasure. In the child it is described as an autoerotic mechanism driven, primarily, by cruelty. Pity develops later. Baby cruelty, though, is preconscious, and in that sense without intentionality or responsibility. What we find in American slavery are conditions of mastery where the instinct remains unchecked. It is an externalized structure that stimulates the option to ill.

bondsman, who had value for his owner, was transformed into a creature of no value. Noble or pitiable was the best paternalism could get you, forget about the forty acres and a mule. Blacks were no longer available as property, but their symbolic stature under Jim Crow was amplified: Slavery is no longer the bête noire, black people are. One's presence is built on a social structure that involves one's absence. In the reconstruction of the invisible black subject—invisible still but no longer a slave, perhaps just a problem—one discovers that the culture needs a solid black surface on which to project itself.

The machine by which blackness is produced in America does not rely on the genitals or teeth or hands but the whole thing. There is no particularity to the object (this shoe or this ribbon or this garter), only the generic position holder of black. Instead of a small thing being substituted for the whole person, as in a normal perversion, in this case the person is shuttered down. Once emancipated, black agency must remain a black-market item in order for mastery to be able to respect itself in the morning. Black agency has historical material impact, yet it is invisible. You can do everything in the world if you are invisible. (Juanita Moore can slip into an all-white fancy theater in *Imitation of Life*. Because no one sees her, she can walk in the front door.) And you can do nothing that remains. When Ralph Ellison writes, "I recognize no American culture which is not the partial creation of black people,"[7] one might understand him literally. The early colonial slave trade was the *key element* in the speed, agricultural choices, development of market, and overall economy of the conquest of the Americas. America might have been found without slaves, but it could not have been conquered. For the history of black people in America to have had profound impact yet to remain profoundly invisible fits again into a pimp economy. It is an economy of pleasure based on an economy of pain.

---

[7] Ralph Ellison, *Ralph Ellison: a Collection of Critical Essays* (Englewood Cliffs, N.J.: Prentice-Hall, 1974), p. 44.

RESISTANCE IS FUTILE: SLAVE FETISH
AND THE URGE TO MASTERY

Black pleasure becomes a real problem for black people when it is generally understood that blacks are always having fun. Black is synonymous with pleasured, rhythmic, cool, and if you can't pull that off while maintaining your day job (chillin'), then you're failing the race. The logic is one of association: black pleasure is more pleasure because black pain has been, systematically, more pain. Black Love and Black Paranoia exist in equal parts, as the dynamics of black mastery are still unreconciled. Even Colin Powell, the dean of mastery, reflects for the country in mixed proportions Black Love and Black Paranoia.

Cultural critic Saidiya Hartman has argued that the black body represents the body in pain. Translated into psychosexual terms, she explains that pain tends to be someone else's pleasure.

> I have chosen not to reproduce [Frederick] Douglass's account of the beating of Aunt Hester in order to call attention to the ease with which such scenes are usually reiterated, the casualness with which they are circulated, and the consequences of this routine display of the slave's ravaged body . . . and especially because they reinforce the spectacular character of black suffering.[8]

Unlike Dietrich, black people are famous for representing suffering. Given those conditions, Hartman refuses to represent. Her argument is that the terms of representation in relation to the history of black people in America are a setup. They have been imposed. In her study she looks at scenes of antebellum black pleasure: the coffle (slave market parades), the plantation

---

[8] Saidiya V. Hartman, *Scenes of Subjection: Terror, Slavery and Self-Making in Nineteenth-Century America* (Oxford: Oxford University Press, 1997), p. 3.

holidays, and minstrelsy. Pleasure, one would think, is for the good of the slave, just like anybody else. Black pleasure, Hartman argues, is subsumed by the pleasure of the master. Hilarity or pain, sexuality or humility, they are interchangeable experiences of terrorism in this economy.

Pimp theory understands that one cannot refuse representation. The scene of mastery in Frederick Douglass's work is required reading, despite Hartman's caution, for it predicts the future that gives us Iceberg Slim, Big Daddy Kane, Too $hort, *Sweet Sweetback, The Mac,* and Pimping Ken. Mastery is a tough job, but somebody's got to do it. The former slave and father of black American public discourse, Douglass would write in 1855, "The slave is a subject, subjected by others; the slaveholder is a subject, but he is the author of his own subjection."[9] Douglass describes a structure of subjectivity by which one comes into being. The terms are emptied of racial category; rather, they are generic. In a sense, anybody could fill either position. In his analysis of authority and authorship, Douglass points to the need for the slave to bend mastery to his service.

Pimp theory is a formal readdress of the mechanism of mastery even as it is a form of repetition compulsion. It relies on the double spin, playing the black fetish. It is a philosophy that states that a priori the consolidation of power happens—with or without your consent. Pimp theory says, "We being an intelligent people, we knew that it was happing any way so we had to benefit from it." After planning an escape by water and land with his comrades on the Freeland plantation, Douglass was finally returned to Baltimore as an overly independent, skilled, difficult Negro. One day he wrote himself a note that explained he was a sailor traveling for his owner along such-and-such a route. He then put on a sailor's uniform and took the train to New York. Pimping it, Douglass rode the wheels of steel to freedom. He went from horsy back to Cadillac.

What one finds in the legacy of African-American letters is an ongoing fascination with the structure of mastery. Ellison's Invisible Man breaks

---

[9] Frederick Douglass, *My Bondage and My Freedom* (New York: Arno Press, 1968), p. 69.

down the social contract: "Responsibility rests upon recognition, and recognition is a form of agreement." All the big dogs understand that rhetorically you're in a double bind when engaging mastery: agency calls for representation in order to be recognized, yet black had no public agency. If you are outside the economy, you are free to play any card in the deck. In the pimp discovery of America, the joker's wild. Pimp theory is to be that thing so thoroughly for your audience (whores, patrons, colleagues) that one is able to rob the man and have him thank you for it. That is the magic trick, the moment of transformation, and that's why he's a Black Nationalist hero. The initiative is to avoid crawling like a dog and, indeed, become the top dog. And now you know why the little girls love L'il Bow Wow. The pimp perfects that peculiarly black American skill to hide in plain sight. One's life becomes quite literary on account of that trait. You are a purloined letter, the missing phallus and missing link, activating the troublesomeness of a sign of a sign. Everyone wants my simian drugs. One exploits perversion and violence, terms that already resonate in the precinct of "black." The pimp by mastering himself is thus free to exploit exploitation. Pimp theory says some forms of adoration are necessary. The serious limitation on pimp theory as a liberation ideology is that it must reproduce the structure from which it hails. Pimping is not the only form of black agency to exist during slavery and to prosper in a nation with a racial policy. It is, though, one of the most famous forms of black representation because it reaffirms the logic of mastery.

5. ThugGods:
Spiritual Darkness and Hip-Hop

BY MELVIN GIBBS

"I am a Thug, my father and grandfather were Thugs, and I have Thugged with many." —BUHRAM JEMADAR, NOTORIOUS THUG LEADER

"The 'Five Percenters' are made up of neighborhood groups of young Negro teenagers who have no respect for law and order." —FROM FBI FILE 157-6-34, DATE 8-26-66

"Everybody knows the devil is black." —SPOKEN TO THE AUTHOR BY SOMEONE WHO SHOULD'VE KNOWN BETTER

WHO OR WHAT IS A THUG? Some would say any generic brown-skinned male with baggy jeans hung low, exposed boxers, a wife-beater T-shirt, and brand-name ghetto gear (FUBU, Wu-Wear, Roc-a-wear, Ecko, etc.).

Others might point out that a thug is a criminal and only a criminal can be a thug but everybody knows all those baggy-pants people standing on the corner or sitting on the stoop are robbing, stealing, and selling drugs so of course they're thugs. Certain lumpen proletarian gatekeepers like to proclaim that while there are many criminals, only the hardest and realest of those doin' hard time can truly be thugs.

From the corner of the room: "On urban radio all you hear is thug this and thug that and how much of a thug everybody says they are and it's so sad that everybody wants to be a thug and dress like a thug." The amen corner chimes in: That baggy-pants style comes from jail, where you're not allowed to have belts. The deconstructive fashionistas remark on the paradox that hip-hop's stereotypical fashion statement comes from jail—men without freedom providing the dress code for men with all the freedom and luxury capital in the world. But we still don't have an answer to our initial question.

So what makes a thug? How do we recognize him? What makes this particular word so resonant for people inside and outside of the African-American community? I suggest that it's not necessarily the gear or the crimes or the music that make a thug, but a thug's relationship to power. Power and power relationships are the root of thug criminality. Criminality is often defined by a power structure that defines who is and who is not a criminal. A person's interaction with a particular power structure creates a way of being—an ontology and philosophy. It was the ontology and philosophy of the Supreme Black Goddess and its relationship to the power structure in India in the mid-1800s that brought the word "thug" into the English language. The "thuggish" view of power is mirrored in America today by those who live the philosophy and ontology of the "Supreme Black God," and the "thuggish" relationship to power is mirrored in their respective histories.

A "Thug" was a heinous robber/murderer, a member of a secret criminal organization said to have existed for at least five hundred years in what is now called India before being eradicated by representatives of the British Empire (the British East India Company) in the mid-1800s. These Thugs were said to be "an organized system of religious and civil polity prepared to receive converts from all religions and sects and to urge them to the murder of their fellow creatures under the assurance of high rewards in this world and the next . . . It is the imperious duty of the Supreme Government of this country to put an end to this dreadful system of murder" (Captain William Sleeman in the *Calcutta Literary Gazette*, October 3, 1830). The word was coined by Sleeman, who "discovered" the Thugs, brought them to the attention of the British authorities. As the head of the Dept. of Thugee and Dacoity, Sleeman spent a large portion of his career "eradicating" them.

What made a Thug a Thug (as opposed to a "normal" robber/murderer or dacoite) was devotion to the goddess Kali—the Black Goddess—who supposedly sanctioned and required murder on her behalf.

The Thugs' center of worship was said to be the village "Bindachul" (Vindhyachal—Vindhya Mountain) on the Ganges, whose temple complex is one of the most ancient and most important centers of goddess worship in India. (The *Mahabharata* mentions Mahadevi, the Great Goddess, as "dwelling in the Vindhyas"). In 1830, then Captain Sleeman wrote, "Kali's temple at Bindachul," a few miles west of Mirzapore on the Ganges, "is constantly filled with murderers from every quarter of India between the rivers Narbada, Ganges and Indus . . . to pull down her temple at Bindachul and hang her priests would no doubt be the wish of every honest Christian . . ." (Sleeman, *Thugs, or a Million Murders*).

The cult of "Thugee" and its practices were revealed through the confessions of informers (known as "approvers"), men who were members of hereditary criminal families spread throughout India. No Thugs were ever caught in the act. All were convicted through the testimony of "approvers" and circumstantial evidence. There was no defense attorney or jury, only a judge and the prosecutor, Sleeman. The lack of hard evidence was buttressed only by Colonel Sleeman's intuition and the perception of the inherent criminality of the accused. Describing the execution of Thugs he states: "They lifted up their hands and shouted 'Bindachel ka jae! Bhawoni ka jae!' Their invocation of Bhowani at the drop [hanging] was a confession of their guilt, for no one in such a situation invokes Bhowani but a Thug, and he invokes no other deity in any situation, whatever his religion or sect. She is worshipped under her four names, Davi, Kali, Doorga and Bhowani."

Who or what was this four-named goddess? What power did she possess and grant that justified, and was said to require, murder?

Devi (spelled Davi above) is a Sanskrit word that means "goddess." In Sanskrit, word gender is signified by an *i* ending for feminine and an *a* ending for masculine. The root *dev* means "god" (literally, "shining," for instance, like the sun), so Devi would be a female god, or goddess. The feminine word endings hold important ontological connotations in Sanskrit. The word for power, for example, is *shakti*, a word with a feminine ending. In Sanskrit (and in Indian religious thought in general) power is regarded as female. This points to the importance of Goddess worship throughout Indian history. A male god can be a *shakta*, or *shaktiman*, holder of power, but the Goddess is *Shakti*, power itself. To go directly to the source of power itself, you have to worship the Goddess. Or, to put it another way, to acquire or hold power in any form you have to worship the Goddess. MahaDevi, or Great Goddess, is the One Great Power.

MahaDevi is also known as the goddess Durga. *Durga* means "inaccessible" in Sanskrit and refers to a well-protected fortress. Durga is MahaShakti's manifestation as pure martial power and as such the goddess Durga is intimately tied to politics in India. Because Durga is power, one could become a *shaktiman* by her grace. (Shakti is also known as *Bhavani*. *Bhavana* means "world" in Sanskrit, so *Bhavani* can be translated as "goddess of the world" or "power of the world." In the twenty-first century the temple of Vindhyachal Devi is still regarded as a mandatory pilgrimage for many of those elected to national office in India, religious and secular alike.

The most important time for Goddess worship is called Navaratra, or nine nights, which takes place in autumn just before harvesttime. During Navaratra manifestations of the Devi (who is the intersection of the highest spiritual and greatest martial power) can take spectacular forms. During the nine-night festival of the goddess Vindhyavasini, devotees possessed by the Goddess pierce themselves with spears through their faces in front of thousands of witnesses without drawing blood or leaving scars afterward to show their devotion to the One Primordial Power. It is also to show that they have manifested the *shakti* (power) of Vindhyachal Devi within themselves.

The day after Navaratra is known as Vijaya. This was the day kings, rulers, and would-be rulers performed elaborate martial ceremonies for the Goddess. These ceremonies showed that the Goddess had descended and manifested in the rulers, and served to solidify their power. By extension, it was also typically a time when military expeditions began. This was also when, according to Colonel Sleeman, the Thugs went on their murderous expeditions.

. . . These pilgrimages to the temple are made generally at the latter end of the rainy season, and while on the road from their homes to the temple, nothing can ever tempt them to commit a robbery. They are not however, so scrupulous on their way back . . . They attribute their ill success at the present to their neglect of certain religious ceremonies and processions which formerly used to be performed with great pomp and splendour, but which cannot be so now without attracting the attention of the British authorities.

Here lies the thread that when pulled unravels Sleeman's conception of the Thugs. At this point one might ask how the idea of a secret criminal society jibes with performing ceremonies with "great pomp and splendour." Further reflection calls the "criminality" of the Thugs into question. If they were performing ceremonies, this wouldn't have gone unnoticed, especially by those who would have been performing their own ceremonies, the kings, rulers, and would-be rulers. One would imagine if the Thugs were truly considered criminals, those in power would have mounted a military expedition against them. How could an organization that announced its "power" in a manifestly martial context continue to exist for five hundred years? One would have to conclude that the Thugs were deeply involved in the political systems and economies of the various kingdoms that existed at that time. The fact that certain bands of Thugs gave a percentage of their loot to the kings of the territories where they committed their "crimes" was known by Sleeman, and therefore by the Crown. To say these kings and their governments were corrupt would be to miss the mechanics of power accumulation of that time as well as British efforts to impose their will in the territories that became India. To say that Bhowani kept her followers from making a slip-up for five hundred years might be good enough for her devotees and made for excellent propaganda back home, but surely couldn't have been good enough for the Christians responsible for the security of the East India Company.

Sleeman, writing about his progress in eradicating the Thug gangs in 1839, said,

Except for the parts I have mentioned, and in Oudh, I believe the roads are now, from one end of India to the other, free from the depredations of Thug gangs; but there are many leaders and leading members of the old gangs still at large; and some of them may perhaps be in situations which enable them occasionally to destroy solitary travelers, though they have—for the most part I believe—found service with the military and police establishments of the native chiefs.

The fact that the Thugs still at large (of which there were many) were absorbed into the military and the police, and not the penal system, is eye-opening: it shows that they were already regarded as military men by the territorial rulers before the British moved to suppress them. They were regarded as *shaktiman* by other holders of power and respected as such. Their relationship to Vindhyachal Devi both caused and reflected this. She gives Shakti-Power in all its forms. Vindhyachal Devi was and still is today regarded as Adishakti—the One Primordial Power of the Universe. It was the connection with this power and the sanction of this power that elevated a Thug to something beyond the common order of criminal. The ontology of the One Primordial Power is what made a Thug a threat to the empire.

> *"From 1964 up until now, people said 'you are a gang, you are a*
> *splinter group.' Why? Because we did not go according to the*
> *norm of what people were talking about. You have young men and*
> *women waking the street saying 'There is no God in the sky. God*
> *is within me.' "* —DUMAR WA'DE NATIONAL REPRESENTATIVE
> FOR THE NATION OF GODS AND EARTHS, 1998;
> WWW.ALLAHSNATION.NET

Common New York City street slang reveals that the worldview of many African Americans points to a philosophy of the One Primordial Power hidden below the surface. Use of words like "S(u)n" and "God" for man and "Build" for speech reveals a worldview that embraces the unity of humans and the One Primordial Power. Hit records played regularly on commercial radio hide in plain sight the religious mode of being and the metaphysics that are today's counterpart to the religious devotion of the original Thugs. This modern thug's metaphysics comes from the group commonly known as the Five Percenters. It was started in 1964 by Clarence 13X Smith, a former member of the Nation of Islam, who is known to his followers as Father Allah. Clarence 13X (who was also known as "Puddin" because of his smooth speaking style) had been a student minister at Malcolm X's Mosque No. 7 in Harlem before leaving the Nation of Islam. He had also been an officer in the Fruit of Islam, the paramilitary wing of the NOI where he was in charge of martial arts instruction. The term "Five Percenter" is derived from the Lost and Found Muslim Lessons, which were written in the form of questions posed by Fard Muhammad, the founder of the NOI, and answered by Elijah Muhammad. One of the questions Fard asked was "Who are the five percent?" Elijah explained that the five percent were the percentage of the population that were "poor righteous teachers," those who knew and understood the "true" knowledge of God. He goes on to explain that 10 percent of the population have knowledge, but use their knowledge and the power they amass through it to exploit and confuse the masses by teaching them to eat improperly and to worship a "mystery god" in the sky. The remaining 85 percent are the confused, exploited masses without knowledge of who they really are. The lessons state that "the Original Man is Allah, the Supreme Being, the Blackman. The Asiatic black man is the original man, the ruler of the universe . . . Islam is the true religion. A religion which can be proved by Mathematics in a limit of time."

The NOI teaches that Fard Muhammad was Allah and that he came to teach in the wilderness of North America. Clarence 13X's study of the lessons brought him to the realization that being an Original Man, he was Allah as well. He began teaching his doctrine of Godhood at the mosque and quickly came into conflict with the mosque hierarchy. He was asked to leave, it was said, because of his self-avowed love of shooting dice. When he left the mosque he took the Lessons. These included the most esoteric NOI teachings and contained information which up until that time had been taught only to the upper echelon of the NOI. Clarence 13X taught them directly to the youth of Harlem. In addition, he created his own innovative teachings, the Supreme Mathematics and Supreme Alphabet, which illustrate the principles of Godhood through cabalistic breakdown of the numbers 0 to 9 and the Western alphabet. The nascent organization and its members came to be known as the Poor Righteous Teachers, or Five Percenters. The males of the organization referred to themselves as Gods and the females referred to themselves as Earths. The Nation of Gods and Earths is now the official name of the organization started by Clarence 13X Smith. His teachings are part of the African-American Islamic tradition that has its roots in the Moorish Science Temple of Noble Drew Ali, which included Fard Muhammad among its members. Ali applied the prophetic impulse of African-American religious practice to the religion of Islam. He wrote many tracts, including his own "Koran." Ali taught that the so-called Negro was in fact "Moorish," and "Asiatic," and had a spiritual commonality with all "Eastern" (non-European) people. He taught that the terms "negro," "colored," and "black" were constructed definitions imposed on the exported Africans and not true ones. In his "Koran," v. 47 17, it says, "the nationality of the Moors was taken away from them in 1774 and the word negro, black, and colored, was given to the Asiatics of America who were of Moorish descent . . ." He wrote, "Come all ye Asiatics of America and hear the truth about your nationality and birthrights, because you are not negroes."

The teachings of the Moorish Science Temple can be seen as an African-American spiritualization and recuperation of the "one drop of black blood" concept of racial identification so central to the construction of race in the United States. "One drop," as followed by custom and later codified by law, is the idea that any person who possesses even one drop of African blood should be considered "colored," "negro," or "black" and subjected accordingly to the laws and customs that governed African Americans. To put it another way, you could be 99 percent "white" but that 1 percent "colored" would define you as colored under law and custom. The fact that this concept was born of a desire to enforce a radical separation between "whites" and "nonwhites" is self-evident. The primordial peoples of

America and the Chinese population of the American West, the other main "nonwhite" populations of the United States, were subject to laws and treatment analogous to that of African Americans. It is not a stretch to say that when it came to civil rights and legal protections, until the 1960s America operated under a two-caste system. "Whites," who were supposed to be of 100 percent European ancestry, were the higher caste, and "colored," meaning everyone else, was the lower caste. Ali took the American idea of "colored" peoples as out-caste and inverted it. He fought against the imposed racial categories of his time. He wrote, "According to all true and divine records of the human race there is no negro, black, or colored race attached to the human family, because all the inhabitants of Africa were and are of the human race . . ."

Ali took the reductive American construct of "colored" people and expanded it through the idea of the worldwide "Asiatic" race, who were the creators of "Moorish Science." The "one-drop" cultural construction posited the "negro, black, or colored" as irredeemably other and therefore living in cultural and spiritual darkness. The Moorish Science Temple created a cultural space that allowed the "Asiatics of America" an alternative, a "dark" spirituality and culture. The radical opposition of "white" and "colored," dark and light, was reconfigured in terms of East and West. Ali's "Koran" says, "The key of civilization was and is in the hands of the Asiatic nations. Asia, the East, the place where the sun rises is the place of origin and home of the Moors."

In African-American Islam it is taught that "Asiatic" derives from the Sanskrit word *usaa*, meaning "dawn" and "to rise." So those in whom knowledge dawns and rises are said to be "Asiatic." The worship of Kali, the Black One, goddess of the Thugs, is literally a "dark" spirituality, developed by the sages of primordial South Asia to illuminate and facilitate the passage to the highest levels of consciousness and deepest levels of spiritual power as well as the techniques for manifesting that consciousness.

To the Five Percenters "Asiatic" is a state of being as well as a physical description. The Five Percenters teach that those in whom knowledge dawns, rises, and completes itself are "gods," are "Asiatic," are "suns" (hence the greeting "What up, Sun?"). Clarence 13X Smith taught that the sun as emitter of light is symbolic of knowledge and the black man who is God. In his teachings, the moon is seen as a receiver and emitter of reflected light. The earth, as the foundation of known lives, is symbolic of the black woman. As the earth needs the sun to enable and complete the life process, the black woman needs the black man to enable and complete herself. When the two create a child, bring forth a "seed," or "star," they create a "u-n-I-verse." Clarence 13X prophesized that these u-n-I-verses would become a "Nation of Gods and Earths." As the sun is the dominant body in this solar system, the black male, in Clarence 13X's belief, is the dominant body in day-to-day life. All his "first born," meaning original disciples, were therefore "suns."

> What We Teach: (1) That black people are the original people of the planet earth. (2) That black people are the mothers and fathers of civilization. (3) That the Science of Supreme Mathematics is the key to understanding man's relationship to the universe. (4) Islam is a way of life, not a religion. (5) That education should be fashioned to enable us to be self-sufficient as a people. (6) That each one should teach one according to their knowledge. (7) That the blackman is god and his proper name is ALLAH. Arm, Leg, Leg, Arm, Head. (8) That our children are our link to the future and they must be nurtured, respected, loved, protected, and educated. (9) That the unified black family is the vital building black of the nation. From 5% Web—Nation of Gods and Earths
>
> —www.allahsnation.net

Five Percenter teachings tend to be transmitted informally in school yards, on basketball courts, and in school lunchrooms. "Ciphers," or circles where Five Percenters can "show and prove"—meaning where Five Percenter knowledge can be exchanged and tested—can be formed wherever and whenever there are "gods" willing to do so. Information exchange commonly takes a question-and-answer form, emulating the Lost-Found

Muslim Lessons. A typical starting point for informal ciphers would be the question "What's today's mathematics?" meaning "What is the breakdown of the numbers making up today's date in the terms of the Supreme Mathematics and Supreme Alphabet?" This would lead to a "build" or discussion illustrating the principles relating to the mathematics of the day. From there a knowledgeable "god" might well relate the discussion to relevant parts of the Lessons. The Lessons, the body of esoteric teachings received from the NOI, are not sold or disseminated in book form, but are given to those deemed worthy of having them by those who already have them in the form of Xeroxed notes and are supposed to be memorized. Memorization of the entire corpus of the Lessons is considered one of the pinnacles of Five Percenter study. A cipher can and usually will get as esoteric as the most esoteric "God" in it. Scientific facts gleaned from the Lessons relating to the composition of the solar system are broken down by the Supreme Mathematics and then combined with etymologies and mystic interpretations of words learned from elders (I Stimulate Light And Matter, i.e., Islam knowledge or "know-the-ledge"). Other ideas are spontaneously generated using the Supreme Alphabet and are calculated to produce what could be considered Tantric enlightenment (similar to Zen satori but using the tools of African-American cultural experience).

Five Percenter praxis is relentlessly individualist. Each man is Allah and controller of his own Cipher. One of the characteristics of Allah is that he absorbs and emits knowledge. This allows for highly innovative and idiosyncratic religious expression. No one person's interpretation of the faith is accepted as valid for anyone one other than himself.

All "Asiatic," or non-European, mystic thought that is found to agree with the Supreme Mathematics is regarded as Islam and therefore regarded as part of the Five Percenter canon. The same goes for all scientific research that supports the content of the Lessons. A casual search of links from the Nation of Gods and Earths website led to websites of Black Hebrews, Egyptian meditation organizations, sites containing transcriptions of *The Art of War* and *The Book of Five Rings*. Not to mention sites containing info on current scientific data on our solar system and research on naturally occurring nuclear reactors in Africa. All these are considered to be within the cipher, or circle, of Five Percenter knowledge.

Each person does his own research, completes his own cipher of wisdom, and comes up with his own "Koran," that is, his own personal revelation, expressing the knowledge he has amassed using the tenets of the Supreme Mathematics and the Supreme Alphabet, and his knowledge of the Lessons.

Where did Father Allah find his su(o)ns? When Father Allah left Mosque No. 7 he took his teachings directly to the streets, to those who he felt needed it most: the youth of Harlem who had been marginalized and criminalized. In the words of Dumar Wa'de, "When we first started teaching these teachings in 1964, in Harlem, New York people had the same misconceptions they do today. You are a gang. Why? Because this was a group of young men, hardly coming onto ourselves. We were cutthroats, we were thieves, drug-sellers, you name it, we were that. But, Our Father who we bear witness to as Allah, came and taught us that crime does not pay. That we could not live this way of life, if we are going to be able to change ourselves, thus change the world . . ."

This effort to reach out to the criminalized is at the root of the Five Percenters' problems with the authorities. Because they provide an organized context for criminals to meet and interact, they are considered a criminal organization. Their efforts to return a criminal to his original condition are considered irrelevant.

Today, as African Americans still struggle through "Asiatic" cultural definitions to overcome their caste status, the thug icon is the reigning cultural symbol of black culture among hip-hop's white devotees. The hip-hop cultural space is where the thug icon lives and exists as an inverted caricature of American values. This is a conservative cultural space that updates and maintains the African-American role as a radical negative. America's nihilistic relationship to "Negro" life is modulated in the thug-life stereotype. The thug icon highlights African-American youths' existence as a criminal caste enabling (in the codependent sense) American nihilism. The "Asiatic" cultural space is where the thug exists as an iconic figure of an alternative "dark" ontology that teaches alternative methods of cultural and spiritual transcendence. The battle between the two takes place in the shifting space where power in America defines criminality and criminality defines power.

For the British the metaphysical implications of Kali, the Thug goddess irreconcilably clashed with her image and worship. A dark goddess, worshiped by dark-skinned people with "dark" rites, could be nothing other than the devil. The identity of black godhood and the devil in "white" American thought can be illustrated through an example that highlights the American construction of the "colored" identity as a radical negative.

Robert Johnson, arguably the greatest of the Delta bluesmen, was reputed to have acquired his legendary musical prowess after making a deal with the devil. According to one popular version of the story, he couldn't play at all until he decided to sell his soul to the devil, also described as a "Big Black Man." In interviews with so-called conjure men and root doctors, the spiritual descendants of West African spiritual healers in the southern United States, they explain that to gain musical talent you must take your guitar to a crossroads and eventually a Big Black Man will show up. When he walks up to you, you shouldn't be afraid. He'll ask to pick up your guitar. He'll play it, and when he hands it back to you, you'll get the power of musical mastery. The word "devil" is never used in any description of the Big Black Man by the conjure men interviewed. The fact that the Big Black Man became the devil illustrates how "dark," "Asiatic" spirituality and spiritual power becomes reconfigured as "spiritual darkness" in "white" thought and culture. The Big Black Man, a figure of spiritual transcendence, an archangel of an alternative "dark" spirituality, becomes reconfigured by whites as an opposing spiritual force.

Surveys have established that approximately 70 percent of hip-hop music sales are to the white community. Keeping this in mind, what conclusion should we draw about the seeming omnipresence of the thug icon at this stage of development in hip-hop? It has been suggested that white America's battle against its own nihilism is what drives its youth's engagement with hip-hop and thug culture.

America's nihilistic relationship to the Negro and the particularly American form of nihilism has its roots in the theology of John Calvin. Calvinist theology is the progenitor of American Protestantism. Although often seen as synonymous with Puritanism, its influence is woven into all forms of what's considered American Christianity. The concept of unconditional election, one of the "five points of Calvinism," along with its allied concepts of reprobation and predestination, is particularly relevant to this discussion.

Unconditional election asserts that God has chosen a group of people as his own, his "elect." Those who are not elect are the reprobate, and God has chosen to "ordain them to dishonor and wrath" (Westminster Confession). Predestination means these choices have been made before creation and are unalterable. This means it is impossible for the elect to lose their elected status and it is impossible for the reprobate to escape their damnation. Election creates a community of individuals who are the embodiment of God's grace and will. Reprobation defines the unelected as a people "in sin" (Five Points of Calvinism) and subject to the wrath of God as expressed through his elect.

The European Protestants who colonized what became the United States took the reprobation of the uncivilized colonies as a given. The morality of the predestined elect was the morality of the conquest of America. The conquest of the predestined elect over the utterly irredeemable goes beyond subjugation to annihilation. The nihilistic conquest of the reprobate by the elected is the ethic that informs what is called American morality. The perfect certainty of moral righteousness combined with the ethical justification for the annihilation of all that is "unelected" in American life is the definition of American nihilism.

When the early Americans applied the concepts of predestination and election to race they created the logic of race relations in America. Over time the concept of predestination has largely lost credibility, but the concept of moral election has survived. It is, in fact, what sustains American nihilism. The elected still strive to eradicate reprobation through annihilation wherever they see it. The unelected may no longer be utterly, irredeemably damned, but they're still damned nonetheless. And they're still subject to the process of eradication through annihilation.

The proto-American ethic is categorically binary, either/or, elected/damned. The elect had a justification, in fact an obligation, to eliminate the damned. But since they couldn't assimilate the damned, they had to either banish or annihilate them. With a weakening of the power of predestination, a third option became possible: transformation. This transformation consists of the repudiation and renunciation of the reprobate's previous existence and the reprobate's reification by and through the elect. It should be added that the either/or, elected/damned binary choice held for cultures as well as individuals. The culture of European Protestantism was the elected culture. All other cultures and races were reprobate and were subject to repudiation, banishment, and annihilation.

The death of cultural predestination as signified by the civil rights movement has created cracks in the either/or cultural wall that kept American nihilism from becoming cannibalism. The death of the inherent reprobation of the Negro also signified the death of the inherent election of the white. But the no longer inherently damned Negro is still damned nonetheless. Politically speaking, to paraphrase the reggae group Steel Pulse, Babylon still makes the rules.

Asiatic cultural production fights this process by revealing and engaging the sublated process of framing and destruction. Five Percenter praxis was developed as an Asiatic engagement of the totality of conditions that prevent African-American youth from maximizing their potential. As the Wu-Tang Clan's Method Man said, "Ni**az is foul in this duck season . . . We at odds until we even" ("Duck Season," *Wu-Tang Forever*).

The confrontation with America's nihilism in its macro and micro forms is one of the main struggles of all youth in America. The dissonance between what America seems to be and how teenagers want it to be is what fuels America's teenage angst. The struggle of white teenagers in America since the civil rights era may well bear an analogy to the Asiatic struggle. It could also be argued that since white America has been unable to radically export its nihilistic impulses toward blacks, to the rest of the colored world it has started to absorb them. One might even say America in a sense has become colored—susceptible to cultural ills that were formerly the sole province of the Negro.

White America's (and the rest of the white world's) fledgling attempts to develop a dark spirituality in order to contest those forces attempting to conserve white spirituality drive its engagement with African-American culture. Whites have always used African-American culture to dialogue with their own culture—usually by positing the category "Negro" as a radical negative. But the identification of African-American culture with the most destructive aspects of American culture no longer fully masks African America's constructed role as a radically negative other. Nor does it mask white America as a generator of nihilism. This "slippage of the mask" of American culture, so to speak, has created the space where white culture engages Asiatic culture. The multilevel battle at the crossroads between the dark spirituality of the Asiatics and the spiritual darkness of the constructed Negro is creating new cultural permutations as white American youth take on hip-hop personas.

One road sadly taken (or perhaps, more correctly, one travel sadly ended) was the one taken by John Walker Lindh, the "American Taliban." The spiritual journey that led Lindh to fundamentalist Islam and Afghanistan first passed through the Asiatic teachings of Malcolm X and the dark spirituality of "conscious" hip-hop. Lindh wrote conscious battle rhymes, questioned the rapper Nas's right to call himself a god, and opined on the use of the N word while attempting to cross the one-drop line by taking on a virtual identity as an African American on the Internet. One could say his predicament illustrates the radical nature of the choices a white person has to make when they attempt to question whiteness as a category.

What drew Lindh to hip-hop and African-American culture was obviously its dark spirituality, its Asiatic ontology. What pushed him away was its spiritual darkness, the part of hip-hop implicated in the construction of a white America. It's ironic that his embracing of fundamentalist Islam, and consequent rejection of Western values happened because of his reading *The Autobiography of Malcolm X*. Malcolm's trip to Mecca led him to drop his belief that the white man was the devil. In his Asiatic repudiation of the one-drop construct, Malcolm made the conceptual leap, still rare in American life, of seeing all people as "Moors." He found a universal dark spirituality.

It seems Lindh was unable to make that same conceptual and existential leap. Although he was able to disengage from his whiteness and able to take on a virtual black persona that was convincing enough to gain praise from a member of the Nation of Gods and Earths, he was unable to dismantle his whiteness and recuperate it. Reading of Malcolm's travel to Mecca and his epiphanies there regarding the all-inclusive nature of Islam, John Walker Lindh decided, like Malcolm, to become an orthodox Muslim. Unlike Malcolm, however, he was unable to execute a quantum leap over the American racial construct. He could not embrace a universal dark spirituality. Being all too aware of America's spiritual darkness, he rejected America altogether.

He gained his infamy as Abdul Hamid, a jihadist fighting with the Harkat-ul-Mujahideen, Pakistani allies of Osama Bin Laden's al-Queda. It has been said that he went to Pakistan at the urging of his mentor, Khizar Hiyat, whom he met in the Bay Area, where he and Lindh (then known as Sulayman al-Faris) were both members of the Tablighi Jamaat (Preaching Society)—a large and well-respected sect of charismatic Islamic proselytizers based in Pakistan. In recent years they have been considered by antiterrorism officials as the major recruiting pool for the Harkat-ul-Mujahideen, but they are historically known among Muslims as an apolitical group who stress personal responsibility and adherence to the teachings of the Koran. Among its millions of members are included Yusef Islam, formerly the singer Cat Stevens, and, it is said, the current head of the Nation of Islam, Louis Farrakhan. Before going to Pakistan he lived in Yemen, studying Arabic and Salafi Islam, an ultraconservative pacifist form of Islam. He affected a sort of "wigger" version of an Arabic persona, speaking broken English with a fake Arabic accent. Apparently it wasn't as effective as his virtual black persona, and he managed to offend quite a few people before leaving. (In an ironic circularity, John Walker Lindh's seal of approval as a virtual "conscious" black man came from a member of the quintessential "Thug" organization, the Nation of Gods and Earths. When Lindh, as "John Doe," posted one of his raps on the rec.music.hip-hop newsgroup he got the reply, "You bad You bad! Go head, Go head!" from Jahzid Allah, a god who is author of a lot of the "Plus Info" on the NOG&E website.)

White engagement with the thug icon can thus be seen as taking a parallel track with the African-American engagement of same. In the same way that Asiatic cultural production moves toward nullifying the Negro, white engagement with Asiatic cultural production is an attempt to nullify the exclusionary cultural category white. The current widespread cultural drift of thug iconography is a part of a larger, evolutionary process: the colorization of one-drop white America.

6. Yoked in Gowanus

BY JONATHAN LETHEM

IN EACH OF THE THREE DECADES of my more-or-less adult life I've moved away from the neighborhood of Gowanus in Brooklyn, where I was raised and where I kept returning. At eighteen I embarked for college in Vermont; at twenty-two I ran away to California; just now, at thirty-six, I've emigrated to Toronto. Here the question has surfaced again, as it did twice before. It's a question which comes at nervous moments, a nervous question, though often tossed off, jocular: *Ever been mugged?* The question's asker is usually a little breathless, despite himself, wanting that confirmation or consolation for his fantasies and prejudices.

Now, New Yorkers away from New York slowly grasp how pervasive, how penetrating, a certain image of New York City life has become, one derived from television and film and a half-decade of *New Yorker* cartoons. Recall Jack Benny's famous reply to "Your money or your life?": fifteen seconds of thoughtful silence. Picture a man with a gun emerging from an alley (never mind that New York mostly hasn't alleys) to interrupt a single man or a couple on their way home from a night's entertainment, and you've pictured New York City. That's how Batman's parents lost their lives, for crying out loud, and we all know that Gotham City is actually New York. Add the name "Brooklyn"—which like "Harlem" or "Hell's Kitchen" evokes a Jimmy Cagney–Barbara Stanwyck blue-collar or ethnic underside—and you've begged the question that much harder.

My old neighborhood is now fashionable, mostly white, and renamed: Boerum Hill. In the early seventies, though, it was a weird patchwork, middle class and welfare class, black, Hispanic, and an early wave of gentrifying whites, housing projects, and historically landmarked brownstones side by side. In the public schools I attended, I was part of a tiny minority, and, well, stuff happened to me, stuff I wouldn't wish on those asking me that curious question, or anyone.

But as to that question, I lacked an answer, a clear yes or no. Like my questioners, I was slave to the archetype—the grown-up gun-brandishing bandit who'd stand toe-to-toe and ask his victims to raise their hands. I knew that that unnamed script was what they had in mind, and that it hadn't happened to me. But I couldn't say *no* either. My real experiences drifted in a hinterland of childhood and were troubled on every side by racial guilt and apprehension. The fact that these moments, the ones which I might be tempted to call mugging, had instead no clear name—or that the name they had would be meaningless to my questioner—wasn't incidental. The odd unnameability which gave these experiences such a transitory quality was an essential part of their nature.

In a recent manuscript, I've been reaching for this material, from the point of view of a kid like myself:

Sixth grade. The year of the headlock, the year of the *yoke*, Dylan's heat-flushed cheeks wedged into one or another black kid's elbow, bookbag skidding to the gutter, pockets rapidly, easily frisked for lunch money or a bus pass. "Yoke him, man," they'd say, exhorting. He was the object, the occasion, it was irrelevant what he overheard. "Yoke the white boy. *Do* it, nigger."

He might be yoked low, bent over, hugged to someone's hip, then spun on release like a human top, legs buckling, crossing at the ankles. Or from behind, never sure by who once the headlock popped loose and three or four guys stood around, witnesses with hard eyes, shaking their heads at the sheer dumb luck of being white. It was routine as laughter. *Yoking* erupted spontaneously, a joke of fear, a piece of kidding.

He was dismissed from it as from an episode of light street theater. "Nobody hurt you, man. It ain't for real. You know we was just fooling with you, right?" They'd spring away, leave him tottering, hyperventilating, while they high-fived, more like amazed spectators than anything else. If Dylan choked or whined they were perplexed and slightly disappointed at the white boy's too-ready hysteria. Dylan didn't quite get it, hadn't learned his role. On those occasions they'd pick up' his books or hat and press them on him, tuck him back together. A ghost of fondness lived in a headlock's shadow. *Yoker* and *yokee* had forged a funny secret.

You regularly promised your enemies that what you did together had no name.

And so on.

Now, I suppose my answer to the question could have been "No, not mugged. Only yoked, but that a few dozen times at least." It's odd to think where that conversation might have led, but shame and confusion along with ordinary reticence made it impossible. The shame was in being such a routine victim of racial hazing, as though it would be a racist act to ever mention it—perhaps even retroactive confirmation that the difference between me and my tormentors did matter, a possibility I struggled against and still do. These questions are too big to take up here, as they would have been and continue to be in the circumstances when I've found myself asked the question. I'm writing a novel now in an attempt to contend with this material, and I only hope I get it right enough in the hundreds of pages the attempt demands.

Something I learned recently, though, casts a funny sidelight on the question which had always stymied me. Strangely, the clue came by way of Humphrey Bogart. In Nicholas Ray's *In a Lonely Place* Bogart is suspected of a murder by a chief of police. Bogart plays a World War II veteran who's something of a connoisseur of violence, and he takes an unseemly pleasure in taunting the police with the possibility he may be the killer. During an interrogation the cop asks Bogart if he's heard how the girl was killed—in fact she was choked, then thrown into a ravine. Bogart grins, then makes a fist and curls his arm so that his elbow is thrust forward in emphasis. "Sure," he says, "mugged."

Unmistakably, Bogart has mimed a "yoking"—the grasping of a neck in a vise of forearm and bicep. And equally unmistakably, the urban lingo of the time—1953—regards this act as synonymous with the word "mugging."

I wasn't surprised, though, that Bogart hadn't said the word "yoked." I'd always thought, wrongly it turned out, that "yoking" was a term both local to Gowanus and pretty new. It seemed specifically black because I associated it with the word "yo" (I also associated it, weirdly, with the raw eggs which were thrown with tremendous force on Halloween, as though everything wrong with my life at that point could be summed up as *various yo's yoking and yolking me*). But Bogart's pantomime sent me scurrying to a reference shelf.

From *The Facts on File Encyclopedia of Word and Phrase Origins* (1997), by Robert Hendrickson:

Mugging seems first to have been New York City slang for what was called "yoking" in other parts of the country, that is, robbery committed by two holdup men, one clasping the victim around the neck from behind while the other ransacks his pockets. The term either derives from the "mugs" who commit such crimes or the expression on the victim's face as he is brutally yoked, which can appear as if he is mugging, grimacing, or making a funny face. The term is now well-known throughout the country. As often as not the mugger acts alone today, and mugging has become a synonym for holding someone up. The spelling "mugg" seems to be yielding to "mug." The word "mug," for "a grimace," was introduced to England by gypsies and may derive from the Sanskrit word "mukka," a face.

From *The Dictionary of American Slang* (1995), by Robert Chapman:

To assault and injure someone in the course of a robbery (probably from drinking mugs made to resemble grotesque human faces); the sense of the violent assault comes from mid-1800s British specialization of the term "to rob with strangulation," probably from "mug-hunter," "a thief who seeks out victims who are mugs" (easy targets).

And from *The City in Slang: New York Life and Popular Speech* (1993), by Irving Lewis Allen:

> An early pugilistic sense of the verb to mug was "to strike in the face." Mug, in the nounal sense of a person's face but more proximately in the verbal sense of hitting someone in the face, is the source for the 1840s term mugging—the act of criminal assault and robbery in city streets. Mugging then originally meant the act of striking a victim in the face or mug. Thus, street criminals, sometimes working in small gangs and who robbed people with violence or with the threat of violence, came to be called muggers, regardless of exactly how they did it. An alternative technique of mugging, grasping the victim from behind and around the neck in an armlock, or sometimes using a rope or a stick, and choking him into submission, was in other cities called yoking.

You see the irony: my hesitation to call my experience mugging concealed a divorce of the word from its origins, and a crucial one, I think. Mugging was something that happened to adults and involved a gun and was incontrovertibly crime; I'd only been yoked and had nothing to complain about or even confidently describe. A mugging you reported to Kojak or Batman; a yoking you didn't even mention to your parents. One was the city on television and in the *New Yorker* cartoons, the other the dystopian racial miasma of real experience. But, go figure, that question had an answer all along: I've never been robbed at gunpoint or punched in the face, but mugged? You bet, a few dozen times at least. It's easier than it looks.

Postscript, two years later: When Greg Tate asked if I might write an essay for *Everything but the Burden*, I feared I'd be forced to beg off because of my deep immersion in the novel project mentioned above. Then I thought to offer this, a slightly flippant riff I'd written as a kind of momentary antidote to the long emotional voyage of the novel itself. The book's main character, Dylan Ebdus, is more obsessed with yoking than I purport to be in "Yoked in Gowanus"—in fact for him that experience, of being thrown in a headlock and frisked for pocket change, is a kind of Proust's madeleine, that cookie whose perfume triggered the whole Flashback of Things Past. Nevertheless, the question this piece frames is the same for Dylan as it was for me: Why did the experience of "racial hazing," as I called in it "Yoked," trigger a welter of guilt and yearning in my adult self, rather than the reactionary swerve proposed in the formulation "a conservative is a liberal who's been mugged"?

Apart from the fact that I was too young to be "liberal," or anything else, the answer is difficult—hence a seven-hundred-page novel. One part *is* political: my parents were basically hippies, with an avowed bohemian-egalitarian take on race. I was always sent to public school, and I was taught to assertively ignore difference. When my grandmother pointed out that my best friend was black—she meant to congratulate me on it—I was embarrassed for her at her self-consciousness in even thinking it was a thing to congratulate. Because I was a child, I bought my parents' utopian assertions wholesale. *They* were the last generation that would even notice race, and I was part of the first that would sail past it. So when I was old enough to begin to be bullied, in fifth or sixth grade, being tarred (as it were) with the epithet "white boy" was awfully confusing for me: Hadn't we struck a great deal not to mention that kind of thing?

See, I had also absorbed enough of my parents' deep liberalism to be guilty. I might be a minority here, but my "oppressors" were working out their own rage, so I figured out how to feel better about being bullied by feeling sorry for them. Does this "identifying with the oppressor" remind you of anything? It does me, now. Did all this lead, in turn, to a kind of buried rage at my parents for putting me in this position, and for having ideals I so wished to protect that I couldn't bring myself to describe the problem to them? Yup. Hence, as I say, a seven-hundred-page novel.

But it's worth saying that along with this level of pretentious, patronizing guilt and pity, another, more tender factor modulated the experience of being yoked/mugged. That was a kind of closeness in the act, its weird intimacy, its dailiness. We were in it together, like every bunch of miserable kids anywhere. We were making community and conversation, even if it cost me my bus pass every thirty days. Yeah, it was a difficult conversation—shouldn't it have been? The lives of the black kids around me meant something to me, and I didn't only identify in a baroque and self-loathing way, but in a fine one as well.

These were the birth days of hip-hop, after all. Some of the other white boys being yoked in my neighborhood went on to become the Beastie Boys—one didn't preclude the other. My own brother was in an early version of what became 3rd Base, and if you find the back issue of *Rolling Stone* which includes a "Timeline of White Rap" (culminating you-know-where), he's there, the very first entry: Lord Scotch, named for my father's Midwestern Scotch-English roots.

So I say to you now: Yo, you got a dollar you could lend me?

7. The New Mythology
Began Without Me

BY MICHAEL C. LADD

FOR SEVERAL YEARS I HAVE BEEN developing a series of poems
that concentrate on creating a new mythology for the United States. It is a
mythology that acknowledges the overwhelming influence of Black American culture within United States culture. The criteria for each poem are:
one "founding father," one old-world technology that we take for granted,
i.e., electricity, and one Yoroba deity (deities which have been heavily embraced and, at times, appropriated by African America). The following
poem represents a culmination of events in United States popular culture
that have rendered my little exercise irrelevant. The rapid proliferation of
the multitude of myths that are created or resurrected in American culture
is equal to the amount of "outside" cultures that feed this one. During this
exchange, two phenomena have occurred. New immigrant cultures in recent years have mimicked Black American aspects of U.S. culture, and
white Americans have proved to be the blackest white people in the world.
They are enjoying this role more and more; call a young white man "your
nigger" and watch him beam from ear to ear. But the seemingly hegemonic
success of Black popular culture is not without an additional price for the
Diaspora. I always believed in the Funky Trinity—James Brown, Sly Stone,
and George Clinton. However, the members of the dominant Trinity—
Michael Jackson, Biggie, and Tupac—are much more complex. New gods
are created every TV season in this country, living, mythological characters.

Viewing celebrities in this way is not new. But viewing celebrities who have been executed, or physically reconstructed, seemed to be a true embrace of a post-futurist perspective with all its horror and promise.

THE NEW MYTHOLOGY BEGAN WITHOUT ME

Just as I had gathered my words and my clay
I walked past the Sony screen on the way home
Times Square covered with chicken feathers
Red candles on dripping streets
Broadway ribbed with waves painted black and green
With diamonds
Cross Colors were back in style with sea shells

A statue of Biggie storied to sky
His body made of flash bulbs like Christo built sequins
His eyes were police lights that whirl gaze south
Where Tupac held the torch in the harbor

Down on the street the humidity thumped
Squeezing my body like walking through a heart
Lexus's were set aflame on an altar
Digital clocks flipped forward and back
Their triangled lines
Spinning off like shrapnel falling to the ground
A snow storm of fireflies

Young monks in bell bottoms and back packs
Chant the four elements
Moon walking to Internet sweatshops
To do throw-ups on web sites
For Microhiphopsoft and Krupps

Huge inflatable cathedrals house bouncing worshipers
A blimp flies a sign "Jes Grew done grown"

On top of the ATMs stand little deities
In Barbie sized outfits designed by Ramm:Ell:Zee and
    Flash
They talk loud with batteries
Farting brands of incense
"Nubian Midnight" and "Money"

For fifty dollars a clone of George Washington will personally
    apologize
And rename your children
Babies toddle of newly dubbed
Shock dizza, Boogie NukNuk and Mo'

Japanese members of The National Front for African Dance
    Class
Pass out palm pilot flyers
With Malcolm X quotes
Break dancing tips
And casual shots of blacks on vacation

I find myself in the procession
Pinning dollar bills on the virgin Johnny Cochran, wishing for
    Nat Turner
And hey watch us walk through the anti-shadow of
    ultravisibility
With the ability to divide into invisibility again

The sewer remains safe passage to God
For my new destroyer has three heads

Scary Spice, Coretta Scott King, and a composite of seven fly
    Italian housewives over forty
Sally forthing, hemming Obatalla's cumulus robes

I find the lead float
The size of a city block
I clamber the disco balls

Believe it or not
I meet the Messiah
Chilling in a hot tub
His face slipping off
Smiling like a cheese melt
The omnipotent one
The powdered sugar walker
Lord of the Ferris wheel
And genetic no nos
The prodigal son
Hallelujah, hallelujah
Michael Jackson

We quake in our Nikes before thee
For we know not what we do
Hallelujah, Hallelujah

The new mythology began without me
Oh spirits relieve we from these lonely thrones
—BRONX, 2001

8. Steely Dan: Understood as the Redemption of the White Negro

A CONVERSATION BETWEEN
GREG TATE AND VERNON REID

GT: What does Steely Dan have to say to the Black man?

VR: Steely Dan is the manifestation of the white Negro made rock, made jazz, made pop. They embody the subversive idea of the Below Radar Against the Wall Outsider. In their aesthetic they're masters of the kind of crafty bad-is-good linguistic doublespeak realized in their blues. The name Steely Dan is itself a simultaneous tribute to Beat outsiders like Burroughs, who coined the phrase, and a huge nudge and wink at the mainstream American pop audience, most of whom have no idea what a Steely Dan is. Steely Dan is the ultimate jaded-hipster/post-beatnik clique whose songs are an oblique catalog of obsessions, twisted lives, the pleasures and dangers of underground economics. They probably have the most hit songs devoted to a life of crime outside of hip-hop in pop. They also chronicle a kind of noirish disillusionment with the romance of the American ideal: like Bogart playing Philip Marlowe, or Otis, "Sitting on the Dock of the Bay"; forever brokenhearted and forever haunted. Their song "Any Major Dude" is about a more experienced hustler having the compassion to share the dark knowledge any hustler would.

GT: You see them as a redemption of the white Negro. I always saw them as descendants of Frank Zappa in that regard.

VR: Absolutely, but their humor is much more subtle, much more sly, much more self-deprecating and world-weary. Did they just say that? If there's one failing with Zappa, it's that he could be egregiously broad in terms of humor. But Steely Dan held the line. They are the hipster establishment, in a funny way, with the complex arrangements which are kind of jazz-esque. They're arrangements which say, "We are a very sophisticated band and we can hire the best." Which is again the outsider-elite thing. Like being an actor who only does independent films but has I. M. Pei or Frank Gehry design his house. Outsider status has been very good to them.

GT: Is it all a pose, or does authenticity even matter?

VR: Well, rock and roll doesn't work without a certain amount of pretension. Saying, "My thing is gritty and real" is a pose. The pose is in the claim. Being informs everything, but the pose of "I'm a working-class joe" is exactly that. Steely Dan doesn't pretend that, though a lot of what they talk about are people who are marginalized, grifters searching for an angle but unable to find it. Hustlers who are running out of time. The best line in "Kid Charlemagne" is "You are obsolete / Look at all the white men on the street." Your success leads to your obsolescence.

GT: What's their debt to Black culture, and do they owe anything to Black culture?

VR: They've taken certain lifestyle things and turned them into archetypes, and they use those archetypes to people their songs. Like for me, one of the clearest examples of that is in the chorus of "Deacon Blues": "Learn to play the saxophone / I'll just play what I feel like. / Drink Scotch whiskey all night long / and die behind the wheel." They've synthesized a certain idea of the jazz life. They project a certain archetypal and stereotypical idea of the jazz musician's life circa 1950s, 1940s. The whole idea of libations and sensations that stagger the mind. This whole romanticized life of the music and the notion that the discipline of learning the saxophone will lead to unimagined hedonistic pleasures. Steely Dan takes on the world of the outsider as the only place left for them to go—any world I'm welcome to is better than the one I come from. They're looking for a way out of entitlement but, ironically, their success is a soundtrack to many white males, I would say, who were smart enough to know there's a man behind the curtains. Their success allows them to be aesthetes. And they talk about that. Their early records like *Can't Buy a Thrill* and *Katy Lied* are about being an outsider. By the time you get to *Gaucho*, you're talking about the other side of that—of having been the hipster and "Please take me along when you slide on down." It's very much about the lion in winter, and the hipster in decline. But in terms of what they owe, I think there have been little homages along the way—like when they did Duke Ellington's "East St. Louis Toodle-Oo." I think simply by the fact that they lived their peculiar kind of "truth" and have been unflinching, I think that's tribute enough. The fact that there's so much about the American racial dynamic in their music is a great gift. It chronicles a certain complicated relationship to the perceived outsider, the perceived minority. They touch on all of these different taboos, like "Haitian Divorce," about a cat who wants to get away from his wife. And the rub is what happens when they come home. She gets pregnant and the end of the song says, "It changed / it grew / and everybody knew / Semi-mojo / Who's this kinky so and so?" And that was the Pyrrhic victory for the man who wanted a Haitian divorce. Because it's often said that when you enter the realm of the Santeria and voodoo, to make things happen you have to be very careful. If you employ the spirits, know they're very restless and there is a price you will have to pay.

Looking at Becker & Fagen's solo records is very interesting. Looking at Fagen's romantic idea of a hipster deejay, kinda burned out, in *The Nightfly* as opposed to Becker's totally underrated *11 Tracks of Whack*. The harder edge has evidently been Becker's contribution, so the combination of the two has been very fruitful. There's brilliant things in their most recent record too. One of the great motifs they use is the character who's working at the Strand and sees his old girlfriend and she's doing really, really well. I wonder which one of them went into the Strand bookstore and said, Oh yeah, these people are it, man.

Their music is rich in literary allusions. There are whole websites devoted to deconstructing the lyrics. "We've got your skinny girls here at the Western world"—the idea of the West as a whorehouse is brilliant.

They went about this ongoing critique of Western values while simultaneously benefiting from those values. You can't get much more American than that to me. The fact that they got "Chasing the Dragon" on the radio was amazing to me because chasing the dragon is about doing heroin. There's stuff like that all through their music. They're one of America's great culturally significant pop-rock musical institutions. And with more consistency than most.

GT: Given what you say about their use of subterfuge and masking, it's interesting to look at Steely Dan in light of hip-hop's reinvention of the hipster archetype. Hip-hop brought a whole new notion of a player with a sense of play to the table.

VR: I think hip-hop is a music that's very young, and its very success threatens it as an art form. I think the first two A Tribe Called Quest and De La Soul records speak to that. It's interesting to look at the Beatnigs and the Disposable Heroes of HipHoprisy in light of that success too. William Burroughs seized upon the Disposable Heroes as one of his favorite groups before he passed because there was an ongoing critique of the Black left: "HipHoprisy is the greatest luxury." But no other music is as peer-pressure-intensive as hip-hop. It's music that constantly refers to itself and other practitioners. Hip-hop is built upon itself. It digests and regurgitates itself. At the beginning the material seemed very fresh, but even Outkast, one of the most artistically successful groups today, is doing P-funk. It's dope and, well, it is P-funk in an archetypal way . . .

GT: Somebody has to be the trickster. The culture always needs those jokesters that stand right in the forefront of Black entertainment.

VR: Busta Rhymes looked like he was going to be that, and then all of a sudden it was one guest appearance too many.

GT: He also got a crew, the death knell of expression in hip-hop. It became about trying to sell the flip mode squad and a clothing line, it became about entrepreneurship.

VR: Here's the difference about Steely Dan, and it's a damning thing to say, but Steely Dan survived their success artistically in a way that hip-hop is unable to do.

GT: De La Soul had to live down their artistry to survive in hip-hop.

VR: When they made a record defending themselves, it was in reaction to things that were being said about them that the public didn't even know. The record *De La Soul Is Dead* produced one great song, "Ring, Ring, Ring," but in that song lay the seeds for the demise of their first epoch. Public Enemy's "Welcome to the Terrordome"—the same thing.

GT: But in "Ring, Ring, Ring" they really established the line no artist in hip-hop can cross in terms of separating themselves from any kid on the street. Because they're really telling it like it is: "This hip-hop shit is just hoop dreams, and don't expect that because you give me your tape in a hotel lobby it's going to save you." It's a critique of the hip-hop fan who wants to be down, but it also establishes the line you can't cross in alienating that listener. The people who define hip-hop are really all the hangers-on. All the guys you make your friends because otherwise they will be your haters.

VR: It's a great song, no question about it, but the nature of the complaint—the whole idea of claiming to have haters—y'all all jealous of my skills, y'all, y'all, y'all. It's kind of about the whole need to show out in the neighborhood. Part of it is that you really *want* people to be green with envy. You want people to notice you got a fly car, but then you turn around and complain because at least it gives you something to talk about. The fact that you lack an internal life or other references is the great danger of what has happened to hip-hop.

GT: It's like when you see Cash Money Boys or whoever on MTV's *Cribs* and they're saying, "Our fans want to see us living large with diamond-fronts and tricked-out Bentleys, but they also got sixty cats from the neighborhood on the payroll because the fans also want you to share the wealth too.

VR: What hip-hop needs right now is a Clint Eastwood character—a man with no name who rolls with no crew. And has got some backup like Ennio Morricone. The brilliance of Steely Dan is that they benefited materially from the outsider thing, but the characters that inhabit their stories and their goals are not resolvable. Human nature is not a resolvable thing . . .

GT: Steely Dan also don't labor under the burden on keeping it real and representing.

VR: It takes courage, and not giving a fuck. Too many people in hip-hop say they don't give a fuck, but they really do.

9. A Pryor Love: The Life and Times of America's Comic Prophet of Race

BY HILTON ALS

WINTER, 1973. LATE AFTERNOON: the *entr'acte* between dusk and darkness, when the people who conduct their business in the street— numbers runners in gray Chesterfields, out-of-work barmaids playing the dozens, adolescents cultivating their cigarette jones and lust, small-time hustlers selling "authentic" gold wristwatches that are platinum bright— look for a place to roost and to drink in the day's sin. Young black guy, looks like the comedian Richard Pryor, walks into one of his hangouts, Opal's Silver Spoon Café. A greasy dive with an R&B jukebox, it could be in Detroit or in New York, could be anywhere. Opal's has a proprietor— Opal, a young and wise black woman, who looks like the comedian Lily Tomlin—and a little bell over the door that goes *tink-a-link,* announcing all the handouts and gimmes who come to sit at Opal's counter and talk about how needy their respective asses are.

Black guy sits at the counter, and Opal offers him some potato soup— "something nourishing," she says. Black guy has moist, on-the-verge-of-lying-or-crying eyes and a raggedy Afro. He wears a green fatigue jacket, the kind of jacket brothers brought home from Nam, which guys like this guy continue to wear long after they've returned home, too shell-shocked or stoned to care much about their haberdashery. Juke—that's the black guy's name—is Opal's baby, flopping about in all them narcotics he's trying to get off of by taking that methadone, which Juke and Opal pronounce "methadon"—the way two old-timey Southerners would, the way Juke and Opal's elders might have, if they knew what that shit was, or was for.

Juke and Opal express their feelings for each other, their shared view of the world, in a lyrical language, a colored people's language, which tries to atomize their anger and their depression. Sometimes their anger is wry: Opal is tired of hearing about Juke's efforts to get a job, and tells him so. "Hand me that jive about job training," she says. "You're trained, all right. You highly skilled at not working." But that's not entirely true. Juke has submitted himself to the rigors of "rehabilitation." "I was down there for about three weeks, at that place, working," Juke says. "Had on a suit, tie. Shaving. Acting crazy. Looked just like a fool in the circus." Pause. "And I'm fed up with it." Pause. "Now I know how to do a job that don't know how to be done no more." Opal's face fills with sadness. Looking at her face can fill your mind with sadness. She says, "For real?" It's a rhetorical question that black people have always asked each other or themselves when they're handed more hopelessness: Is this for real?

Night is beginning to spread all over Juke and Opal's street; it is the color of a thousand secrets combined. The bell rings, and a delivery man comes in, carting pies. Juke decides that everyone should chill out—he'll play the jukebox, they'll all get down. Al Green singing "Let's Stay Together" makes the pie man and Juke do a little finger-snapping, a little jive. Opal hesitates, says, "Naw," but then dances anyway, and her shyness is just part of the fabric of the day, as uneventful as the delivery man leaving to finish up his rounds, or Opal and Juke standing alone in this little restaurant, a society unto themselves.

The doorbell's tiny peal. Two white people—a man and a woman, social workers—enter Opal's. Youngish, trench-coated. And the minute the white people enter, something terrible happens, from an aesthetic point of view. They alienate everything. They fracture our suspended disbelief. They interrupt our identification with the protagonists of the TV show we've been watching, which becomes TV only when those social workers start hassling our Juke, our Opal, equal halves of the same resilient black body. When we see those white people, we start thinking about things like credits, and remember that this is a television play, after all, written by the brilliant Jane Wagner, and played with astonishing alacrity and compassion by Richard

Pryor and Lily Tomlin on *Lily*, Tomlin's second variety special, which aired on CBS in 1973, and which remains, a little over a quarter of a century later, the most profound meditation on race and class that I have ever seen on a major network.

"We're doing some community research and we'd like to ask you a few questions," the white-woman social worker declares as soon as she enters Opal's. Juke and Opal are more than familiar with this line of inquiry, which presumes that people like them are always available for questioning—servants of the liberal cause. "I wonder if you can tell me, have you ever been addicted to drugs?" the woman asks Juke.

Pryor-as-Juke responds instantly. "Yeah, I been addicted," he says. "I'm addicted right now—don't write it down, man, be cool, it's not for the public. I mean, what I go through is private." He is incapable of making "Fuck you" his first response—or even his first thought. Being black has taught him how to allow white people their innocence. For black people, being around white people is sometimes like taking care of babies you don't like, babies who throw up on you again and again, but whom you cannot punish, because they're babies. Eventually, you direct that anger at yourself—it has nowhere else to go. Juke tries to turn the questioning around a little, through humor, which is part of his pathos. "I have some questions," he tells the community researchers, then tries to approximate their straight, white tone: "Who's Pigmeat Markham's mama?" he asks. "Wilt Chamberlain the tallest colored chap you ever saw?"

When the white people have left and Juke is about to leave, wrapped in his thin jacket, he turns to Opal and says, "You sweet. You a sweet woman . . . I'll think aboutcha." His eyes are wide with love and need, and maybe fear or madness. "Be glad when it's spring," he says to Opal. Pause. "Flower!"

Lily was never shown again on network television, which is not surprising, given that part of its radicalism is based on the fact that it features a white female star who tries to embody a black woman while communicating with a black man about substantive emotional matters, and who never wears anything as theatrically simple as blackface to do it; Tomlin plays

Opal in whiteface, as it were. Nevertheless, "Juke and Opal," which lasts all of nine minutes and twenty-five seconds, and aired in the same season in which *Hawaii Five-O, The Waltons,* and *Ironside* were among television's top-rated shows, remains historically significant for reasons other than the skin game.

As Juke, Richard Pryor gave one of his relatively few great performances in a project that he had not written or directed. He made use of the poignancy that marks all of his great comedic and dramatic performances, and of the vulnerability—the pathos cradling his sharp wit—that had seduced people into loving him in the first place. Tomlin kept Pryor on the show over objections from certain of the network's executives, and it may have been her belief in him as a performer, combined with the high standards she set for herself and others, that spurred on the competitive-minded Pryor. His language in this scene feels improvised, confessional, and so internalized that it's practically nonverbal: not unlike the best of Pryor's own writing—the stories he tells when he talks shit into a microphone, doing standup. And as he sits at Opal's counter we can see him falling in love with Tomlin's passion for her work, recognizing it as the passion he feels when he peoples the stage with characters who might love him as much as Tomlin-as-Opal seems to now.

Although Richard Pryor was more or less forced to retire in 1994, eight years after he discovered that he had multiple sclerosis ("It's the stuff God hits your ass with when he doesn't want to kill ya—just slow ya down," he told *Entertainment Weekly* in 1993), his work as a comedian, a writer, an actor, and a director amounts to a significant chapter not only in late twentieth-century American comedy but in American entertainment in general. Pryor is best known now for his work in the lackadaisical Gene Wilder buddy movies or for abominations like *The Toy.* But far more important was the prescient commentary on the issues of race and sex in America that he presented through standup and sketches like "Juke and Opal"—the heartfelt and acute social observation, the comedy that littered the stage with the trash of the quotidian as it was sifted through his harsh and poetic imagination, and that changed the very definition of the word "entertainment," particularly for a black entertainer.

The subject of blackness has taken a strange and unsatisfying journey through American thought: first, because blackness has almost always had to explain itself to a largely white audience in order to be heard, and, second, because it has generally been assumed to have only one story to tell—a story of oppression that plays on liberal guilt. The writers behind the collective modern ur-text of blackness—James Baldwin, Richard Wright, and Ralph Ellison—all performed some variation on the theme. Angry but distanced, their rage blanketed by charm, they lived and wrote to be liked. Ultimately, whether they wanted to or not, they in some way embodied the readers who appreciated them most—white liberals.

Richard Pryor was the first black American spoken-word artist to avoid this. Although he reprised the history of black American comedy—picking what he wanted from the work of great storytellers like Bert Williams, Redd Foxx, Moms Mabley, Nipsey Russell, LaWanda Page, and Flip Wilson—he also pushed everything one step further. Instead of adapting to the white perspective, he forced white audiences to follow him into his own experience. Pryor didn't manipulate his audiences' white guilt or their black moral outrage. If he played the race card, it was only to show how funny he looked when he tried to shuffle the deck. And as he made blackness an acknowledged part of the American atmosphere he also brought the issue of interracial love into the country's discourse. In a culture whose successful male Negro authors wrote about interracial sex with a combination of reverence and disgust, Pryor's gleeful "fuck it" attitude had an effect on the general population which Wright's *Native Son* or Baldwin's *Another Country* had not had. His best work showed us that black men like him and the white women they loved were united in their disenfranchisement; in his life and onstage, he performed the great, largely unspoken story of America.

. . .

"I love Lily," Pryor said in a *Rolling Stone* interview with David Felton in 1974, after "Juke and Opal" had aired and he and Tomlin had moved on to other things. "I have a thing about her, a little crush . . . I get in awe of her. I'd seen her on *Laugh-In* and shit, and something about her is very sensual, isn't it?"

Sensuality implies a certain physical abandonment, an acknowledgment of the emotional mess that oozes out between the seams that hold our public selves together—and an understanding of the metaphors that illustrate that disjunction. (One of Tomlin's early audition techniques was to tap-dance with taps taped to the soles of her bare feet.) It is difficult to find that human untidiness—what Pryor called "the madness" of everyday life—in the formulaic work now being done by the performers who ostensibly work in the same vein as Pryor and Tomlin. Compare the rawness of the four episodes of a television show that Pryor cowrote and starred in for NBC in 1977 with any contemporary HBO show by Tracey Ullman (who needs blackface to play a black woman): the first Pryor special opens with a close-up of his face as he announces that he has not had to compromise himself to appear on a network-sponsored show. The camera then pulls back to reveal Pryor seemingly nude but with his genitalia missing.

Cut to . . .

In September 1977, Lily Tomlin asked Pryor to be part of a benefit at the Hollywood Bowl to oppose Proposition Six, a California anti-gay initiative. Onstage, Pryor started doing a routine about the first time he'd sucked dick. The primarily gay members of the audience hooted at first—but they didn't respond well to Pryor's frequent use of the word "faggot." Pryor's rhythm was thrown off. "Shit . . . this is really weird," he exploded. "This is an evening about human rights. And I am a human being . . . I just wanted to test you to your motherfucking soul. I'm doing this shit for nuthin'. . . . When the niggers was burning down Watts, you motherfuckers was doin' what you wanted to do on Hollywood Boulevard . . . didn't give a shit about it." And as he walked off stage: "You Hollywood faggots can kiss my happy, rich black ass."

Cut to . . .

"Was that corny?" Lily Tomlin said to me one afternoon last winter when I told her I'd heard that certain CBS executives hadn't wanted her to kiss Pryor good night at the close of *Lily,* back in 1973. After all, Pryor was then a disreputable black comic with an infamous foul mouth, and Lily Tomlin had just come from *Laugh-In,* where she had attracted nationwide attention. Tomlin kissed him anyway, and it was, I think, the first time I had ever seen a white woman kiss a black man—I was twelve—and it was almost certainly the first time I had ever seen Richard Pryor.

Tomlin and I were sitting with Jane Wagner, her partner and writer for thirty years, in a Cuban restaurant—one of their favorite places in Los Angeles. Tomlin and Wagner were the only white people there.

"We just loved Richard," Tomlin told me. "He was the only one who could move you to tears. No one was funnier, dearer, darker, heavier, stronger, more radical. He was everything. And his humanity was just glorious."

"What a miracle 'Juke and Opal' got on," Wagner said. "The network treated us as if we were total political radicals. I guess we were. And they hated Richard. They were so threatened by him."

CBS had insisted that Tomlin and Wagner move "Juke and Opal" to the end of the show, so that people wouldn't switch channels in the middle, bringing down the ratings. "It threw the whole shape of the show off," Tomlin recalled in a 1974 interview. "It made 'Juke and Opal' seem like some sort of Big Message, which is not what I intended . . . I wasn't out to make any, uh, heavy statements, any real judgments."

"Everybody kept saying it wasn't funny, but we wanted to do little poems. I mean, when you think of doing a drug addict in prime time!" Wagner told me. And what they did is a poem, of sorts. It was one of the all too few opportunities that Tomlin had to showcase, on national television, the kind of performance she and Pryor pioneered.

"Lily and Richard were a revolution, because they based what they did on real life, its possibilities," Lorne Michaels, the producer of *Saturday Night Live,* told me. "You couldn't do that kind of work now on network television, because no one would understand it . . . Lily and Richard were the exemplars of a kind of craft. They told us there was a revolution coming in the field of entertainment, and we kept looking to the left, and it didn't come."

10. The Beautiful Ones

BY MICHAELA ANGELA DAVIS

HERS WAS AN OTHER BEAUTY, UNMOLESTED and misunderstood. I'm sure I can't recall whether I was the prey or the predator; no matter, ours was a mangled and stunning love. In the beginning I measured her, compared her, feared her, hated, punished, and pitied her. But so much more than that, I craved her, privately, silently. I needed her savagely. I could not resist her swollen breasts of sweet juice and juju. I nursed from her with inevitable greed. Wedged between each labored gasp were pitiful whimpers begging her to be other than this other she was. Though through the sorrowful pleading I would continue to feed. Her flavor, a delicious toxicant for me, like a rare and precious nectar far too exquisite and complex for what my degenerated taste buds had come to accept. But still from her I drank, drank to misremembered drunkenness. I did not know my penchants had been so ruthlessly deformed by cultural appropriation and intellectual embezzlement. I had been rendered completely ignorant to the certainty that it was precisely her otherness that made her taste magnificent, bewitching. She was the absolute provider, the ever-constant and forgiving muse. She was other and like no other.

Madonna watched Marilyn Monroe and Marilyn watched Marlene Dietrich and Marlene watched her. The whole world watched as this ripe brown lush and strange woman cropped and lacquered her hair, donned tails and a top hat in a time when women were barely allowed to speak to men in public, let alone make a parody of their sexuality. She, before them all, produced a never-thought-of freedom, a stylistic vocabulary that would vibrate from her time throughout all time. Madame Josephine Baker was the natural birth mother to androgyny as a conscious critical act of glamour. She was also that little black girl from St. Louis in Paris, the belly of modern fashion dictator-ship, who raised the status of showgirl costumes to haute couture. Josephine's dancer's split is the international starting line for contemporary cutting-edge style and lifestyle. It was the former white folk's maid, who, while nude under a fur coat, slow-dragged with Ernest Hemingway at a party. She is the one who made nakedness the indispensable fashion acces-sory to nearly every twentieth century female performance icon. But yet it is Marlene's tuxedo I most remember as the example of cross-dressing chic. It is Marilyn's legs under a billowing cloud of white chiffon I see when I search for an illustration of the epitome of risqué glamour. Madonna's arms of black rubber bangles are my paradigm for an ingenious fashion trend. Josephine was an other beauty. She has been immortalized in the minds of much of white culture as an eccentric hypersexual exotic, not a style revolutionary. And my mind too has been sabotaged and remembrances and accolades di-luted by the relentless repetitious un-otherness I have seen.

As a small child morning was met with the hideous hope that this day was the chosen day, justice day. The day God would finally answer my plea and cleanse me of the exquisite scourge. On top of the cool toilet seat I'd stand in front of it, stiff, at attention like a toy soldier, eyes clenched like fists. Slowly I'd gather my nightgown up to my shoulders, exhale the tight knot that once was my face, then open. Oh shit, still there. Shit. Quick. Kill it. Before the next breath, the sharp merciless blade of judgment slashed my less-than-seven-year-old self-portrait. Compared to all I'd seen and studied in all the sources I believed to be important glamorous and true, reflected in that icy slab was a mis-colored, misshapen haphazard collection of parts em-bellished with mix-matched features topped off with some mad ridiculous fuzz. The whole thing looked wrong, lopsided and wrong and I couldn't stop staring. I couldn't control my comparing. What I saw was a foreign little hybrid that was sure to grow stronger, bigger, and much more strange. I be-lieved it inevitable that when the transient compassionate veil of childhood dropped she'd be exposed. Unprotected by the universal armor of sweet pig-tails and ankle socks surely she'd be a perfect target for the ignorant bullets of ridicule. Only a sliver of time staved off the discovery of her immunity to the dictatorship of popular tastes and intelligence. Even then tightly wrapped in my plump little girl ness, she was advanced in the art of experience and the craft of pleasure. And that I knew was dangerous. Her ancient innocence mesmerized and threatened me. She belonged to me. She was mine and I wanted to keep her, make her my beloved. But the staring, the comparing wouldn't stop. She was mine and maybe she could have grown strong and more beautiful but I had no history, no technique for how to care for her. I was sure I couldn't protect her. She alone possessed my deepest devotion and undying dread. I was her mother and I was her child. I could not bear the thought of her being slowly devoured by years of isolation and vandalism, appropriation with no appreciation. There was no other choice but to kill her. She was my precious tiny self-image and I stabbed her to death each morning before I brushed my teeth. Swiftly and unceremoniously I buried her, stuffed her in the hole I inherited in my head. That muddy ditch that no forty acres and a mule could fill, the unquenchable abyss so many acquired in that long ago long boat ride. Then I washed my face, smashed down my frontal hair fuzz with water and grease, put on a crisp white blouse and pleated skirt and skipped off to school. On each corner stood one of my girls. By the time I made it the few blocks to the playground we were a full on collective, scrubbed shiny, joyously ignorant of future cultural assaults and ready to play. I'd blaze through polyrhythmic hand games with riveting speed and fiercely jump several rounds of double-dutch, never letting on I was the victim and criminal of a senseless bloodless murder before the sound of the first bell.

The essence of cool. Duke Ellington once said she was the *essence* of cool. She listened to Louis Armstrong, took his genius brand of blaring coolness and smoothed it out into a caramel colored butter of a sound. Yes, she listened to ol' Satchmo and picked the sweetest peaches off his melodic tree and made warm sticky cobbler. And some one was listening to her, watching her, picking on and off of her too. She the one with the name of a man, but ever the lady, the lady of the day, Billie Holiday. If jazz is the nativity of cool then Billie Holiday was the immaculate conception. Billie had so much style, not meaning she merely had high style, she had style in abundance. She had so many different looks and faces mainstream media had to reduce it down to one white flower in an attempt to comprehend her incomprehensible range. She wore black velvet turbans, chic suits with cinch belts, fingerless full-length gloves, Grecian gowns and sported little dogs on bejeweled leashes. She had that other kind of style and most probably the most other kind of sound in vocal jazz history. Damn right she was cool, damn cool. And there was some one looking at her listening to her, she and all her super cool friends, like Lester Young and Count Basie. Yet, it is not she America heralds as the coolest of them all. I have been taught to look at the looker, to listen to the listener. Picture this, a black and white photo, a singer, quietly stylishly dressed, at a microphone, the background is dark, a smoldering cigarette and a scotch on the rocks provide shy illumination, the singer completely composed and on the brink of collapse. I have been taught to look at that image and think, now that's a cool cat. Frank Sinatra was a good listener, a good looker, very good indeed. I have also been taught to look at Lady Day in the same scenario and think what a pitiful addict, remarkably talented yes, but oh what a pitiful shameful waste. I have been taught to pity her more then admire her, she, the essence of cool. But surely, surely, he is not the coolest. And yet I have been taught by the repetition to see his tipped black hat not her arched black eyebrows as the epithet of cool. The lookers and the listeners, they too have fallen but I have been taught to remember their contributions and not their limitations. So many epitaphs of other beautiful ones. Bird, Jimi, Jean-Michel, are caste in too much pity and too little brilliance. This is how I've seen them teach us to see them. This is what I've seen, what I've been taught.

Me and my girls, me and my girls were a dazzling eclectic bouquet of young gifted and black flowers. Our bodies, long and lanky, round and ripe. Skin sweet smooth and fertile, spanning shades from dark like moist South Carolina rice field soil to light as warm handmade butter cream. Our features mapped the journeys of our ancestors, Nigerian noses, Ethiopian eyes, and cheekbones from the Congo. And our hair, oh our hair said more about our lives, our souls, our politics and our passions than any quilt, photograph or family bible or tree ever could. Our head tales were filled with intense imagination, revolution, pain and satisfaction. They spoke in tongues of large bulbous afros, shiny spring curls, intricately woven cornrows and fat wooly plaits. They spoke in colors of black like Mississippi molasses, gingerbread brown, and blonde like creamed corn. We wore our hairstyles like Irish fisherman wore their sweaters, signifying to whom we belonged. We presented the shape and texture as badges of honor. Living proof that we had made it through the slaughter of the attack on our beauty. We were scarred and crippled but not torn from our obsession for expression. We had no ebony to carve, no vibrant threads to weave or glass beads to string, but we had what we ourselves could produce as our medium. It was right there on our heads, a never ending supply, and we carved and weaved and spun resplendent crowns. Crowns they envied, crowns they could never re-create or remove.

I loved him. I loved him first. I loved him with more devotion than I could control. I loved his face. I loved his face so much. His face was permanently plastered to the insides of my eyelids, his face. I saw his face every time I closed my eyes, beautiful, his beautiful sweet face. He had the sweetest face and the sweetest voice. When he sang everything became beautiful and sweet, the air, the fights down the hall, my face, nothing ugly or limited could live in the wake of his sweet voice, he made everything beautiful and sweet and I loved him for that. No one was as good as he was, no one. He was so good at being beautiful, better than anyone. He was so brave to be openly that good, that beautiful. There were four more with him, handsome and talented, but he was the other one. I knew I was not the only one who loved him, I knew because my girlfriend cut out pictures of him from *Right On* magazine and taped them to her afro puffs, a genuine sign of love for his beauty yes, but I loved his strength as well. I loved his courage not to murder himself, to fully expose his otherness when he must have known one day they would tear at his skin like hungry vultures leaving him naked and deformed. I'm certain he knew they would swarm him with illusions of the superiority of their plainness, suck his originality, siphon his vitality like starving ghosts. I saw he and the other four do it anyway. They created the perfect combination of song, dance, showmanship and style, a formula so many would attempt to imitate. There will never be another boy-group like that, like them. There will never be an other like him, no other face like that beautiful face. Michael Jackson was my first love. I bought every teen-zine that covered him and every 45 record of his Motown pressed. But I longed to see that sweet voice come from his mouth, watch him move smooth and check his fabulous outfits. I could not wait for the occasional Jackson 5 special on the special show at a special hour. I even detected a hint of satisfaction with the short-lived Saturday morning cartoon of his face. Once there was a regular variety show where I could hear his sweet, sweet voice, for one season. He was the best at being the best and yet I always had to wait to see him but could see one of the imitators every week through all seasons. Same station, same time in the flesh, no caricatures. The Osmonds, the bland and the boring brothers, could be seen regularly, with repetition, weekly on my TV. The Osmond Brothers were the Jackson 5 drowned in bleach, all color and flavor removed and yet they were granted the honor to be seen live, over and over again. I could never love Donny Osmond. He was not brave. He was not beautiful. His voice was not sweet and his feet could not fly smooth. I could never remember what Donny Osmond wore. But Michael Jackson's purple velvet gold brocaded vest and bellbottoms with the paisley bell sleeved shirt still flashes past my eyes. I could never love Donny Osmond. I could never sing with him. I could never remember his songs. I could never love Donny Osmond. He did not make me forget my parents forgot me at night. I could not love Donny Osmond though my TV tried to teach me to. I loved Michael Jackson first and he would be the last like him I would love. And more came, New Edition. And more imitators followed, New Kids on the Block. And the imitators still got more time in my TV, on magazines, billboards, and posters in the record store. The white boys have watched long enough and have eventually learned how to dress sing and dance like the black boy groups, but they will never reach what that one beautiful black boy reached. And though he did not die it happened anyway. They convinced him too with the attack of stolen images that their beauty was the beauty of the beautiful people. They taught him too that his other is unacceptable in the land of the glamorous. He who was once so beautiful sacrificed his face for me. He did not kill but he burned and mutilated beyond recognition his beautiful face. He tried to white out the other. And like the others, Michael Jackson is known and understood more as a freak than a genius. Michael Jackson, my first love, messiah to my fear, deliverer to my disease.

Throughout grade school my bi-polar self-image experience continued undetected and untreated. My compulsion to scrutinize my body and face developed into an addiction. What was once a single morning sacrifice became a habit that I would hit at least five times a day. The urge to look at myself and compare came more often than the dawn. I would excuse myself from class feigning legitimate bathroom needs only to race to the mirror to see if I had changed, if I looked a little more like them. I looked at me. I looked at my girls, my people and I looked at them. Them in those fashion magazines. According to these observations I was odd and too flavorful and undoubtedly flawed. My people were marvelous, industrious, entertaining even, but they too seemed wanting compared to them in those pages. Fashion magazines were the place where everything was perfect and where we weren't. There were no nappy edges in those pages, just life in high gloss and high contrast. My desire to devour the images of the beautiful ones in those pages was only surpassed by their creator's desire to devour me.

And why were the names Farrah Fawcett and Cheryl Tiegs so familiar to me and not Naomi Sims or Beverly Johnson? I knew them. I knew their straight bodies and their straight faces and their straight hair. I knew them. I knew them because I saw them everywhere, not just on the covers and in the glossy magazines, but on my TV. How was I to know that the stunning Naomi Sims was the first black woman on the cover of a national magazine? In 1968, though still so young I wanted to see the lush life, I was looking at *Vogue*. So when that one historic cover for that one historic month of *Ladies' Home Journal* came out I missed it. And again, when she was on the cover of *Life* in 1969 for the week, I was checking *Glamour*. I didn't know her because she was not where I was or where I wanted to be. And she was certainly not on my TV. I didn't find any of the other beauties in the beautiful magazines until 1974, when Beverly Johnson made the cover of *Vogue,* I remember that. I remember that one. I had an impression that there must have been more to come. I knew ever so vaguely of Barbara Smith, Billie Blair, and Yves Saint Laurent's muse Mounia. But they were so few and far between and so rarely in those places I was looking. I didn't know about model Pat Evans being so bold, if I had known she was brave enough to be black and bald in a time when everyone was white and whipping blonde hair maybe I would have seen things differently. Seen me differently. And yes I began to see Iman in some of those places, she was so often removed from the attractive environments. She so dignified, so regularly shown in wild clothes with wild animals, she like a queen, made queen of the jungle. I did know her. And she became the chosen other for so long. The only other allowed to be seen repeatedly. I saw how they saw her. I saw how they wanted us to see her, isolated, exotic, a beautiful mistake.

It wasn't until I reached high school that I realized the siphoning. My habit of peering at myself and wanting had subsided yet I knew my self-perception after all those crimes of passion was deformed at the core. I wanted to heal. I wanted to understand why. Why I judged myself so mercilessly. Why I prayed to change and why I looked at my people with equal devotion and dementia. I had seen too much and too little, I was programmed with too many conflicting ideas. I had to understand so I began to study fashion pages instead of just staring, wanting, and comparing. Soon I could see we really were where I believed we were not. We were all in it. Our impulses our vibrations the specific way we cocked our hats were there. We were there but we were not. It took some time but I realized they saw us and they studied us, they had been studying us a long time. They've always seen us. They've seen us be avoided, chained, hanged, and burned by their hands. And as a result of the rape came the birth of a new emotion called the blues that we allowed them to rock and to hold. And they needed that. They've been able to go anywhere we were yet we could only see of them that which they choose to show. Therein lies what separates us. Their ability to infiltrate versus our irresistible compulsion to create. Yes I do believe white people needed the blues more than us blues people.

In America, white people need black people to create define and validate American style. We never needed them and there's no fury like a lover scorned or ignored. When it comes to style and flavor America always had to love black people. Not only did we not need their love, we appeared not to be damaged by their spiritual abuse and violence. We were beautiful without them. We were more beautiful without them. That was dangerous.

What we did and what we wore was ours, pure and rarely simple. They *had* to look at us. They had no choice. We used their discarded materials and built us a culture rich and impenetrable. We could drink from the same well and taste the waters differently, vividly, more refreshingly. Never was it enough for us to walk into a general store, purchase a pair of jeans, and merely put them on. Just as it was never enough to be given the entrails of a hog and just eat them. We added our color spice and soul and organized their rubbish into an incomprehensively delicious down-home delicacy. We are the beautiful people, the same beautiful people who scooped mud from the red earth and molded our hair into sculptures that inspired and educated their masters. We are the beautiful ones who took what they saw as only a tablecloth and wear it as skirt then as a shawl, then a gown then a crown, then at day's end use it as tablecloth and dine naked in our loveliness. We are those people, those beautiful ones. So to us, what's a pair of jeans but another canvas on which to paint our portrait or another page of a journal to write our endless memoirs? We never saw what they let us have as scraps. It was all tools, raw materials we could use to make something beautiful, something new without them. We turned all their punishment and persecution into possibility.

When I reached college I knew without a doubt me and my girls had power in the fashion world. Not only did we have power, we were a phenomenon, a driving force directing and forecasting the future. Obviously, for much of what was done out of an organic genetic obligation to self-express, our natural impulses found their way manipulated onto those glossy pages several beats behind their original time. Black style, our style was crucial to the survival of mainstream American style. We were a valuable relentless source of inspiration. Like American music, black people gave American style culture, depth, and spirit. We gave it life and global value, respect. And still our faces were never or rarely seen in their documentation. On that rare occasion when we did find our way into their perfect glossy world we were isolated. The lone exotic native, stunned, just picked from the bush, wearing animal prints, barefoot with bones in our noses holding a monkey to our bosom like a child. Black models in mainstream fashion have traditionally been shown in an untouchable aesthetic set aside from the desirables. Our vibrant spirit was completely misunderstood by the white medias' puppeteers. We radiated an energy so ancient and so futuristic they could not comprehend, and alas, for their comfort's sake they made us freaks. We were never credited for how our vibration influenced the entire American look. It was our exclusion from the society of mainstream media that fueled our talent. Improvisation, ingenuity, and innovation were our reparations.

Improvisation, another distinction between them and us, perhaps the most underestimated and the most significant. Improvisation is most openly expressed in music, like jazz, and in sports, like basketball. Billie Holiday swung a never heard time into time when time had seemed to run out. Miles Davis blew a strange no sound into sound creating a new sound standard. Michael Jordan moved space into no space and proved that people could fly. This we have seen. This we know. Yet the artful instinct of improvisation in our style, manifested in mainstream American fashion until recently, has been much more subversive, more sublime. You had to be looking for it, and sure enough, I was. I could see the draping of the Kush, ancient Egyptians before the coming of the Greeks, in the "innovative" gowns of Halston and Giorgio D'Sant Angelo. The impermanent permanent waves in their pale hair, the blue eyes laced with kohl, the desperate tans, the beads, the Bo

Derek in "their" beauty. I could see moves taken from one of our more public catwalks known as the Soul Train line, moving through their bodies on Paris runways and of course on them glossy pages. I could see. I could see they knew how to steal the way we looked, but had no clue how or where to find or define how the way we looked made us feel. What was worse they couldn't understand how the way we looked made them feel. We were so fine we caused dangerous stirrings in their perfect world. We were so sexy they caught a contact. Black beauty made the whole world feel high.

For all their espionage and all their resources and numbers, for all their striving for perfection they could not see the most perfect part of our beauty. Not once did I see them, them in those glossy pages look as if they felt the ecstasy of me and my girls when we freaked to "Give Up The Funk" or the eroticism when we grinded to "Love Won't Let Me Wait." Them on those pages looked like they've never been able to access our feelings. The more I looked at them the more *they* looked wanting. Hungry, starving, desiring our feelings even more than our hairdos but they couldn't get at them. Couldn't appropriate them. Couldn't even comprehend them. It was the funk that made us look like us. It was our funky ass feelings that activated our style, gave us a context in which we could emotionally survive. That was it and it was that which eluded them. That was it and it was that part of her they craved more savagely than I.

They could pray for her under the blaze of the sun and under the hot hat of a hair dryer but still they were much too cold and dehydrated for her to enter. By walking page by page year after year through the freezing desert of those perfect glossy magazines I had discovered I already had it. I had that *it* that I hungered for and rejected. I had it. I was it. It was the feeling and the feeling was the funk. I was the most desired. I was not separated from her, just forgotten, just distracted by the glare from the gloss. This feeling that produces this look, this style, our style, black style was all we ever were. Funk, the blues, jazz improvisation was the beauty. We protected it nurtured it and allowed it to live through all their atrocities and all our comparisons. We were it. And our spirit our emotions were so big and so deep we made an ocean of style for the whole world to swim in and dip from. Me and my girls had the *it,* were the *it* they could never have. And sometimes, just some-times I feel sorry for them.

Understand, I could buy their dresses if I wanted. I could straighten, bleach my hair if I wanted. I could have or buy blue eyes. I could have or buy a sharp nose. I could have, do, buy, or duplicate the absolute best they ever had to offer. And they could not even understand why I could take their best and be better at it, be better at being them. I could be them and just add the funk. They could never taste that flavor. Them with all their stuff could never feel just how delicious it feels to be black. And for that I pity them, sometimes, and if they only knew, that could be the most dangerous of all.

11. Skinned

BY CASSANDRA LANE

I'VE GOT TWENTY-NINE YEARS OF Louisiana in my blood. Its heat, its sheer heat, and the hairy mosquitoes and invisible gnats that needle my skin. Enough to poison me. I know intimately the weather's oppressiveness: rashes on the back of my neck and in the crook of my arm. I've been scratching at those tiny bumps for so long, they are part of my skin's makeup, my expectations of summer.

Growing up, each year was a long string of months where everything was sticky: the wooly, circular rug in my grandmother's den, its center gummy with Kool-Aid stains; our bare feet, caked with dirt on the balls and heels, sometimes catching on tiny splinters in the kitchen floor.

My sister Dena was seven and I was eight when an unusually frigid winter hit DeRidder. White stuff fell from the sky in hesitant flakes and settled like torn cotton balls against the ground. A thin layer of ice covered the browned grass. I thought of how that ice had choked the green life out of our yard and wondered if the grass would ever be able to revive itself. A row of icicles hung from our low-hanging, lean-to tin roof. Dena said it was all so so pretty. In my favorite black-and-white horror movies, Dracula's fingers looked like those icicles, long and bloodless.

Grandmama walked into the kitchen and stood over me at the window. "Ain't never seen nothing like that before, have you?"

I shook my head.

"Well, the weather's changed patterns over the years," she said. "It snowed and iced over like this in DeRidder a bunch of times when your mama was a girl. They put thick socks on their hands to keep them warm when they walked to school."

Mama had told us a version of the story before. "We smeared our faces with Vaseline and walked backwards to keep those winds from slicing our faces." Later, much later, she would tell us how, every day, a golden bus filled with white children drove right past her and her brothers, Billy Joe and James, as they neared their school. The tires, taller than any they'd ever seen, spewed clouds of snow into the air around them. The children looked down at my mother and her brothers. They stuck their heads out the open windows and sang, their voices buzzing like a thousand angry bees, *"Nigger, nigger, nigger!"*

One day, Mama and her brothers were ready for them. They held their heads down so the kids couldn't see their grins. The bus's windows shot up and the kids' tongues pressed against the back of their upper teeth, poised for that vicious chant. Mama, Billy Joe, and James brought their hands from behind their backs with as much force as they could, slinging rocks toward those scrunched up faces.

"I tell you one thing," Mama would say, "Next time that bus passed us, those windows stayed up and those faces just kept looking straight ahead. Like they were the ones driving the bus." Mama would laugh and I would laugh too. Proud. Vindicated.

Grandmama told Dena and me we could go on outdoors and play in the snow. I was content to stay by the heat of the oven. Dena, as usual, was eager to get outside. A tomboy, she climbed trees and beat up the neighborhood bully while I hid behind curtains and read or lay flat on my back on a quilt between overgrown fig trees.

"Do I have to go out, Grandmama?" I whined.

"Gal, get your overcoat on and get your behind out there. Here, take this bucket and bring me back some of that snow. I'll make ya'll some sweet ice cream like I used to for your mama and uncles."

We pulled on our sweater hats and zipped up the flannel-lined coats Mama had bought on sale at Kmart. Dena hurried down the back steps and started snatching icicles from a fig tree that was just a mess of gray sticks. I followed slowly, the empty plastic ice cream bucket in my right hand. My feet slipped on the slickness and the bucket went flying. I broke my fall with my palms, face inches from the ground, harder and colder than cement. The impact was so shocking it stopped the blood in my hands. I got up and ran back into the kitchen, sobbing, not realizing my palms were bleeding until I held my hands to my face. I spent the next few weeks praying for spring to hurry up.

It gets chilly in New Orleans, where I live now, but the chill never lasts long and I certainly never have to walk in it. I jump from my porch to my car and then inside the doors of wherever I'm going. I keep a heater under my desk in the gray newsroom, blast it on high until my toes itch with heat. Each winter passes quickly, fading into my memories until the next year. A stranger to true, lasting cold, I cling to what I know.

My husband is a different story. Born in January at Harlem Hospital, Ric lived in New York all his life until five years ago, when he moved to New Orleans to take a job as a staff photographer at the daily newspaper. He told his coworkers: "If I come back with a twang, shoot me." He didn't realize there are various dialects in the South, that people in Chalmette, one suburb of New Orleans, sound like folks in Brooklyn.

October 31, 2000. New York City. Thirty-two degrees and getting colder. We're here on vacation, and Ric is feeling nostalgic. I've sworn to him that I'll never live anywhere north of Georgia. I like baring my skin year-round. I love New York, but after this trip swear to visit only during the summers.

All the same, it's Saturday and I want to go out. To pull these coats and scarves off inside a nightclub and dance and sweat and dance some more. I don't care if my underwear gets soaked. On the subway, I flip through the pages of the *Village Voice,* come across the description of a nightclub that's supposed to be hot and soulful.

"You ain't gonna be able to pull me from the dance floor tonight. I need this," I tell Ric as we get off the train and walk to yet another shoe store— our sixth today.

"You need it, huh?" Ric has always laughed at my low tolerance for cold. "You look like you're in pain," he'd told me the first time we met. A winter night in New Orleans—sixty degrees.

Now, I walk with my shoulders as hunched into my chest as possible. My chin, my lips, my nose are wrapped in a thick chenille scarf that looks like moss.

"Yeah, I need it. I've been eating like a hog here. And anyway, if I gotta shake in this doggone city, I want to be responsible for some of it."

"Oooo, you sound country."

"Look, you ain't but one removed from the South your damn self," I say through the tiny holes in the woven scarf. "And your mama didn't leave her ways in South Carolina." We finish shopping as the sun and its feeble warmth retreats. On the way back to Ric's mother's apartment in Washington Heights, a young black woman stops me. "I love your Afro puff," she says, her eyes absorbing my hair, my face. Her hair is bone-straight, the way I wore mine a year ago before finding the nerve to let the chemicals wear out. My weak strands reverted to their natural state, became tightly coiled and strong. But my acceptance of this new, natural me didn't purge me of insecurities.

Back at Bernice's apartment, I eat a few spoonfuls of the heavy, fat-laden food she has prepared for us. Twice-baked macaroni-and-cheese, candied yams, rice and gravy, apple pie. I feel my stomach expanding and I panic. After talking for a few hours with Bernice and Ric in the living room, I leave to shower and get dressed in the back bedroom. Using a green and magenta scarf, I tie my hair, soft and shiny from the shower's humidity, into a tight ball. I blend powder into my face, dip my forefinger in light-bronze eye shadow and graze it across the skin directly under my arched eyebrows. Dabbing a brush in black orchid shadow, I then dust the rest of my lids, blinking when a grain of powder falls into one eye.

From the mirror, I can see the perfectly lined eight-by-ten-framed photographs of Bernice's three granddaughters. They cover the entire length of the wall behind me.

I turn to inspect them closely. Natalie and Ashley, identical twins. And here, Debbie, their youngest sister, whose skin glows like polished oak under the camera's lights. Debbie's skin is two shades darker than her sisters'. While the girls' mother is Puerto Rican, Debbie's father, Ric's brother, is black. I stare long and hard until the varying shades of skin become one. The eyes and smiles, multiplied a dozen times, are haunting, hopeful.

Earlier, Ric joked about the eeriness of it all. "Why in the world did she put up so many pictures of them?"

"Aw, she just wanted to make sure they knew they were beautiful."

I drag my gaze from the photographs, slip on my shoes, and head for the living room.

"Girl, you better put some clothes on." Bernice fusses over me as though I'm one of her granddaughters, and I let her. Her eyes linger on my backless black dress and strappy black heels. She gets up and goes to her bedroom. "Here," she says forcefully when she emerges, pushing toward me a mawmaw-looking garment that would, if I dared drape it on, brush the hem of my skirt and camouflage any hint of my subtle curves.

"Oh, I'm wearing my leather jacket over this." I cock my head to the side and finger her sweater in what I hope appears to be a grateful gesture. "Thanks, though. That looks real warm."

"Not sexy enough, huh?" She rolls her eyes behind her bifocals and folds the thick red sweater over her flaccid arms. The fine-tooth plastic comb she was using to scratch her scalp, easily visible under her fine, auburn-dyed hair, still rests there.

"Umph, ya'll too much for me," she says, and I can tell she's glad we're here, reminding her of the days of her youth, our laughter filling the quiet apartment.

"You look good," she says. "And you, too, son. Both of you look real good."

We feel good, too.

On the subway—*again*—I wait until we're close to our stop in Greenwich Village before easing a plum gloss over my lips.

Ric watches me as I frown into the compact mirror. "You look fantastic."

"Really? I look okay?" At my worst, I feel like that same skinny, knock-kneed girl with the flat forehead and wide nose like my daddy's. "The only thing saving you is that you got them Chinese eyes," Uncle Billy Joe used to tease.

In nightclubs I've been to, everybody's competing. With each turn of his head, I have feared my husband's eyes might follow a woman who's more attractive and naturally voluptuous. It's the same fear I've carried into each of my relationships. Mama always implied that men leave women for more beautiful women, and I've looked for signs before they begin. My insecurities drive Ric crazy. "You make me feel like I'm on trial for a crime I don't know anything about," he said once, and I felt guilty.

Now, he looks at me with soft eyes.

"How many times do I have you tell you? You're beautiful."

I snap the compact closed and beam at him. "You're the one who's beautiful."

We get off the subway at Astor Place and walk four blocks. As we round the corner and draw nearer the line outside the club, I nudge Ric. I am shocked to see a string of white people waiting to get in.

"Looks like we're the only black people here, babe."

The blurb in the paper had definitely said "live deejay playing R&B and hip-hop." We fled New Orleans, a mostly black city, to get away from our oppressive, mostly white work environment. We promised not to speak of the editor who narrows his blue eyes at me and makes crude jokes about black and Latino students; the photographers who believe Ric's appointment has blocked other white photographers from that opportunity, even though Ric and another guy are the only black photographers on a staff of twenty-six; the reporters who spend their time gossiping, tearing apart other writers' stories behind their backs, and complaining about affirmative action just because, every purple moon, a black reporter is hired.

"I don't know, Ric." My words are slow, careful. "I don't feel like partying with just white people. I really want to have fun. I really want to dance."

"Well, we're here now," Ric says as I shiver a few feet behind the last person in line. "Maybe we should go in and get out of this weather. Let's just go in and have fun."

I twist my mouth to one side. "Sure we can't find another place around here?" Competition aside, I want to look upon other black women, see their outfits, study their hairstyles. I want to relish, while pretending not to notice, other black men's silent appraisal of my looks. I want the men and women to acknowledge Ric and me on the dance floor, to marvel at the energy that would shimmy between us.

"We could go find a paper and look for something else. Maybe that reggae place in Brooklyn that you read about."

"More walking? More subways?"

I contemplate leaving, but rebellion strikes me. Why should we be the ones to leave while they use our rhythm and our blues as their entertainment?

"You're right, Ric, you're right. Let's just see. If we don't like it we can leave. Besides, maybe the black people are already inside, where it's warm."

We go in and there are white people everywhere. In feathers and furs and striped tights. In wigs and fake eyelashes and glitter. It is, after all, Halloween. We walk upstairs to the coat check, where there's another dance floor with the same scene.

"Do you want to leave?" Ric asks after looking around. I remind him that we've paid twenty bucks apiece to come in here. Maybe it'll get better.

A black deejay with skinny, jaw-length dreadlocks plays a mixture of house music and hip-hop. The dance floor is packed with gyrating pelvises.

"Do you want something to drink?" Ric has asked me more than once. "Do you want to dance?"

"No."

The minutes drag on, an hour. I cannot move. My immobility has kept Ric, too, frozen to a spot in the corner of the club. "You've spoiled what could have been a perfectly good night," he says finally, angry and frustrated.

We stand against a wall by the ladies' room. The long line of alcohol-filled women waiting outside the door seems not to be moving. My arms are locked across my chest.

"Sand, we're here now. I am begging you, why can't you just try to have fun? Forget about them. We're here to enjoy each other and the music.

These white people have a power over you. They're in here having fun and look at you. You're not hurting them, you're hurting us. They could care less."

And that's the problem, I think, but I keep my teeth clamped.

It is as though these people are all the white teachers, bosses, landlords, clothing store clerks, and smug-looking magazine models who have, with their words, their squints, their icy smiles, made me feel ignorant, invisible, incompetent, illegal.

I cannot forgive them. I am Houston Buckley's granddaughter.

Papa, my mother's father, was a boy when a gang of white men lynched his biological father, Burt Bridges, in Mississippi. "They said my daddy was a uppity nigger. They said they was going to show him who was boss," Papa would say, sitting in his worn recliner, clenching and unclenching his strong hands.

"Houston, you got to learn to forgive," Grandmama would plead with him. "Don't let white folks keep you out of heaven."

"Hmph," he'd answer, his chest all puffed out.

The women standing in the bathroom line are giggling and gossiping and straining to hold in their pee. Through a wetness like onion juice in my nostrils, I breathe. "I hate those stupid bitches. I just hate them."

Ric coughs out an incredulous, joyless laugh. He runs a hand over his closely shaved head, tries to smooth patience into his voice. "Sand, the white people in this club have done nothing to you. You can't hate all of them because of what some of them do. White people are a fact, babe. They will always be in power in this country. You're either going to learn to live with them or you won't get too far."

I want to hurt him for speaking the truth and making me hurt, making me feel powerless and outdated and unsophisticated. I want to hurt him for being so adaptable. Him, who has seethed with hatred for them, too. Who has, because of his experiences with many of them, made generalizations about the entire race, too. Maybe he's good at playing the chameleon game. He has been able to embrace some white people as friends—and as lovers. I hate him for that part. I want to suck the life from him, all his reasoning and maturity and acceptance.

"Oh, I can take them in doses, all right. I just don't want them in my dance club." My eyes leave the women and rest on his. I speak in a low, deliberately slow growl. "And, unlike you, I don't want them in my bedroom."

His nostrils swell before he pushes his long, thin face in mine, his shiny, near-black skin darkening to purple underneath. His pupils glitter like a piece of granite in the sun. They grow harder, blacker, until they look like they'll explode. For a second I wish he'd slap me. I need a reason to scream. I have brought up an old argument. *How could he have slept with one of them—a white woman?*

"I have told you, I do *not* have to justify my past to you. I don't have a problem with white people who don't have a problem with *me*. You have no right to judge me. No right." He straightens and his eyes flash from me to the line of women outside the bathroom then back to me again. "You've got a real problem, Sand. A real problem, and you need to get help."

Tears and makeup slide down my cheeks and over my collarbone, so bony, protruding almost abnormally from my chest. *Was he tender when he kissed the white woman there?* I yearn to be kissed on my collarbone right now, to feel the hard smoothness of his teeth sinking there, into my skin, underneath my bone.

Ric looks at me with disgust. "Let's go. Sand, let's go."

I want to take it all back. I want to go back to that corner before we turned and saw the club. I want to keep walking arm in arm with Ric, confidently. To make a small joke about being the only black people. To acknowledge it, shake our heads, wonder where the black people are partying tonight. Maybe pause to see if we'd like to go through the trouble of finding somewhere else to go, then quickly change our minds because we've come all this way, because it feels like somebody's pricking my toes with frozen needles, and because we don't know where else to go anyway. "We're going to have fun here," I'd say assuredly. And we would.

I want to take it all back. I can't take it back.

It didn't start here, in this dark, pumping club.

It didn't start on the corner.

It didn't start tonight.

. . .

Nineteen fifty. Kurtwood, Louisiana.

Papa is nearly sent to prison for killing a white man.

It happened this way. Papa is driving his old pickup truck down a dirt road. Grandmama sits on the passenger side, holding their sixth child, James. Another truck comes barreling down a side street and slams into Papa's truck at an intersection. The baby falls from Grandmama's lap. The three of them are okay, just slightly bruised and badly shaken. Grandmama and Papa stumble from the truck, dazed. Glass and torn metal everywhere. With baby James safely clutched to her bosom, Grandmama listens closely to a low moan, an "oh, oh, oh," coming over and over again. She drags her feet to the sound and looks down to where the driver of the other truck lay flat-back in a ditch, covered in his blood. The impact of the crash had sent him through the windshield.

When Mama tells me the story of my grandparents' accident, I try to imagine Grandmama walking over to that ditch, drawing closer to the source of that awful moaning, crossing over to that white man.

"When she looked down, she saw that something had torn off that man's face—glass, metal, something," Mama says as if she were there. "Something had peeled the skin from that man's face. Daddy told me they couldn't get Mama to stop screaming. She just kept screaming and screaming."

The man dies and Papa is charged with manslaughter. It is the man's wife who saves Papa from prison. On the day of the accident, she was riding on the passenger side of her husband's truck. "It wasn't Mr. Buckley's fault," the woman cries at the trial. "My husband, my husband was sloppy drunk. I begged him not to get behind that wheel."

I am angry when my mother first tells me this story. Angry that the white man, even in his death, was given the benefit of the doubt while Papa was immediately incriminated. That his selfishness and drunkenness could have sent Papa to jail, left Grandmama without a husband and their children without a father for who knows how long. Even worse, that his carelessness could have killed them all—Papa, Grandmama, my uncle James. My mother, who was born in 1953, would not have been. I would not be. This story *is* mine.

When I beg Mama to repeat it, Papa and Grandmama have been dead for years. I am an adult, filled with my papa's pride and traces of his daddy's ghost. My great-grandfather, Burt Bridges.

Burt Bridges.

I imagine the faces of the people who hanged him—and the faces of those who watched with glee. Only a few of my acquaintances are white. I don't let them get too close to me. Their flesh is always a reminder that I'm on the other side.

In elementary school, everything I aspired to had a white face on it. Bionic Woman. Jessica Savitch. Wonder Woman. Barbie. The softly painted women on the covers of my mother's romance novels.

My very first best friend was white. Melissa Gill. She had see-through skin and big gray eyes with specks of green and orange burning from the centers. Little gold hoops glistened against the red of her small ears.

We played together every day in Mrs. Crain's third-grade class; we were, as a couple, loners. No one came near us, we went near no one. We dreamed of growing up and one day marrying Tom Selleck, of living in a three-story house with gingerbread trimming. As we strolled together on the playground, our shadows followed alongside us, oversized, dark copies of our legs cutting across each other like scissors. One day, I see Melissa talking to some other white girls. They ignore me when I stand behind her, waiting for her to turn to me, grab my hand, and take off skipping with me in the hallway beyond these silly girls.

She turns around. "Oh."

The other girls look away. I follow Melissa into the hall.

"What's wrong?" I ask.

She drops her head, her straw hair falling to cover her pink cheeks.

"My mother says I can't be friends with you anymore."

The truth is on the tip of my tongue before it has a chance to lodge uncertainly within my chest. "It's because I'm black, isn't it?"

She hangs her head lower, burdened with something too big, too old, too confusing for her young neck.

I don't know how I knew the answer. I didn't understand. I simply knew, even though my family members, when I was that age, never talked about racism at home. The adults, except Papa (whose outbursts became more frequent and more coherent to me as I got older), hardly talked about white people at all. Religion was the main topic in our home, preparing for the afterlife instead of getting caught up in the worldly one.

My friendship with Melissa does not gradually fade—it stops abruptly. One day we're playing together, the next day I'm sitting alone at recess and Melissa's playing with her new white girlfriends.

At the open house for parents, I search for the woman who will be holding Melissa's hand, I search for the woman who has never seen me but hates me so much. Who has ruined my recesses.

She is tall and big-bellied with an unfriendly face, bluntly cut chestnut hair. Obsessed, my eyes follow her movements around the room. Trembling, I stare at her chalky skin, at her side profile, at her wide back. Her eyes flicker over me coldly as she passes. Melissa sticks to her side.

After Melissa, I won't have another white friend. In fourth grade, I will befriend the new girl that year, Aronna Phrasavath, whose family escaped from Laos. When she absorbs into a group of white girls the next year, I'll be alone again. Over the years, I'll insulate myself with a few other black students in a way that leaves no room for even the interest of any Britneys or Christinas. Not that any of them were looking my way. Voluntary segregation for us was easy. The norm.

I tell myself that Melissa doesn't exist for me, that I will look through her like she's glass, as easy to pluck and discard as the icicles Dena pulled from the fig tree. I will never forget her mother. I stare at her and promise to get her back someday, somehow.

My own mother laughs and talks with Mrs. Crain. She is used to my silences, my deep retreats within myself. She doesn't ask me what's wrong. I don't know how to find the words to describe to her how I feel: small and ugly. I don't know she's felt this way many times herself, and that she still does.

. . .

When Dena and I were teenagers, Mama, her tense eyes boring into us, tried to protect us from boys and men. Her prophesies were as doomful as those my uncle Junior handed down in church about the end of the world. "Men are dogs," she said. "They will use you up and throw you away." She said black men always want white women, or the next best thing: a combination of big breasts, long flowing hair, and light skin. The lighter the better.

I had none of that. My skin was neither white or light. My breasts neither big or even medium-sized. My hair neither long or straight. My skin was the color of maple syrup, my breasts shaped like pine cones, my hair coarse and slow to grow. While my parents were both in their early twenties and still married, Daddy used to keep a Polaroid shot of his white girlfriend stashed in his Mustang's glove compartment. He proudly showed it to Dena and me once when Mama wasn't around. Just four and five years old, Dena and I stared, gape-mouthed, at the woman's pale, scrawny arms, at the bright rouge staining her cheeks. *Who was she? Why did Daddy like her more than Mama?*

But when *I* got ready for love, Mama's pain didn't matter. I had to believe she was wrong about men. I had to believe I was as worthy, as sexy, as beautiful as the women I looked nothing like. And I had to believe there were men who would appreciate me the way I was. More than that—one who would make me, as Midnight Star sang, the *object* of his desire.

The day Ric told me he'd once slept with white women, we had been dating for several months, had fallen in love, and had no intention of turning back. For the first time, I felt I could tell a man anything about me without him judging me. For the first time, he'd allowed himself to be vulnerable enough to open up to love. He, too, felt he could trust me not to judge him. He was wrong.

"Would you ever date a white person?" I ask one morning as we are lying in bed, talking about our pasts.

"I never really dated them. I have had sex with them, though."

My body numbs. I make my voice flat.

"Really? How many?"

"Two. What about you?"

"Oh *no.*" My voice rises, dripping with scorn. "I've never been interested in white men." I'd felt my insides cringing when a white man, a fiftyish British man I was interviewing for a story, couldn't recall my name but told me he was "dying to kiss my hot chocolate cheeks." He'd desired my skin while disregarding my self. This, after a history of enslavement and rape of brown women.

Ric strokes my stomach gently, ignoring my stiffness. *Get your hands off me,* I feel like screaming. After all his talk, I think. All his talk about discrimination and white privilege. All his talks about how he grew up in Harlem hating the messages and the messengers who painted such horrific images of his world. How, even now, white people—especially the men—often enrage him, how a fury rises up in him sometimes when they challenge his right to success. A white coworker once damaged his photo equipment when no one was watching. We had been one—I thought—in our views. These days, we joke, people are quick to say race is only skin-deep, that color doesn't matter, so get over it. But Ric and I knew it wasn't a lack of education or finances or professionalism that kept me from getting the cute apartment with hardwood floors on Dumaine Street. The culprit was my dark skin. We both knew it wasn't that he was speeding or running a stop sign when cops pulled him over to search him and his sports car. The culprit was his dark skin.

"I wish every white person could be transformed into a black person for a little while," Ric had said once while we were watching a science fiction flick. And I had not needed to ask why.

That morning in the bedroom, I sit up and face him, not caring if the hurt and betrayal and fury churning inside me shows in my eyes. "How—how could you lay with the enemy? Yes, they'll have sex with *you,* but they can't stand *me.*" Every time yet another famous, wealthy black man marries a white woman, I believe she has won in this long and silent battle between her and the black woman. *See,* she can say—and often her hard toss of her hair does say—*I am his biggest fantasy. He wants me more than he will ever want you.*

"How can black men fall into that trap?"

"It wasn't about that for me. And I think you'll find that white women feel just as, if not more, insecure about black women."

"That's such bullshit. They don't have to put up with the messages we've been fed all our natural-born lives." Spit flies from my mouth and lands on his arm. He doesn't wipe; he just listens.

"They're supposedly so beautiful, so pure, so fucking desirable." My voice sounds hysterical. I can't make full sense of what I'm feeling. It feels like something has long been forming within me, without my knowing. Something as hard and sharp as a jagged rock, twisting my intestines around its edges. I refuse to kiss Ric. I keep thinking of his brown lips curving over a pink nipple. How could he have opened himself to it, to skin so cold, so foreign to us.

I imagine a white woman's silky golden hair, spread on Ric's pillow like in the commercials, in the movies. I see his face in it, him opening his mouth to a strand of it, and all of a sudden my mouth is dry and I'm coughing, crying. I can't stop. I'm straining to tell him how I've spent years trying to accept myself as beautiful. Beautiful, yes, beautiful. Mostly, by refusing to be inferior to the skin that rejected mine, ignored mine. So I gave as good as I got. That skin didn't want to brush my hand when I paid for my groceries, I didn't want ungloved white fingers making my sandwiches. Didn't want naked white breasts dominating my movie screen. For every negative connotation of the word "dark," I had one for the word "white," an adjective often misused to describe purity. I chose, instead, pale, generic, bland, ghostly, evil, sickly. For the words "brown" or "black," I thought of comfort, peace, warmth, safety. A velvet slip dress. My favorite oak. Bayou St. John. Mama's arms encircling me.

Ric's revelation shoots down my defenses. His silence infuriates me, frightens me. "So Mama was right after all?" I ask. "It *is* true that white women are more beautiful, more desirable, that all black men want them, at least secretly? That they are the ultimate objects of desire?"

"No, it's not true. I'm with *you*. I love *you*. I know some black men can't wait to get them a white woman first chance they get, no matter what she looks like. It wasn't that way for me. I was working in an all-white environment. At that time in my life, that was my circle. Those women were friends who wound up becoming more than that. Both situations were just casual." He goes on, "Still, I do think people can simply fall in love, despite their race."

I feel sick to my stomach and fall against the headboard.

"Why do I tell you things if you're going to judge me and get angry with me? My past has nothing to do with you."

"It has everything to do with me," I yell. "I can't make you understand because you are not a black woman."

"But I'm a black man and you know what I've been through." The anger he's kept contained begins to seep into his tone, into the air, into me.

I know he knows how it feels to have skin that is judged, rejected. To internalize past experiences so that even when you're not being discriminated against, you believe that you are. Always, I am conscious that I'm brown. In meetings and classrooms where I am the minority saddled with stereotypes, my tongue turns to brown, my teeth, the inside of my throat. My words tangle in the muddiness. They slip and slide around my mouth, slamming against the inside of my cheeks. The intelligence and confidence I'd had moments before melt into self-doubt. Sediment.

I feel desperate to make Ric see why I feel betrayed, I keep reaching. "You are not a black woman from the South. You—you are feared. I am worse. I am nothing. I wish you could get inside my skin, get inside me."

Ric and I get over that day in the bedroom, that night in the club, the few heated arguments that follow. For the time being anyway. I try to see things from his point of view, my grandmother's. I wonder what would happen if we *could* turn skin inside out, to its underbelly.

Grandmama saw underneath that white man's skin. She saw how, in suffering and death, we are all the same. But it wasn't Grandmama who had the power to save her husband from prison; it was the white woman, who simply did what she was supposed to do: told the truth.

Even if history didn't impact us, the knowledge that we are all the same underneath doesn't erase present-day injustices. And if I were blinded and could no longer see my skin, it wouldn't erase fears I've held that white women in a club or white men in a meeting could snatch something away from me. It wouldn't erase the hate these fears stir inside me.

12. Ali, Foreman, Mailer, and Me

BY TONY GREEN

I STARTED THINKING ABOUT NORMAN MAILER while stuck in rush-hour traffic on Pinellas County, Florida's stretch of U.S. 19, while eyeing the "What Would Jesus Do" sticker on the car in front of me. As a white radio deejay spewed frat-house hip-hop lingo over a Ludacris track, I imagined the sticker morphing into "What Would Norman Mailer Say?" The churchgoing Baptist in me doled out a matronly head slap, and I obligingly banished the image.

But it did cause food for thought. What would the author of "The White Negro" think of modern sports/pop culture? What would he have made of, say, Michael Jordan's triumphant return from retirement? The Cherica Adams trial? Lawrence Taylor? Or, more provocatively, what would the Mailer of "The Fight" have to say about George Foreman? Could he, a quarter of a century ago, have predicted that the sullen engine of destruction (whose self-contained silences caused Mailer to speculate on the hidden power of catatonics) would be playing a burger-grilling Shazann for the post-boomer crowd? That he would manage to have not only regained the heavyweight title, but have managed to erase his reputation as a thug, bully, and clay-footed, slow witted musclehead? I could feel the image of the Mailer bumper sticker slowly coming into focus again. After all, no one has more willingly sacrificed himself on the race-cultural cross, dying for the future gaffes of his fellow Caucasian thinkers and scholars. But then again, Mailer is too obviously flawed to be called a martyr. Maybe he is, as a professor friend of mine opined, like an enemy POW testing out a minefield ahead of his captors, managing to stay on his feet just long enough to detonate every booby trap.

"I mean," my friend told me, "he made every possible mistake before everybody else. I read some of his stuff and I'm like, man, I'm glad he said this before I did."

Despite this, I love to read Mailer on boxing. I remember absorbing the paperback version of his "King of the Hill" essay on the first Ali-Frazier fight. An early writer, I had already done my requisite turn as the poetically inclined, vocabulary word–spewing black kid at my predominantly white elementary school. My father had me reading vocabulary workbooks and listening to 33-rpm audio courses on language (remember those Morris Schreiber packages?), so writing wasn't that new. What struck me most about that book was that it hinted at the hidden world of athletic competition, the one that existed in the minds of the athletes. That it came closest to mapping the hyper-speed collision among strategy, reason, emotion, and reaction that too many writers have termed "instinct" (I told one sportswriting colleague that athletic feats seem like instinct to him because the athletes were just thinking faster than him; he, naturally, laughed). That isn't to say that I felt he got it right; even then his racial signifying made me feel kinda queasy. I was just impressed that he acknowledged the existence of something that the average box-score–junkie sportswriter of the time wasn't willing to. My addiction to "King of the Hill," in retrospect, happened because it was the only piece of writing I had read that made me feel the same way I did when I was trying to gauge the trajectory of a fly ball, man-cover a quick guard, or fake out a tackler in youth-league competition. Long, hyperthyroid prose and exclamatory decorations ("Ho! How his timing was off"), I admired him, yet still with reservations, the same way I would have admired Jack London had I been exposed to his anti–Jack Johnson rhetoric at the same time I was absorbing "The Most Dangerous Game." Or reading James Lincoln Collier's *The History of Jazz,* in which Collier undid his jazz scholarship with oddball musings and armchair psychology. Mailer could convey the spirit of the athletic mind in a lot of ways, even the workings of it, yet it was often through sheer force of craft—Mailer channeling his own pugnacious spirit through his protean writing skills. While he often made brilliant observations of the fighters' technical nuances and how their per-sonalities played out during the arc of a fight or training session, their in-ner motivations—the spiritual/psychological latticework that backdropped their quicksilver decisions and actions—seemed impenetrably opaque, leaving Mailer reading his own reflection in their actions and thoughts. Describing Frazier as a racial archetype—"the son of the hardworking black woman whom white employers would describe as 'deserving some-thing better in her life'"—did a disservice to Frazier's obviously complex nature. For me, a lifelong athlete (football, wrestling, track, weight-lifting, martial arts), reading Mailer has often been a way of preparing myself for my real-life interactions. If, as my friend suggested, his writing is a road map to white America's racial id, then it's helpful to know what you're up against.

Ever since he came on the scene, George Foreman has always fasci-nated me. Capable of lifting grown men off the ground with an uppercut (as he did to Joe Frazier in their first fight), he was the kind of exclamation-point athlete that, more than the swift and fanciful, appealed to me.

I grew up on a group home in Yonkers, New York, where my father worked as a cottage parent. Which put me in an odd position, shuttling among the black and Hispanic friends I spent most of my time with, my working-class Irish, Italian, and WASP elementary school mates (and sports league teammates), and, later, my upper-class private school bud-dies. Among other things, it gave me a chance to see how a large athletic black man would get along in several different settings, and gave me a bit of appreciation for what I would later see as the George Foreman catch-22.

After a pickup game, me and my group-home friends would sit around after the Little League season and recount some great move that the Gi-ants' Ron Johnson had put on somebody during the season, while I would be secretly hoping somebody would bring up the hit Jack Tatum put on

Frenchy Fuqua on the famous "Immaculate Reception"—so ferocious that it sent the ball flying some twenty yards across the field—so that I would have something really interesting to talk about.

As I grew bigger and stockier, I became less the swift dodger I had been as a kid, more gravity-centered earthmover. By age thirteen I had outgrown my age-group weight limit and wound up a lineman on the youth league's varsity. I played well, but back home, I had nothing to tell my buddies. Nobody wanted to hear about hard tackles or good blocks. They wanted to hear about touchdowns, caught passes. Or more to the point, nice moves. Fake-outs. Burns. Outrunning some hapless fool in the open field in front of everybody, or making him grab air on a sweep. By that time I had started private school I had started getting "white boy" treatment. Not because of my brains (contrary to public perception, my peers respected me for being smart), but because of my style; I was slower, gruntier, and decidedly less flashy than my boys. White, like the working kids who populated my Little League. To whom I was the hard-working, upstanding black scholar/athlete (a decade or so later, when I ran into a couple of them in a bar in the Bronx, they praised me as a local kid who went to private school and "beat up the rich Jew boys").

On the other hand, around my private school friends (I actually shared a class with one of Mailer's kids) I was the bad ass. The black kid who would run right over you if he had a chance in pickup games, or was a good enforcer to have on your side when somebody owed you lunch money. I was the resident expert on "jive," and whether a Jimmie Walker imitation was good or not. Which was cool, except when it came time to get called on in spelling contests (I was, after all, a city champ in elementary school), or to talk about books, activities I found myself left out of. I got tired of explaining to kids in gym class why I wore Afro Sheen, or why I wore dress shoes and Ban-Lons to school (my pop had some out-of-touch ideas about what was hip in upper-class circles). I became sullen and uncommunicative. My inner life, I felt, was beyond the understanding of all but a few of my classmates, so I slipped into the easy roles of bully, clown, and hell-raiser. The kind who tipped over teachers' desks in empty classrooms on a dare. Which was good except when I got in a play-fight with one of my homeboys who had also come up from our Yonkers hood. He leaned against the science building wall in a rope-a-dope and shouted, in a voice that would make Billy Crystal go home and get it right: "You too slow, Joe. You too slow, Joe! I'm the greatessstttt."

Aaargh!!!!

So when I read Mailer's take on Foreman, I understood a lot. First, about how I must have seemed to many of my friends, the more genuine of which I still talk with. But also, how Foreman must have felt in Zaire, facing outsider status from Africans and African Americans (one speaker in the documentary *When We Were Kings* declared that fans in Zaire didn't care that Ali was "less black" than Foreman—he was more "genuine"), misunderstood by the white press corps ("black folks don't fear black folks the way white folks fear black folks," Ali would say), and fetishized by the white intellectual elite. Mailer described Foreman's press conference demeanor as resembling "a huge black chorus."

"The word 'murderous intent' does not quite apply," Mailer said in *When We Were Kings*. "Foreman was awesome." Howard Cosell, in his funereal prefight elegy to Ali, spoke of Foreman in the kind of hushed tones reserved for conquering armies.

When Foreman lined up to fight Muhammad Ali in 1974, I was hoping for a Big George knockout. For me, it would be black strength's ultimate victory over black speed and flash. The ordinary black athlete's victory over the front-runner, who captured the imagination of everyone from the hood to Park Avenue. When Foreman lost, was knocked out, on top of it all it was devastating to me. Not so much because I was the only dude in my clique who was rooting for him, but because, it seemed I was the only one in the entire world who was rooting for him, who knew that there were more George Foremans in the world than there were Alis.

In "No One Knows My Name" James Baldwin pricks Mailer's inability to recognize the need for black men to create their own identity, faced with a society bent on assigning them one. One of the lessons of "The White Negro" is that a black athlete, more than any other, has to be careful when selecting his public persona, since he, more than other athletes, exists as an archetype. Especially in these endorsement-happy times, in which offending an archconservative media company shareholder can determine whether you build your second house in Mississippi or Milan.

Opting to simply be yourself is chancy, though possible to pull off (as Bill Russell demonstrated) since the public often has a hard time reconciling the seemingly contradictory nature of a black athlete's true persona. I remember one sports fan lamenting, for example, that "Hank Aaron is such a nice, hardworking guy, you wonder why he can't just let all that race stuff go." And Barry Bonds would fit the classic romantic definition of an "introspective, temperamental artist" were he anything but a ballplayer. Foreman's Staggolee-ish identity through the Ali fight was pretty stock, as was his reaction to loss. Bullies tend to disintegrate after being proven beatable, and Foreman reacted in type. He was sullen and bitter, paranoid even. In a *Sports Illustrated* article, he accused Ali of having "his people" loosen the ropes so that the challenger could rope-a-dope more easily. In another, ten years after the fight, he still claimed that this loss was the result of intrigue: he said the water that his trainer had given him had tasted strange. He wondered why his adviser, Archie Moore (every bit the ring genius Ali was), had kept advising him to keep slugging, playing into Ali's strategy.

He could be brilliant or buffoonish in the ring. He destroyed Joe Frazier for a second time, and registered a now classic slugfest win over Ron Lyle. On the other side, he resorted to a circuslike bout against five fighters, during which he argued with a ringside Ali while clumsily attempting to show off his footwork. Then after a twelve-round decision loss to Jimmy Young, he went into a heat-exhaustion-fueled delirium, and retired from boxing for ten years. That's the official version. Foreman's is essentially the same, except that he claimed to have seen the Lord.

I, for one, have always believed his religious and personal conversion.

From all accounts, even Mailer's Foreman was a genial, personable sort when not swallowed up by the boxing hype machine. Even in his previous life as a thug, Foreman was a failure as a purse-snatcher because he kept returning purses to women who called out to the Lord.

Still, if I and others have trouble completely accepting him as the changed Big George, it's because it just happened to be the only role he could have reasonably assumed, in the wake of the loss, were he interested in entering public life after the loss.

The list of available identities for black athletes has always been kind of spare. The Bill Russells and Archie Moores, truth be told, are more common than one would think, yet thoughtful sorts like Alan Page and Calvin Hill have always seemed to exist somewhere on the margins of the pop-sports radar. Then there was the "Ali opponent" stigma. Ali's boxing genius was rivaled (surpassed, some say) by his ability to affect context, to determine the grounds on which every aspect of the fight would be fought, keenly cognizant not only of the perceptions of his black constituency, but of white onlookers. Bill Russell, in his biography, provides a graphic demonstration of this ultimate power: A man is choking another in public, but when others try to intervene, the choker claims that his victim is a Nazi. The focus then shifts from the attack to Nazis; since most people have trouble with the moral quandaries presented by offering help to someone who is the incarnation of evil, the victim has to then prove that he is not a Nazi before he suffocates. Ali/Russell chokeholded his opponents as a matter of course. Athletes like Frazier, Larry Holmes, Sonny Liston, Ken Norton, and Earnie Shavers had the misfortune of entering the game during the Ali era, which meant that their own talents went unappreciated. This, in a roundabout way, served to underscore Ali's prowess as a fighter showman and tactician—only an individual of his spectacular talents could have reduced arguably the toughest group of heavyweights in history to costars in his traveling show.

One way he did this was by making them fight his fight out of and in the ring. In the ring, by forcing them to contend with his overwhelming abilities. And out of it by dictating the grounds on which any discussions of a fight would be framed. Opponents were often peppered with questions not about themselves or about their abilities, but about what Ali said about them. Sometimes they asked for it. Floyd Patterson, in his lack of regard for Ali's religious and political beliefs, practically sized himself up for the "sellout" treatment, as well as a ferociously sadistic in-ring beating. Other times they didn't. Sonny Liston was definitely menacing, but not "ugly," as Ali characterized him.

Fighters who tried to buck the Ali stigma often found themselves running headlong into concrete roadblocks. Joe Frazier filled the role of eternal foil pretty nicely. Frazier has in the past confessed an anthracite hatred of Ali, still demanding satisfaction for decades-old slights, finding solace in jabs at Ali's health ("he was the one calling me stupid. Me or him, who talks better now?"). And with good reason: Who can forget Ali pummeling a tar-black rubber gorilla in a prefight press conference before their third and final fight in Manila? Frazier was so irate, said his then trainer Eddie Futch, that he scrapped his strategy (one Futch said would have won him the fight) and tried to take Ali's head off.

Larry Holmes, a decent, working-class type from Easton, Pennsylvania, felt rightfully unappreciated in his role as the dominant post-Ali heavyweight, and got branded as a bitter, acerbic malcontent for his trouble. Which isn't to say that he wasn't bitter, it's just that years of living in the shadow of his former sparring partner gave him every right to be. Just as beating every fighter put in front of him gave him, on many levels, the right to bristle at being compared to a thirty-pounds-lighter, five-inches-shorter former champion (Marciano). Assuming that Foreman was inclined to think in terms of cultural strategy (and there is no reason to assume that he isn't), he would realize a couple of things pretty quickly. First, that he couldn't milk his association with Ali, since the Champ's self-made mythology wasn't hearing nothing about polytheism. And George was smart enough not to play the clichéd "lemme teach these youngsters something" oldster.

So when he resurfaced in 1987, it was as a comebacking, overweight thirty-eight-year-old, bent on regaining the title with a smile and a blessing instead of a scowl and an uppercut. Not entirely contrived, to be sure, but right on time.

He was, predictably, ridiculed, even through a gallant decision loss to then-champ Evander Holyfield in 1991. His other fights were less spectacular. He was outboxed and beaten up in a decision win over Alex Stewart in 1991, and outpointed by overhyped white hope Tommy Morrison in 1992. Finally, in 1994 he regained the heavyweight title by knocking out Michael Moorer, who, after outboxing Foreman for most of the fight, was stupid enough to offer the then forty-five-year-old slugger a stationary target in the bout's waning moments. Onlookers marveled at how he had softened his edges, how he carried himself with an avuncular cuddliness, proclaiming his love for cheeseburgers and pummeling himself with good-natured fat jokes.

A skeptic would carp that it all worked out too perfectly. Everything falling into place the way it did, Foreman reinventing himself as the one Black Man that he could have, winning the title, becoming a brand name. It had to be planned. I, for one, believe it was God. Had to be, since only one truly born again could resist the temptation to rub the world's faces in his success. The fact that Big George hasn't makes me believe he is a much better man than me, than nearly all of us, for that matter. I imagine myself at his age, financially secure and happy after being spectacularly humiliated before the world, being the butt of "slow and dumb" jokes by sportswriters and even handlers. I'd spend my days thinking of ways to tell folks to kiss my ass instead of marketing electric grill machines to bad techno music.

George, despite all his success, is kind of a disappointment to me. The more you scratch the surface of the New George, the more you realize that it doesn't explode the limits of his original fetishization, it validates them. George's current incarnation wouldn't work without the original perception of him as a merciless engine of destruction. The gentle, avuncular George is merely a variation on the original, not a transformation. It seems like a transformation compared with some of the sports world's more notorious one-note virtuosos: Lawrence Taylor, who seems determined to play the out-of-control raw dog until he's on a respirator. Or Roberto Duran, who, in continuing to box into the half-century mark, gives the appearance of someone incapable of accepting any other role than that of fighter.

But the real reason Foreman's cuddly black man routine drives me nuts is because, deep down, I suspect that this is his real persona. You can't deride him as a charlatan, nor can you even wish a fantasy ass-kicking on him (you know the kind you wish on, say, Barney). I mean, this is George Foreman, after all. And you have to give it up to him.

A friend of mine once waggisly claimed that he could actually hear the sighs of relief whenever New George opened his mouth, a result of yet another assurance that he was not a threat to anyone, anytime, despite appearances to the contrary. There is evidence that the old bad ass survived into the nineties—he just let him out on the relatively safe cultural targets that got set in front of him inside the ring. His famous uppercut contemptuously stretched washed-up white-hope Gerry Cooney. An almost casual left hook nearly beheaded Adilson Rodrigues, who had managed to give then champion Holyfield a considerably tougher time (Rodrigues told about how seconds later, they had to prop Rodrigues up from behind the ring apron so he wouldn't topple into the seats). He wasn't above resorting to some strategic low blows to slow down a more nimble Alex Stewart in 1992. Or, claiming that he had received permission from God to kill then champ Michael Moorer, whom he eventually knocked out to regain the heavyweight belt (well, at least one of them, boxing being what it was, and is).

Part of me wants to rage at the institutionally racist problems mainstream society has with aggressive black men (see the softening of MLK and Ali's pop-culture personae). The other part of me, the ex-middle guard and wrestler, to paraphrase the Fantastic Four's Ben Grimm, "wants somethin' to hit."

I'm in my mind's eye again, this time watching Big George rehearse a burger commercial with a short, pudgy, slightly elderly white sidekick, mugging, throwing fake punches. "Come on, Big George," the sidekick says, "show me what you got. I'm too pretty; I'm too fast, rope-a-dope! Rope a dope." At which point George throws a lazy straight right, playful, gentle. At the last minute, he snaps his half-fist into a clench, bends his fight knee, and, almost indiscernibly, rotates his fist forty-five degrees. The sidekick crumples to the ground. Blood flies. The crew gasps.

"Oh man, I'm so soooorrrrry."

13. The 1960s in Bamako:
Malick Sidibé and James Brown

BY MANTHIA DIAWARA

I WAS LOOKING AT A BOOK OF Malick Sidibé's photographs, put together by André Magnin (Scala Press, 1998), with my friend Diafode, who has been living in France since 1979. As we flipped through the black-and-white photos of our teenage years in Bamako, Diafode's attention was suddenly drawn by a photo of a group of boys entitled "Friends, 1969." *"Les Beatles!"* he exclaimed, and added, putting his index finger on the photo, *"Voilà les Beatles."* ("The Beatles, there are the Beatles.") I looked closely at it, and before I could even say a word, Diafode started identifying them one by one: there was John Lennon, Ringo Starr, and all the other members of the Beatles of Medina-Coura, one of the hip neighborhoods of Bamako in those days.

Diafode and I spent that evening in my Paris apartment, looking at the Beatles of Medina-Coura and reminiscing about our youth in Bamako. Sure enough, I now could see Nuhun, a.k.a. John Lennon. He's wearing a "Col Mao" jacket with six buttons, just like the one John Lennon wore on the cover of one of the Beatles' albums. Nuhun now lives in Canada. And there's Cissé, a.k.a. "Paris," with his arm on Nuhun's shoulder. He's wearing a tight-fitting shirt, with a scarf à la Elvis Presley, a large belt, and bell-bottom pants. We used to call him Paris because he was so elegant and smooth. When he used to live in Bamako-Coura—a neighborhood on the southern tip of the commercial center—and did not have a motorcycle to come to Medina-Coura on the north side, he would walk for forty-five minutes to cross the busy commercial center, under the hot sun at two o'clock, to join the group at Nuhun's house to listen to music, play cards, and drink tea.

The elegance of Paris's style was also marked by a pack of Craven A cigarettes, which he placed in his shirt pocket while holding one unlit cigarette between his lips. He walked slowly through the busy crowd of the market and across the railway, without losing his rhythm and without sweating a drop. When he arrived at Nuhun's place, his shoes were always shiny and his face was as fresh as ever. He would always say, *"Salut, les copains,"* before taking a napkin out of his pocket, wiping off a chair, and sitting down. We used to say that one day, Paris would surely leave Bamako for Europe. With his Craven A cigarette and tailored shirts, he looked like the actors from the Italian photonovellas. Paris now lives in Canada too.

Other guys in the photo reminded Diafode and me of more Bamako stories. There is Addy, who went to Switzerland to study hotel management and returned to Bamako in 1970 with the first copy of the *Four-Way Street* album by Crosby, Stills, Nash and Young. We had organized "Woodstock in Bamako" with Addy's record collection. Since then, Addy had worked for hotels in Abidjan and Bamako before opening his own business in Bamako. That one over there is Niare, who's sitting on the floor and holding the album by Sly and the Family Stone that contains "I Wanna Take You Higher." Niare now works for the Malian government as an accountant. And in the back there, we have Amara, a.k.a. "Harley-Davidson," who is wearing a flowered shirt. In those days, everybody had to have a flowered shirt to feel part of the youth culture, not only in Bamako, but also in Paris, London, and Amsterdam. Harley, who is now an abstract painter and conceptual artist in Bamako, was even in those days a dreamer and a little bit on the wild side. He was convinced that he would seize history one day and become the center of it.

Malick Sidibé's photographs enable us to revisit the youth culture of the 1960s and our teenage years in Bamako. They show exactly how the young people in Bamako had embraced rock and roll as a liberation movement, adopted the consumer habits of an international youth culture, and developed a rebellious attitude toward all forms of established authority. The black-and-white photographs reflect how far the youth in Bamako had gone in their imitation of the worldview and dress style of popular music stars.

Malick Sidibé's photographic art was talked about in every conversation, along with the design of popular magazines, album covers, and movie posters of the time. To say that Bamako's youth were on the same page as the youth in London and Paris in the 1960s and 1970s is also to acknowledge Malick Sidibé's role in shaping and expanding that culture.

To the youth in Bamako, Malick Sidibé was the James Brown of photography: the godfather whose clichés described the total energy of the time. Inasmuch as today there is a desire to go back to the music and film of the 1960s and 1970s in order to give a meaning to that culture, we can also go back to Malick Sidibé's photographs to gain access to the style, vibrancy, and ethos of those times in Africa.

So implicated are his photographs in the culture of the 1960s that when we look at them, our youth comes back to life. They are the gateway to everything that was fashionable then, everything that constituted our modernism. They are a document through which one can see the passage of time in Bamako as marked by dress style (from B-boys to hippies), music appreciation (from Latin beat to James Brown), movies (from westerns to *Easy Rider*), hairstyle (from Patrice Lumumba and Marlon Brando to the Afro), and dance moves (from the Twist to the Camel Walk).

In Sidibé's photographs, one can see the turbulence of youth and the generational conflict that characterized the 1960s. The desires of youth are inscribed in most of the photos as a determined break with tradition and as a transformation of the meaning of the decolonization movements of the 1960s into a rock and roll revolution. It is clear from his photographs that what the youth in Bamako wanted most in those days was James Brown and the freedom and existential subjectivity that linked independence to the universal youth movement of the 1960s. The photographs show that, in attempting to be like James Brown, Jimi Hendrix, the Beatles, and the Rolling Stones, they were also revealing their impatience with the political teachings of the nationalist state and the spirit of decolonization.

As Diafode and I looked at these photographs now, more than a quarter of a century later, I felt a strange familiarity, a simultaneous desire and repulsion. I looked intently at every photograph in the book, each more than once, looking for myself, but at the same time dreading the possibility of finding myself there. These photographs are speaking to me now, not only as important aesthetic documents on the culture of the 1960s, but also as documents that both problematized the narrow meaning of nationalism at that time, and opened the door for a Pan-African and diasporic aesthetics through rock and roll.

I am proposing here to go beyond the nostalgic function that the photographs served for my friend Diafode and me that night in Paris. This is not to underrate nostalgia as a significant element in photography and the other arts. On the contrary, photo albums and home videos of weddings and naming celebrations play an important role in the lives of African immigrants in Paris and elsewhere. They protect them from the effects of segregation in the host country by providing entertainment and pleasure. They also constitute a link between the immigrants and their original homes, and thus foster a sense of community culture.

But to understand the conditions of emergence and evolution of Sidibé's formal style in these photographs, it is important to place him in the social and historical context of the 1960s in Bamako. Malick Sidibé was one of the first studio photographers in Bamako to take a lighter and cheaper 35 mm camera outside, to house parties and picnics, in order to take pictures of young people. As he followed the youth, who themselves were following a universal youth movement, he discovered his style in photography, which I will call rhythmic or motion photography. But how did we arrive at the finished product that we have in this book today? How did the bodily dispositions and the structure of feeling of the subjects in Sidibé's photography change from those in the work of his predecessor Seydou Keita?

It is important to understand that at the time they were taking people's pictures in Bamako, neither Malick Sidibé nor Seydou Keita considered himself an artist. It is also important to understand that the types of photos each took and the perfection they both achieved in their work were a condition of the demand that existed at their respective times. Photographers in Bamako were no different than the barbers or tailors—they all beautified their clients or provided them with styles for the visual pleasure of people in

Bamako. Their success depended on word of mouth, which contributed, as Pierre Bourdieu would put it, to increasing their symbolic capitals. They only became artists by first pleasing their customers, by providing them with the best hairstyles, dresses, and photographs.

Seydou Keita's photography was both enhanced and limited by the economic, social, and cultural conditions prevailing in Bamako between 1945 and 1964, when he had to close his studio and become a civil servant for the socialist government in Mali. The people he photographed in his studio were from the middle class. They were from traditional Bamako families—businessmen and their wives, landlords, and civil servants (schoolteachers, soldiers, and clerks for the colonial administration). As a photographer, Seydou Keita's role was to make his subjects look like they belonged to the bourgeoisie and middle class of Bamako, to make them feel modern and Bamakois. The women were very beautiful, with their hair braided and decorated with gold rings, and their long dresses with embroidery at the neck. The men wore European suits or traditional boubous, and they exhibited their watches, radios, or cars. Seydou Keita produced artifice through studio mise-en-scène and makeup to ensure that every one of his subjects looked like an ideal Bamakois, a bourgeois nobleman or -woman, or a civil servant invested with the authority of the colonial administration.

When independence arrived in 1960 and the colonial administration had to cede its place to the new government of Mali, people's relation to photography, as to many other things in Bamako, began to change. Civil servants were no longer content with their intermediary roles between whites and Africans; they were now competing with the traditional leaders for control of the country. They no longer wanted to mimic the colonial administrator in Seydou Keita's studio; they wanted to be seen occupying the colonial master's chair at his office, his house, and his places of leisure. As these patterns of life changed in Bamako, new structures of feeling emerged and studio photography became devalorized as something conservative and artificial. Soon the studio's customers would be largely composed of people who needed passport and identification photos and visitors from rural areas. Seydou Keita's reaction to the changes was also conservative: not only did he have problems with the new socialist government, but he also found women in pants, miniskirts, and Afro hairdos to be neither beautiful nor religiously acceptable in a predominantly Muslim country.

Thus, the change in power from a colonial system to an independent state brought about a profound transformation in people's sense of aesthetics in photography. Young people especially began to look upon studio photography as old-fashioned or as something reserved for those who were pretending to be Bamakois: to be photographed in the studio was associated with being a fake and a powerless pretender. In other words, studio photography was seen as unreal, whereas realism had become the criterion for defining the new aesthetics of Bamakois photography. By insisting on realism, people were demanding a new photography that portrayed them as actors in situations, a photography that was neither a studio reenactment nor an imitation of something previously done. The new Bamakois wanted to be filmed while he or she took the center of the action that was unfolding. Photographers, therefore, had to come out of the studio and follow the action wherever it was taking place.

It was these limitations of studio photography—a genre fostered by colonialism—that led to Malick Sidibé's emergence as the photographer of the young generation. While maintaining his studio—largely for passport photos and camera repair—Sidibé took his camera to where the youth were and photographed them there. I will therefore define the youth's sense of a new realism in photography less as an absence of artifice, mise-en-scène, and mimicry, then as something tied to the location and historical action of the subjects in the photos. In other words, each photo tells a story located in space and time that serves to empower the subject. The emphasis on action was meant to bring photography as close to live action as possible.

There is, however, another problem related to a change in power relations in Bamako that needs to be addressed when discussing Sidibé's photography. It would seem that his photos of young Bamakois are in contradiction not only with colonial-era studio photography, but also with the patterns of life that one would expect in a decolonized state. According to the famous theses on culture developed by Aimé Césaire and Frantz

Fanon, it is not only impossible to create a national culture under colonialism, but it is also equally evident that artifacts like these photos are signs of neocolonialism and Western imperialism. Writing about African independence in the 1960s, Césaire stated that whereas the colonial era was characterized by the "reification" of the African, the transition to independence would give rise to a revival of his creative energies, and a recovery of his authentic ways of being that had been forbidden by the colonizer. Independence would awaken in the individual the African personality that had for so long been suppressed. For Césaire, "after the 'moment' of precolonial Africa, a moment of 'immediate truth,' and the colonial 'moment,' a moment of the shattered African consciousness, independence inaugurates a third dialectical 'moment,' which must correspond with a reconciliation of the mind with its own consciousness and the reconquest of a plenitude" ("La pensée politique de Sékou Touré," *Présence Africaine* 29 [December 1959–January 1960], 67).

For theoretical purposes, it is important to retain Césaire's use of the terms "moment," "immediate truth," "own consciousness," and "plenitude." All of them refer to independence as an authentic state of being, a state of genuine creative and natural harmony between the precolonial past and the present. In contrast, the colonial and neocolonial state were characterized by assimilation, alienation, and depersonalization of the African. Authors like Césaire expected the continent to create a new man with an African style in politics and culture. Lumumba, Sékou Touré, and Kwame Nkrumah were the prototypes of the ideal post-independence image, and they were all fiercely nationalist, authentic, and anti-imperialist. That the images of the youth in Sidibé's photographs did not seem to reflect the Africa these leaders were attempting to shape has been interpreted as an indication of how alienated the youth were, as a sign that the youth were not in continuity with the political history of the nation. The photos could be said therefore to reveal the presence of neocolonialism among the youth.

Indeed, in Mali, the socialist government created a militia in the mid-1960s to monitor the behavior of the people in conformity with the teachings of socialism. This militia was aimed not only at abolishing traditional chiefs and other tribal customs, but also at correcting the youth's habitus, i.e.: body disposition, style, corporal hexus. In Bamako, curfews were set and youths caught wearing miniskirts, tight skirts, bell-bottom pants, and Afro hairdos were sent to reeducation camps. Their heads were shaved and they were forced to wear traditional clothes. The situation did not get any better for the youth after the military takeover in 1968. Even though the former regime was castigated for taking people's freedom away, for being worse than the colonizer in its destruction of African traditions, and for being against free enterprise, the soldiers who replaced the militia continued to patrol the streets of Bamako in search of rebellious and alienated youth. It was clear, therefore, that to both the independence leaders and the military regime in Bamako, the youth in Sidibé's photographs were not obeying the teachings of independence, nationalism, and tradition. They were mimicking the culture of the colonizer, which shut the door to authentic self-actualization.

Looking at Sidibé's photographs today, it is possible to see what was not visible then on account of the rhetorical teachings of revolution. It is indeed clear to me that the youth's refiguration of the independence movement, their appropriation of the political history of decolonization, and their representation of their freedom were all misrecognized by their elders. According to Bourdieu in his lecture on Edouard Manet at the College de France, 2000, one can obey the past without representing it. In assessing the youth's continuity with and transformation of the political history of independence in Bamako, it is therefore critical to look at the degree to which the youth had internalized and incarnated the lessons of the revolution. The youth had quickly internalized African culture, collapsed the walls of binary opposition between colonizer and colonized, and made connections beyond national frontiers with the Diaspora and international youth movements. That the theory of decolonization could not recognize this at the time as anything but mimicry and assimilation is an indication of its failure to grasp the full complexity of the energies unleashed by independence.

First of all, the youth saw in the departure of the colonizer from Bamako an opportunity to seize the city for themselves, to become the modernizing agents of their hometown, and to occupy its leisure spaces. Independence also enabled them to exhibit African cultures that until then had been for-bidden by the colonizer. Thus, they could go back and forth in history with-out interruption, and without the permission of the new government or the traditional religious and tribal leaders. The youth in Bamako felt free to pick and choose as a prerogative of their new freedom. Their dress style, their point of view, and their corporal hexus constituted a new habitus in Bamako that was misrecognized by their parents. What I call here "change of habi-tus," following Pierre Bourdieu, can also be understood through Raymond Williams's notion of change in patterns of life. For Williams as well, the training of youth in social character and cultural patterns may result in youth's developing its own structures of feeling, which will appear to come out of nowhere: "The new generation responds in its own ways to the unique world it is inheriting, taking up many continuities that can be traced, and re-producing many aspects of the organization, which can be separately de-scribed, yet feeling its whole life in certain ways differently, and its shaping its creative response into a new structure of feeling" (p. 49).

Clearly, what Bourdieu and Williams are saying is that one cannot pre-dict the outcome of a revolution, nor the new habitus that will develop out of power relations, nor from where the youth will draw the resources for their creative and epistemological ideas. As the civil rights leaders in Amer-ica have learned from the generation that succeeded them, it is much easier to liberate people than to tell them how to live their freedom. Unlike revo-lution, freedom cannot be taught—otherwise, it is a freedom that is no longer free, a freedom under siege. The youth in Bamako did not want to be restricted in their freedom, and therefore used it to express the themes and aesthetics of Pan-Africanism, the black Diaspora, and rock and roll—some of which were in continuity with the independence movement, and some in contradiction with it.

If one follows Bourdieu's statement that habitus + capital = action, the challenge in Sidibé's photographs becomes how to describe the components of the youth's actions, the extent to which they represent an accumulation of social and cultural capitals in relation with Diaspora aesthetics and bodily dispositions that Bourdieu terms, appropriately, habitus. (Lecture on Manet).

The youth in Bamako, as in most modern African capitals in the 1960s, began building their social networks in high schools. High schools were important centers of intellectual and cultural life because, in the absence of a university at that time, they constituted the sites where the future elite of the nation gathered. Most young people also met at soccer games organized between schools, before forming their own clubs, or *Grins,* to use the common Bamako term of reference. By the time the high school youth had formed their *Grins,* they had already self-selected among the masses of students, cemented their friendships, and developed attitudes and styles specific to them. They would have already chosen a name—the Rockers, the Temptations, the Rolling Stones, the Soul Brothers, the Beatles—by which they were known, and they spread their reputation throughout Bamako.

The name was not the only important thing about a club; it was also crucial to have a permanent location associated with it—e.g., the Beatles of Medina-Coura—a sort of meeting place or headquarters for the group, with a turntable and a good collection of records, magazines, and detective novels that club members exchanged among themselves. Most *Grins* also had a shortwave radio which received BBC Radio, the Voice of America, and Radio France International. The Beatles of Medina-Coura regularly had the local newspaper, *L'Essor,* and occasionally one could find French papers like *Le Monde* and magazines like *Paris-Match* and *Salut les copains,* from which they removed the posters of the Beatles of Liverpool, Jimi Hendrix, and James Brown to put on the wall. Finally, every *Grin* had green tea, which the members drank while listening to music and debating several topics of the world at the same time. Every club built its reputation and symbolic capital by accumulating these important resources at the headquarters, and by organizing parties and picnics to which rival members of other groups were invited. It has been estimated that by the time Malick Sidibé was at the height of his career, there were more than 250 clubs in Bamako (for examples, see Andre Magnin, *Malick Sidibé*).

Besides debating over favorite rock stars, political discussions constituted an important characteristic of *Grins* in 1960s Bamako. Indeed, the way the youth talked about music, movies, or detective stories was always related to their own condition in Mali. They made a comparison between themselves and the people they saw on album covers, magazines, movie posters, as well as fictional characters in movies and novels. They debated the rock stars' stances against the war in Vietnam, racial discrimination in America, the peace movement associated with Martin Luther King, Jr., and Mahatma Gandhi, and Muhammad Ali as the world's heavyweight boxing champion. Discussion of African politics was generally concerned with the heroes of independence—Sékou Touré, Lumumba, and Nkrumah—who defied France, Belgium, and England respectively. The youth elevated these freedom fighters to the rank of icons like Mao Tse-tung, John F. Kennedy, André Malraux, Marilyn Monroe, James Dean, Malcolm X, Angela Davis, Che Guevara, and Fidel Castro.

The *Grins* were important centers of social criticism about what was lacking and what was needed in Bamako. People talked heatedly about the government, the restriction of people's freedom, and the incapacity of African nations to unite. Some argued that neocolonialism was the reason that the leaders could not get together, and that France and the CIA still had their hands in our affairs. The youths at the *Grins* also saw themselves as rebels against traditional socieities, which wanted to interject more religion into their lives and control the way they dressed and behaved. They thought of themselves as open-minded and tolerant toward each other, regardless of ethnic and caste origins. They therefore did not want to go back to the separation of people by tribe that was encouraged during the colonial era. They defined themselves first of all as Bamakois, Malian, and Pan-African, as opposed to Bambara or Fulani. Not only did the youth in Bamako organize their own Woodstock to listen to music in a public sphere and protest against apartheid in South Africa, Ian Smith's regime in Rhodesia, and the imprisonment of George Jackson and Hurricane Carter in the United States, but they also continued to resist the military dictatorship in Mali until its overthrow by a mass movement in 1992.

When I look at Sidibé's photographs today, I see this political action of the youth of Bamako: the way in which they transformed the themes of independence and adapted them for themselves, to the point of not being recognized by their elders. Because Bamako's youth could not content themselves with the mechanistic application of the political theory of independence, nor return to certain African traditions which would have imposed limits on their freedom, they turned to Pan-Africanism and the African Diaspora as powerful sources for the expression of their freedom.

THE IMPACT OF JAMES BROWN

Looking back at the period between the mid-1960s and the early 1970s in Bamako, it is clear that the single most important factor, after independence, that introduced change into youth's habitus was their exposure to Diaspora aesthetics through rock and roll and the Black Power movement. And in this respect, it is also clear from the visual evidence in Sidibé's photographs that James Brown was one of the most important references that combined the ethos of black pride with the energy of rock and roll. As independence changed power relations in Bamako, the reception of Diaspora aesthetics through popular culture opened the floodgate of youth's energy and creativity. The youth could see themselves more easily in James Brown or in a glossy photograph of a defiant Muhammad Ali than in any other motif of independence at that time.

This enthusiastic embrace of popular culture from the United States may seem odd in a newly independent socialist country like Mali. In Mali, as in other African countries, the U.S. had at that time been identified as the symbol of imperialism and capitalist exploitation. It is therefore crucial to explain what James Brown and other Diaspora aestheticians from North America were able to provide to Bamako's youth that could escape the critical eye of anti-capitalism and anti-imperialism, but that was lacking in the other independence-era social and political formations.

The identification with James Brown was total and uninterrupted; from the way he appeared in album cover photographs—as if caught in the middle of a trance—to the way his music and dance provoked the youth to action, James Brown was captivating. The dress styles that his influence popularized among Bamakois included tight turtleneck shirts with buttons or a zipper, which the local tailors made from looking at the pictures on the album covers. The same tailors also made the "James Brown style" of shorter, above-the-ankle bell-bottom pants, which were thought to enhance one's ability to dance the Jerk or the Mashed Potato.

In 1967, Malick Sidibé photographed two young women holding between them a James Brown album, *Live at the Apollo,* released that same year. I remember that white suits similar to the one James Brown is wearing on the album cover were all the rage at dance parties in Bamako. It is also a measure of the popularity of *Live at the Apollo* that it appears more often than any music album in Malick Sidibé's photography. There were also some songs on it, such as "Cold Sweat," "There Was a Time," "I Got You (I Feel Good)," and "It's a Man's, Man's, Man's World," without which no dance party in Bamako could rise to greatness. These James Brown hits, along with "Papa's Got a Brand New Bag" and "I Got the Feelin'," remained at the top of the charts in Bamako for more than a decade.

One of the girls in the photo is wearing a sleeveless blouse and skin-tight pants, while the other has on a checkered minidress reminiscent of the Supremes. They are both laughing and looking into the camera, each with one knee bent forward and the other leg spread back as if to mark a dance step. The girl on the left, wearing the minidress, is holding the record album in the center, between herself and her friend. The other girl is pressing her body against the album as if she were dancing with it. *Live at the Apollo* thus becomes an important part of the composition of this photo. Inasmuch as James Brown is clearly identifiable here by his picture and by his name, written in big letters on the album, one can say that he has become the third person in the photograph. By putting him in the center against their hearts, the two young girls transform him from a lifeless photo on an album cover to an omnipresence in front of Malick Sidibé's camera. It is as if, in the photo, they were dancing with the "real" James Brown.

It is also important to understand that the presence of the album in the photo helps redefine the young women. By seeing themselves in James Brown, identifying with the *Live at the Apollo* album, and becoming one with their idol through dance, they change themselves. The person looking at the picture also begins to see the two girls differently. For him, they assume a new identity that is secular and cosmopolitan. They are no longer stuck in the Malian identities defined by the tribe or by Islam. For example, in Mali, young women were not allowed to be seen by their parents dressed the way they were in this photo. Such conduct would have been deemed indecent by Islam. When young women went to the *Grin* or to a dance party, they smuggled their pants and miniskirts out the window beforehand, and then walked out the door dressed in traditional clothes. They only changed into their modern outfits once they were far from home and unrecognizable.

Clearly, therefore, Diaspora aesthetics were opposed to the habitus imposed by tradition, home, and Islam, and which sought to control the young girls' bodies. In this sense, identification with James Brown was an indication of where the youth in Bamako wanted to be at the time of independence, and of nationalist leaders' blindness to these desires. In fact, the origin of this photo becomes indeterminate, as the two young women take on this new identity influenced by James Brown and Diaspora aesthetics, one that had begun to emerge at the same time in Zambia, Liberia, Harlem, Senegal, Ghana, etc. The presence of James Brown in this photo helps therefore to explain the new habitus of post-independence, why young people dressed the way they did, and freed their bodies from the limitations imposed by older power relations.

I call this a Diaspora aesthetic, as opposed to a Malian or even an African aesthetic, because it is defined beyond the national boundary and united black youth through a common habitus of black pride, civil rights, and self-determination. The civil rights movement in America and the worldwide movement of decolonization were resources for this new aesthetic, and James Brown was the dominant symbol for the youth.

James Brown, as a figure mediated through civil rights and worldwide decolonization, had become for the youth the link between the new freedom and an African identity that had been repressed by slavery, Islam, and colonialism. By that, I mean that there is a storehouse of African cultural and spiritual practices that had been forced into silence and rendered invisible by colonialism and Islam and that emerge to the surface when the youth enter into contact with his music.

It is no secret that both colonialism and Islam fought hard to rid Africans of their gods, rituals, and cultures. Colonialism imposed itself in a binary manner, its leaders collecting African statues and masks in order to burn them or send them to museums in Europe, and replacing them with the Bible. For both Islam and Christianity, polytheism was the root of evil, and they therefore sought to fill the Africans' need for several gods with one God. In the process, they banned the priests who represented different gods, and left the rituals and dances unattended by an intermediary between the people and their creator. This destruction of the spiritual and technical base of African cultures is eloquently described in masterpiece after masterpiece of the creative writing of Africa and the African Diaspora. In Chinua Achebe's *Arrow of God*, the African priest loses his place in the harvest ritual to the Christian missionary. In Yambo Ouologuem's *Bound to Violence,* the anthropologist assists in the destruction of an African kingdom by collecting the masks and the oral traditions. In Maryse Condé's *Segu*, Elhadji Oumar's army of jihad destroys the Bambara Empire, burns the fetishes, baptizes the king, and puts a Muslim priest in charge of Segu.

By the time of independence in the 1960s, therefore, what we call "African" had been changed through and through by Islam and Christianity. Most important, the connections with the pre-Atlantic-slavery African had been destroyed or forgotten. The rituals seen today, performed for tourists or at the celebrations of the anniversary of independence, are fixed in time and devoid of any spiritual and technical meaning. They can no longer cure an epidemic, nor teach people the meaning of a puzzle. The presence of Islam and Christianity also means that people adopted a different way of praying that excludes dance, as well as a different disposition of the body which involves submission to God rather than an imitation of God through dance. It is therefore safe to say that Africans, who were famous in the literature of primitivism for their sense of rhythm, were without rhythm at the time of independence.

James Brown's music reconnected Bamako's youth to a pre-Atlantic-slavery energy that enabled them to master the language of independence and modernity and to express the return of Africanism to Africa through black aesthetics. The term "Africanism" has been used in a varied manner by Diaspora authors and theorists, including Amiri Baraka (LeRoi Jones) in *Blues People,* Robert Farris Thompson in *Flash of the Spirit,* V. Y. Mudimbe in *The Invention of Africa,* and Toni Morrison in *Playing in the Dark.* My use of "Africanism" here is closer to the way Baraka and Thompson have adopted the term, and to Houston Baker's concept of the "vernacular" in *Blues, Ideology, and Afro-American Literature*—all of which indicate the survival, transformation, and influence of pre-Atlantic-slavery African cultures on modernist cultures. By subverting Christianity and Islam as the spiritual guardians of modernity, Africanism endows itself with distinctive resources that my friend and colleague Clyde Taylor calls "pagan modernism."

To understand the impact of James Brown's music on the youth in Bamako, and what is here called pagan modernism, it is important, first, to make a detour to one of the pre-Atlantic-slavery cultures, which seems to have survived in James Brown's own performance. I refer here to the Dogon of Mali. According to Marcel Griaule, in his classic book *Dieu d'eau,* Dogon cosmology revolved around men and women's desire to be perfect like the Nommo. The Nommo were twin offspring of Amma, the Almighty God. Unlike their older brother, the incestuous jackal, who was ill-conceived through a union between Amma and the Earth, the Nommo were perfect in everything they did. They each had male and female organs, and would therefore reproduce without the other's help. That is why the Dogon refer to the Nommo both as singular and plural; every Nommo is identical to the other, but also depends on the other like the left hand depends on the right. It is through their function in identity and binarism that the Dogon believe the Nommo to be part god and part human, part fluid and part solid, part water and part snake.

The symbol of Nommo—variable and unlimited in Dogon cosmology and iconography—is also the vehicle for language. For the Dogon, the Nommo revealed the secret of language to men in three stages, each corresponding to a specific work and form of prayer. The first language, which is also the most abstract, came with the transformation of baobab barks into fibers with which to clothe the nakedness of the earth. Even today, the Dogon dress their masks and statues with these multicolored fibers that contain the most ancient language of Nommo, which is understood by very few people. The second language was revealed through the technique of weaving, and it was clearer, less sacred, and available to more people. Finally, the third language came with the invention of drums. It was a modern and democratic language understood by all. For the Dogon, mastery of these languages brought men closer to the purity and perfection of Nommo and placed them in control of their environment.

Through imitation of the Nommo's language, men could therefore partake of a divine essence and, like the eight ancestors of the Dogon, become Nommo themselves. If Nommo were in the drums that they had made to teach men language, then men, by beating drums, were speaking the language of Nommo, and they themselves were Nommo at that moment. As Ogotemmeli, Griaule's interlocutor in the book, puts it, men were "learning the new speech, complete and clear, of modern times" (*Dieu d'eau*, p. 74).

When we return to James Brown in the 1960s and consider his impact on the youth of post-independence Africa, we realize his Nommo-like quality: the desire to elevate men and women to perfection. James Brown is a Nommo—known as "shaman" elsewhere in the world—part god and part human, who teaches the world, through his music and dance, the complete and clear language of modern times, and who makes Bamako's youth coincide with the Dogon desire for perfection. Just like the Nommo was one with the drum—the beating of which taught men the language of modernity— James Brown was one with his band, though his was never complete without his red cape and his invitation to the masses to become part of his groove. People often say that James Brown, the hardest-working man in show business, does not say much in his songs, that he is notorious for limiting himself to a few words like "I feel all right," "You've got it, let's go," "Baby, baby, baby." In fact, James Brown, like the Nommo, uses his voice and vital power to imitate the language of his instruments—the trumpet and drums—to make his audiences understand better the appropriate discourse of our modern condition. James Brown's mimicry of the sound of his instruments—letting them speak through him as if he were one with them—communicated more clearly with his audiences the meaning of 1960s social movements than any other language at the time. By subordinating human language to the language of the drums, or the language of Nommo, James Brown was partaking in the universalization of Diaspora aesthetics, the freedom movements, and the discourse of black pride.

The reception of the *Live at the Apollo* album in Bamako was due in part to the fact that it contained a complete and clear language of modernity with which the youth could identify. James Brown's didactic concern with history and the names of dance steps and American cities was an important factor of identification with the album for the youth who knew that their independence was tied to the civil rights gains of people in the Diaspora. If we take, for example, a James Brown song, "I Feel All Right," it is easy to account for its popularity in Bamako. James Brown begins the tune in a ritualistic manner by addressing everybody in the building. Like the high priest in a ritual about to begin, James Brown, calling himself the "groove maker"— as in rainmaker, the priest of a harvest ritual or funeral—makes sure everyone is ready for the amount of soul, or vital energy, that he is about to unleash. He even summons the spirit of the Apollo Theater in these terms: "Building, are you ready? 'Cause we're gonna tear you down. I hope that the building can stand all the soul. You've got a lot of it coming." Then James Brown, at once the son of Nommo and Nommo himself, proceeds to explain the dance steps he is about to teach the world. He performs the dance a few times, asking the audience to repeat after him. Repetition is the key word here for Diaspora aesthetics: it marks the rhythm and accent of this new language. By imitating James Brown, one becomes James Brown, just as the imitation of Nommo's acts brings men closer to him.

Interestingly, as in all rituals, there is the risk of impurity, of something not working properly, and therefore threatening the success of the performance. During the song, we hear James Brown struggling with a man who was not properly following the directions he was giving: "My man always got to get his own extra thing in there," says an amused Brown. But, luckily for the people at the Apollo that evening, the groove prevailed and the ritual was a success, as James Brown screams: "You got it? Yeah, you got it! Now, let's go!" It is at such moments that James Brown reminds us most of Nommo, who could empower men and women and put them in control of their environment.

In Griaule's book, Ogotemmeli states that the first dance ever was a divination dance: "The son of God spoke through dance. His footsteps left marks on the dusty dance floor, which contained the meaning of his words" (198). Ogotemmeli goes on to say that the masked society that performs the dance rituals symbolizes the whole system of the world. When the dancers break onto the scene, they signify the direction in which the world is marching, and predict the future of the world. Similarly, one can say that, in *Live at the Apollo,* James Brown—son of Nommo and Nommo himself—was speaking with his feet and tracing, on the floor of the auditorium, the divination language which contained the future directions of the world. The youth in Bamako as well were interpellated by this movement, the language of which was absent from the other political movements of the time in Mali. They found the political and spiritual articulation of independence through James Brown's music, and thereby could become Nommo themselves; that is to say, connect with the African culture of pre-Atlantic slavery.

Ogotemmeli, the Dogon philosopher, likes to state that, for human beings, articulation is the most important thing. That is why the Nommo provided men and women with joints, so that they can bend down and fold their arms and legs in order to work. According to Dogon cosmology, the Nommo had placed one pebble at every joint—at the waist, the knee, the ankle, the wrist, the elbow, the neck joint, etc.—to symbolize a Dogon ancestor that facilitated the articulation of the joint. The movement of every joint is therefore tied to the presence of Nommo, who blesses and instructs it. The concept of articulation is also important for the system of language that permeates all Dogon activities. Language, for the Dogon, is opposed to silence and nakedness, while being at the same time the essence of action, prayer, and emancipation. Language prolongs action through prayer, and articulation provides every language system with its accent, rhythm, semantic content, and form. Ogotemmeli states that for each one of the eight Dogon ancestors, there is a language which is different from the others, and which is spoken by people in his village. The way a specific language is articulated by a people can also be read through the way they dance and communicate with God. In a word, articulation determines for the Dogon the rhythm of the world by relating, through a system of alliance, left and right, up and down, odd and even, male and female. It is thus easy to see how important the system of articulation was for both communication and aesthetics among the Dogon people. It was that which united opposites and created meaning out of seeming disorder, enabling men and women to enlist the help of their God and prolong their action on earth.

For me, the two components of Diaspora aesthetics—repetition and articulation, in other words, the incessant presence of Nommo and the joining of opposites in time and space—were missing in Bamako before the time of independence. It obviously had been suppressed by colonialism and Judeo-Christian and Islamic religions, which understood modernism as teleological, lacking in repetition and contradiction. To state this differently, before independence the youth in Bamako were mostly Muslim boys and girls without rhythm, because they were detached from Nommo and other pre-Atlantic-slavery cultures.

So imagine James Brown in *Live at the Apollo* when, in a song called "There Was a Time," he invokes Nommo, promising the audience that they haven't seen anything "until you see me do the James Brown!" To "do the James Brown" in this instance is to speak a different language with one's body, to improvise a new dance different from the ones mentioned before, like the Jerk, the Mashed Potato, the Camel Walk, and the Boogaloo. It is to dance with Nommo's feet, and to leave on the dance floor the verb of Nommo, i.e., the complete and clear new speech of modern times. Finally, it is to perform one's own dance of Nommo, without an intermediary, and to become one with Nommo and James Brown.

In Bamako, in those days, James Brown's music had an intoxicating power to make you stand up, forget your religion and your education, and perform a dance move beyond your ordinary capacities. As you move your legs and arms up and down in a scissors step, or slide from one end of the dance floor to another, or imitate the blacksmith's dance with an ax, your steps are being visited by the original dancers of pre-Atlantic-slavery African peoples. The Nommo have given you back all your articulations so that you can predict the future through the divination dance of the ancestors.

For Ogotemmeli, to dance is to pay homage to the ancestors and to use the dance floor as a divination table that contains the secret of the new world system. Clearly, therefore, what James Brown was preparing the world for at the Apollo was the brand-new body language of the sixties: a new habitus that would take its resources from the civil rights movement, black pride, and independence. The catalog of dances that James Brown cites, from the Camel Walk to the Mashed Potato, is composed of dances that the Nommo taught men and women so they could clearly understand the language of civil rights, independence, and freedom.

In Bamako too, young men and women, upon hearing James Brown, performed dances that were imitations of the way Nommo swam in the river, the way the chameleon crawled and changed colors. The sun dance of the great Dogon mask, the thunder dance of the Kanaga mask, and the undulating movement of the snake were included too. In this way, the Bamakois took charge of their new situation, showed how the system worked, and predicted the future. Just as the Mashed Potato or the Camel Walk were coded dances that told different stories of emancipation, the dances the youth performed in Bamako were also expressions of independence and connection with the Diaspora.

James Brown's music and other rock and roll sounds of the sixties were therefore prefiguring the secular language that the youth of Bamako was adapting as their new habitus and as expression of their independence. The sweat on the dance floor, reminiscent of James Brown's sweat at the Apollo—itself reminiscent of the sweat that runs down the body of Dogon dancers possessed by Nommo—is the symbol of the new and clear language pouring out of the body of the dancers. James Brown, with his red cape, heavy breathing, and sweat, is none other than Nommo.

Looking at the Malick Sidibé photograph of the two young girls with the *Live at the Apollo* album, one revisits this new language and habitus of the sixties. Curiously enough, at the same time that Malick Sidibé was taking photographs of the youth in Bamako, Ali Farka Touré, a blues guitarist from the north of Mali, was also imitating the songs from the Diaspora. First, people would gather at night in school yards and cultural centers to dance to his modernized music. Then, Radio Mali in Bamako began to play his music on the air. There is one particular song by Ali Farka Touré from those days, "Agoka," which takes several riffs from James Brown's "There Was a Time." It is therefore obvious that the youth used independence as an opportunity to latch on to Diaspora aesthetics, i.e., a pagan modernist style opposed to religious modernism and the "nationalist" and conversionist modernism of Fanon, Aimé Césaire, and Jean-Paul Sartre—thinkers who could think of post-independence Africans only as part of the proletariat.

COPYING THE COPIERS

In Malick Sidibé's photography, we see an encounter between pre-Atlantic-slavery Africa, the post-civil-rights American culture, and the post-independence youth in Bamako that produces a Diaspora aesthetic. Thus, to say that Sidibé's photographs are "black photographs"—as a photographer friend, Charles Martin, has stated to me—is to affirm his participation in the 1960s in shaping the new and universal look of the youth of African descent. Because Sidibé's photographs made Bamako youth so stylish, au courant, and universal, it was easy to identify with them. The youth in Bamako saw themselves in them, and they wanted to be in them, because the photographs made them look like the rock and roll idols and movie stars they wanted to be.

To say that the youth in Bamako saw themselves in Sidibé's photographs is to state that his style was modern, and that his photographs presented a Bamakois that was beyond tradition. By leaving the studio to follow young people outside, Sidibé was also discovering his style. At the conscious and unconscious levels, his eye was being trained to recognize the youth's favorite movements and postures during dancing, their hairdos, and their dress styles. By following them, he began to acquire their aesthetic taste, instead of imposing old-fashioned photographic models on them. This is why they considered Sidibé's photography to be realistic: he recognized their style and used his camera to immortalize it. Sidibé saw the emergence of a rebellious youth in Bamako, who wanted to demarcate themselves from the rest through their love of rock music, dancing, and dress style. By photographing them in the manner in which they wanted to be seen, Sidibé too was able to distinguish himself from other photographers in the city.

Sidibé, then, copied the youth, who themselves were copying rock stars and movie stars. And if we consider that they acquired their habitus by carefully watching images of James Brown, Jimi Hendrix, James Dean, Angela Davis, Aretha Franklin, and Mick Jagger in glossy magazines and movies and on album covers, it becomes possible to see these media outlets as important sources of Sidibé's style. It is therefore no exaggeration to state that Sidibé, who never attended a photography school, had learned from the best in the field. By following the youth, who were wearing flowered shirts made by famous designers—because they saw their idols wearing them in magazine photos—he was getting trained by great photographers. And by following the copy of the copy, he was internalizing the history of photography without knowing it.

It is possible to see the influence on Sidibé's photography of great contemporary photographers from Richard Avedon to Andy Warhol, as well as that of black-and-white movie images. But what is important about Sidibé's art is its ability to transform the copy into an original and to turn the images of the youth into masterpieces of the sixties' look. Looking at his photographs today, it becomes easier to see how productive they were in the sixties in shaping the youth's worldview and in uniting them into a social movement. In this sense, Sidibé is the James Brown of photography, because he was not only the number-one photographer in Bamako, but his photographs also helped universalize the language of the sixties. Consider his single portraits of young men and women wearing bell-bottom pants, flowered shirts, and tops revealing the navels of the girls. It seems as if the individuals in the portraits define their identities through the outfits they are wearing. The bell-bottoms, in these pictures, become as much a feature of the portrait in claiming its position as a signifier of the sixties and seventies as the person wearing them. In a way, the person wearing the bell-bottoms is, like a model, celebrating the greatness of the pants to the onlooker.

There is one particular portrait of five friends, all of them wearing the same color of shirt and bell-bottom pants. They are standing facing the wall, with their backs to the camera. What dominates the visual field in this portrait are the bright black-and-white-colored pants, which come all the way down to the floor and cover the young models' feet. The rhetoric of the image implies that the five friends are identical and equal in their bell-bottom pants. In fact, this Sidibé masterpiece of the representation of the sixties conveys a sense of redundancy, a mirrorlike excess that keeps multiplying the image until it produces a dizzying, psychedelic effect on the viewer.

This photograph is still remarkable for the youths' daring and eccentricity in wearing the same outfit to a party. The expressionist patterns of their shirts and the black-and-white designs of the pants work together to produce a kitsch presentation, which erases individual identities and replaces them with a group identity. In other words, the portrait creates the illusion that we are looking at a photograph of a painting of five young men in the same outfit, instead of a live photograph. By wearing bell-bottom pants and sacrificing their individual identities for that of the *Grin,* or the new social movement, they were indicating a break with tradition and their commitment to the new ideas symbolized by their eccentric outfits. Sidibé's photograph captures this moment of the sixties as parodied by itself—a moment of humor and kitsch, but also a moment marked by the universalism of its language. In this photograph, we not only see the location of the sixties dress style in kitsch—the artifice associated with bell-bottoms, tight shirts, Afro hair, and high heels—but also the labor that went into getting it right. Sidibé's photography defined bell-bottoms for Bamako's youth and told them that they had to wear them in order to be modern.

I have argued that Sidibé attained mastery of his craft by copying copies; that is, by following Bamako's youth, who were themselves following the black Diaspora and the rock-and-roll social movement. It is now important to point out the significance of movement in his art. We have seen that the youth's desire to have Sidibé follow them at dances and beach parties was based on their belief that studio photos were not real enough. For them, the way they dressed and comported themselves at the *Grin* and the parties was more original in terms of reproducing the energy and savoir faire of the 1960s worldwide than the mise-en-scène of the studio, which was stuck in the past. Sidibé had therefore to capture them in the details of their newly acquired habitus. They wanted to be photographed looking like Jimi Hendrix, dancing like James Brown, and posing like someone in the middle of an action.

The subjects of Sidibé's portraits look like they are posing in the middle of a ritual. Their action can sometimes even reveal the content of the ritual they are performing. It is easy enough to imagine who was photographed in the middle of dancing the Twist, the Jerk, or the Boogaloo. It is even possible to hear certain songs while looking at Sidibé's photographs. In a way, one can say that the postures and the forms of the body's disposition in his portraits contain signifiers specific to youth habitus in the sixties.

Space is most significant in Sidibé's shots, because the subjects are moving in different directions and the camera needs to account for the narrative of their movement in the shot. A depth of field is always required in order to reveal where the dancers are going and where they are coming from. It is therefore through the configurations of space that Sidibé captures rhythm in his photographs. We see the characters leaning backward and forward, pushing each other around, or moving in the same direction to mark the groove, as in a James Brown song. Sidibé's portraits are possessed by the space, which they fill not only with the traces of the great music of the sixties and the symbolic gestures of rock stars, but also with the spirit of great dancers, from Nommo to James Brown.

There is always a narrative going on in Sidibé's group portraits. Instead of the subjects revealing themselves for the camera, they engage in different activities, as if some of them were unaware of the camera's presence. We see this already in shots with three or four people: they treat the camera more as a spectator to an unfolding story than as the reason they are posing. Looking at the images taken on the beach, for example, we can see the complexity of narrative in Sidibé's photography and how the subjects seem to invite the camera to participate in its unfolding. Sometimes, each subject in a portrait acts as if he were the main character in the shot. He attempts to achieve this level of characterization by manipulating the narrative time in the shot through a behavior that differs from the others. In one of the photos at the beach, there are six persons who all seem to be engaged in different activities. First, each individual is defined in space as if he were the focus of the shot and the others were there to enhance the mise-en-scène. Second, the facial expression of each one of the six people invokes a different emotion in the photo—contemplative, self-absorbed, playful, fatigued, or reacting to something off-field. At any rate, each of the characters in this shot seems to occupy a field of his own that is totally independent from the others.

I believe that this predilection for narrative indicates two things in Sidibé's art. First, the characters in his photography pretend to ignore the camera, or not to act for it, or simply to be caught in medias res, because they are posing like their idols on record albums, movie posters, and magazines. They are waiting for the moment of the photo to be like James Brown and Nommo, and to become like gods of entertainment themselves. It is their belief that Sidibé's photos can transform them into stars, make them bigger than life, and that is why they act so dramatically in the photos. Each of Sidibé's portraits looks like an actor in a black-and-white movie who has been asked to carry the action to the next level.

By capturing movement—an action caught in time and space, which here I call narrative—in his portraits, Sidibé also enables each character to tell his own story. This act is political, insofar as it allows the youth in Bamako to seize upon their own individuality, away from tradition and the high modernism of the independence leaders. By looking like the modern black image, deracinated from nation and tribe, the youth in Bamako were also showing their belonging to Pan-Africanism and the African Diaspora. Therefore, to say that Sidibé's photographs reveal Bamako's youth as alienated is to address their politics, which were more aligned with the Diaspora and the universal youth movement.

Finally, as I look at Sidibé's album with my friend Diafode, I think of the pervasive influence of hip-hop in Africa and the rest of the world. The young people participating in the movement today in Bamako are the ages of Diafode's and my children. What Sidibé's photographs achieve is to teach us to be more tolerant of today's youth, to understand that their action is not devoid of politics, and to see in them the triumph of the Diaspora.

SELECTED BIBLIOGRAPHY

Baker, Houston, Jr. *Blues, Ideology, and Afro-American Literature*. Chicago: University of Chicago Press, 1984.

Baraka, Amiri (Leroi Jones). *Blues People*. New York: William Morrow, 1963.

Bourdieu, Pierre. *Seminar at Collège de France: Édouard Manet*. Paris: 2000.

Césaire, Aimé. "La pensée politique de Sékou Touré," *Présence Africaine* 29 (December 1959–January 1960).

Fanon, Frantz. *Les Damnés de la terre*. Paris: Maspero, 1961.

Griaule, Marcel. *Dieu d'eau*. Paris: Fayard, 1966.

Magnin, Andre. *Malick Sidibé*. Zurich: Scalo Press, 1998.

Morrison, Toni. *Playing in the Dark: Whiteness and the Literary Imagination*. New York: Vintage, 1993.

Mudimbe, V. Y. *The Invention of Africa: Gnosis, Philosophy and the Order of Knowledge*. Bloomington: Indiana University Press, 1988.

Sartre, Jean-Paul. "La pensée politique de Patrice Lumumba." *Présence Africaine* 3, no. 47 (1963).

Taylor, Clyde. *The Mask of Art*. Bloomington: Indiana University Press, 1998.

Thompson, Robert Farris. *Flash of the Spirit*. New York: Random House, 1983.

Williams, Raymond. *Marxism and Literature*. Oxford: Oxford University Press, 1977, p. 49

14. The Black Asianphile

BY LATASHA NATASHA DIGGS

"We are the subconscious of the Western mind..." —NTOZAKE SHANGE

ENTER

I like Asian boys. Think they're kinda cute. Sexy if the body is doing justice. They're different than the black male I also dearly lust for. Different than my in-bred notion of Asian men. That notion has been transformed by kung fu into a down-for-whatever desire for some sweet-and-sour-rib-on-my-chocolate-ham-hock. In a phallic and nonpolitically correct mode I am an Asianphile who has only gone there through Hong Kong films, Anime, and Asian fiction. I am a black girl with an Asian male fetish. There lurks within me the desire to converse with the Asian penis.

GAME ONE: THE QUIZ

"Don't think! Feeeeel. It is like a finger pointing away to the moon . . . Don't concentrate on the finger or you will miss all that heavenly glory . . ." —BRUCE LEE FROM *ENTER THE DRAGON* (1973)

What in my previous life made the Asian equation arousing? When is the exact moment I began to wonder if Asian dick was for me?

Was it: When I was twelve years of age and the Chinese spot between 115th and 116th on Seventh Avenue was the nastiest place to get some pork fried rice? I liked the food but there was something else I liked as much: the Chinese boy (or was he Korean?) who worked there was a cutie. He always smiled and said hello and must have given me something free at one point. Or did he accept the food stamps?

Or: When I met Tommy, a fine arts major at my high school, I thought he looked like Officer H. T. Ioki (Dustin Nguyen) from *21 Jump Street* (who's now on *VIP*) or one of the thugs from Mickey Rourke's *Year of the Dragon*.[1] He wore tight acid-washed jeans that made a crease in his balls. Had short and spiky hair on top, long in the back, and a little peach fuzz going on in the face. Umm.

Or: Shaolin Executioner a.k.a. *Executioners from Shaolin* a.k.a. *Executioners of Death* (1977). The Shaolin are attacked by Manchurians. The remaining students "take refuge" on red ships used by the Peking Opera.[2] They travel the southern waterways as theater actors and acrobats with a political statement. The leader, Hung Hsi Kuan (played by Chen Kuan Tai), hooks up with this chick (Lily Li) in a nearby village. He knows tiger style. She knows crane. She flips his whole shit on their wedding night by simply keeping her legs closed. Honestly, I would have given it up. Those lips were just too plump.

Or: Ricky "Data" Wang in *The Goonies* (1985), John Lone in *The Last Emperor* (1987), and those anonymous bad guys in *Big Trouble in Little China* (1986). Something about those three storms—Thunder, Rain, and Lightning—in that corny-ass (but entertaining) Kurt Russell flick. (Like Chinese girls really have jade eyes! The nerve!)

GAME TWO: BABY NAMES

There was always a brother sporting a karate suit and Chinese slippers on the block. Now whether or not bro could actually do something in the

---

[1] Pretty cool website dedicated to the eighties television series about cops with baby faces who go undercover in high schools; *21 Jump Street*, Johnny Depp's road to fame (and self-proclaimed Cherokee-ness), started here. Has neat trivia. *www.angelfire.com/ak/penhall*

[2] Bey Logan, *Hong Kong Action Cinema* (New York: Overlook Press, 1996), p. 48. The guide for any head who wants to know who's who in the history of martial arts flicks.

suit was a complete mystery. He wore it to ensure mofos left him the fuck alone.

Bruce Leroy (Tiamak) had changed everything with *The Last Dragon* (1985). Oh. My. GOD. A brother does something with kung fu (which was really nothing at all) but Jesus he was cute. Had good hair and a chest thing going—a pretty boy who could kick ass. Only . . . why was he in Janet Jackson's "Let's Wait a While" video?

"My interest in martial arts began at the age of four while watching Kato on television in The Green Hornet.*"*[3]—TIAMAK

" 'Cause I like it," said the thick young bro with the newly stitched tattoo down his forearm. The Chinese characters read: "Only God can judge me."

I noted the gel smoothed across the raised skin. The tattoo looked like a good four to five hours of needle poking at flesh.

I take the answer for what it is.

I know what it is to have a simple answer.

I like it.

No deep thirty-page dialogue to validate choosing Chinese characters over English.

Hell, it looks better than standard English anyway.

The number of boys and girls with foreign words scrolled down their arms and across their waists is increasing.

Only God Can Judge Me.

Money, Power, Respect.

Yadayadayada.

Yeah I like it too but I'm not on the hype machine.

Folks are not giving much thought to things these days. They're either spoon-fed or joining the nation of cannibals. Be like him or eat of him, no questions asked.

---

[3] Here's another website: *www.fast-rewind.com/dragon*, dedicated to the eighties cult classic *The Last Dragon*, starring Vanity and Tiamak, a.k.a. Bruce Leroy. heads who loved this movie will get a brief synopsis of the flick and a few press release pics.

• • •

Here's a *true* story. One day a young couple visited their favorite Japanese steak house. After going so many times, they came to see this steak house as more than an eat-out specialty. You see, they were expecting a child. It would be a son and they soon decided, in the old ghetto-Negro custom, the child's name would be one to live forever after this steak house was closed. The couple loved each meal they had there and thought this the right thing to do. The child would go on to be a shining light in the world of slave entertainment. This child's name would be Kobe, after his parents' favorite steak house.[4]

When Wu-Tang Clan came out with *Enter the Wu Tang (36 Chambers)*, I worshiped them. They sampled from the movies I loved to watch on Channel 5 Saturday mornings. They somehow found a way to mention martial arts stars and the various characters without seeming to name-drop. (I am a contradiction.) The Wu were out-to-lunch as hell but I could relate because I was fixated on the same things.

I wanted to study kung fu but resigned myself to just beating up my baby sister. When I was young I had been restricted from jump rope and hand-clap games. When finally allowed to go outside, I suffered the torment of not having the money to afford Red Devils (the ghetto version of Sassoon for all y'all middle-class Negroes). Therefore I had to hone my self-defense tactics. Doing karate chops in kids' throats on the block became an all-time favorite. I made many a four-foot, jawbreaker-eating asshole lose his breath with a swift dart to the Adam's apple.

At that point my interest in martial arts film went a little further than fighting. Due to how they unrepressed my violent instincts, I came to look at them lustfully. Bruce Lee was the first Asian male sex symbol in the New

---

[4] During the NBA playoffs of 2001, one of the announcers spoke of how Kobe Bryant got his name. Now, whether or not it was a joke or straight from Kobe's parents, one will never know. Still, the idea itself is inherently ghetto enough to be mentioned.

World, but it was Chen Kuan Tai (*Shaolin Executioners, Challenge of the Masters*) who got me wet in junior high school.

When Hollywood began to feature more Asian men in the eighties, the roles let me down while still holding me controlled supernaturally. The heroes were always white boys. The Asian dudes always had mushrooms for a haircut and they always looked like little boys. The only sexy ones were the evil-doers or the idiots.

Hollywood made a mockery of the culture: Always mysterious. Always honorable. Always in need of Western guidance. Their culture too archaic to maintain. I ate up every idea and assumed it to be true. I studied the stereotypes. There was no problem with the type-casting of buffoonery, only attraction. I watched *Year of the Dragon* and Michael Douglas's *Black Rain* every time they aired. While Andy Garcia getting his head chopped off hurt me, I wanted the young Japanese counterfeiter to reign supreme. I seriously contemplated pursuing the call-girl business at a Japanese men's club. Here I bestow to you my ignorance.

GAME THREE: SILK COTTON SHIRTS AND STILL LACKING A ZEN MIND-STATE . . .

The latest Asian knockoff in the hood: fake Versace silk shirts cascaded with Japanese/Chinese gun-slinging, sword-fisting Euro-Asian Anime characters (dragons, tigers, and snow-capped mountains!) down the front and back. Sold outside the storefronts of 125th, the fish-eating pigeon gutters of Canal Street, and in front of Mt. Sinai Hospital, these shirts are everywhere. The marketing of these part silk, part cotton, part polyester oversized men's shirts proves that East Asia is in urban style. I am pleased that an interest is brewing among my Harlem countrymen in Asian couture, though I question how genuine it is. Are blacks making a fetish out of Japanese and Chinese fashion or is it capitalism that's making folks believe that what they are wearing is actually something of an import? I am at fault too. I've hunted for the perfect peasant-style straw hat and dreamed of having the figure that could fit into the Shanghai–Suzie Wong–Dragon Lady dress—the cheongsam.[5] There was a time I went to Chinatown every weekend in hopes of finding the perfect martial arts suit. I wanted the getup David Chiang had in *Shaolin Mantis* (1978). Then again, I wanted one of Chiang's in-laws, John Chang, to have me.

I have been as shallow as all you mofos dangling those damn ying-yang pendants from your necks. I have bought into all the commercialized notions and hyphenated stigmas of "the "Orient," making me no different from a number of those *kente*-cloth–wearing, Tibetan silk wrap skirt–chasing, Native American silver bracelets–jangling white women who haunt nomadic, third-world novelty stores in the West Village. Hoping to feel like they're of another world and reality. Dreaming to look "cultured."

Then I look at my bookshelves. If I'm only about a sexual and material attraction to Asian culture, what's with all the Taoist and Zen books? And all the works by Yukio Mishima, Bei Dao, Kazuko Shiraishi (woman poet), Lu Hsun, Richard E. Kim, Yosano Akiko (another girl), Junichiro Tanizaki, etc.? Why is it that I have yet become a calm little Buddha-monk, absent of the temper tantrums from my youth?

As a New World Afrikan I once wanted to believe Asians (including South Asians) had a history and a philosophy not in need of being re-created for the sake of gaining identity, one that was ancient and untouched by white hands, the oldest civilization around. Rock stars and academia alike seemed to embrace this notion too. This being the case meant Asian culture would be modernized and capitalized upon. That it would come to us via Amazon.com as feng shui coffee table books, Shambhala pocket wisdom, and Le Chateau hot shorts made of red Chinese silk. Buddhism can accompany me everywhere in my life. I can read *The Art of War,* go see the Dalai Lama in Central Park, and sport my

---

[5] For those who may not be familiar with the actual name of the dress, the "cheongsam" is usually comprised of a high collar, crossover and side fastening, a slit in the skirt, which (depending on the decade) is either worn long or short in length. The material from which it is made has changed, becoming a sort of East-meets-West fashion. White girls can rock them. For a little more about how the dress became popular, *China Chic: A Visual Memoir of Chinese Style and Culture* (Regan Books, 2000) by Vivienne Tan is pretty good.

Sisqo "Unleash the Dragon" baby tee with no ridicule. It is more readily adapt-able to my comings and goings than the symbols and garb of Afrocentricity.

Kwanzaa is cool. But it's a black thing. Everyone, on the other hand, has an idea about what Zen is and what "karma" does. Kwanzaa is still disputed. It may be Hallmark marketable but it is not the *Tao Te Ching*. It's not even authentically African.

Dogon cosmology is as deep as Buddhism but the word "Dogon" is not at all street lingo like "karma" is to the Dees, Travina's, and Daminen's on Mal-colm X Boulevard. It is also not entirely accepted by the Western big willies as authentically African. The *minds* dispute it, tagging it as something prob-ably influenced by Europeans. We can't even sully it. You can find a Chinese horoscope mug but when have you seen a My First Dogon™ planetary loca-tion kit at your local crystal and astronomy shop on Broadway? I will be long dead before it is referenced in a Sprite commercial.

GAME FOUR: THE MYTH OF THE DICK

"The significance of curvature when length & circumference fall short"—WANDA COLEMAN, "DANGEROUS SUBJECTS" [6]

More movies are made and the characters continue to annoy or entice me. The Van Dammes and Seagals showed us more Asian bad guys, still dumb, rough, and lacking sufficient ass-kicking skills. Actor Cary-Hiroyuki Tagawa, seen in *Mortal Combat* (1995) and *Rising Sun* (1993), may be sly and sexy, but he is always the guy who loses.

Hollywood absurdly wants you to believe the white star can really do kung fu. As if their dicks were even bigger than a black man's. Okay, we're going into genitalia, but this is what it's all about. Penis size.

Hollywood attempted to make you believe that Sean Connery's dick was bigger than Wesley Snipes's in *Rising Sun*. Connery was all-knowing, more

---

[6] Wanda Coleman, *Bath Water Wine* (Santa Rosa, Calif.: Black Sparrow Press, 1998).

knowledgeable of the master-student relationship than the Japanese he intricately mocked. The Japanese were depicted as extreme in their habits and doings but dickless despite a reversal of power roles at the end of the flick. Wesley was made even smaller when he tried to get in the pants of Tia Carrere's character—a half-black/half-Japanese outcast with a horrible accent (can you believe they crimped her hair to give it a "nappy" look?), who is Connery's lover. "Just like a black man" and "just LIKE a black man." All in all, the idea of the small-dicked Asian man remains intact with Wesley as a stand-in for the black male myth (now chopped down to size) and the already foreshortened Asian phallus.

Despite Hollywood's feeble attempts at making white dicks look bigger, I remain attracted to something of proposed less volume. Some logic for this can be found in Asian-American homosexual texts on rice queens and gay porno. Richard Fung's essay "Looking for My Penis"[7] reveals that, surprisingly, Asian men were seen as a sexual threat during the twenties in Hollywood. The image of the Asian male as egghead/wimp, the clumsy personage jerking off while in hiding as they watch girls undress came later. Nothing sexy about these boys. Yet, according to Fung, once upon a time my Asian crushes were oversexed. Whoa! Once they were mythologically half black and half Japanese too?!

In the porn/horror genre of Anime flicks which I love, black men, I argue, are being meta-morphed into Japanese monsters. This can be seen in characters depicted in *Legend of the Overfiend* (1989), *Legend of the Demon Womb* (1991), *Wicked City* (1989, 1992), and *Guyver*. In one scene of *Overfiend*, the monster known as the Chojin relishes having some "delicious pussy after three thousand years . . ." The size of the monster, the voice in English dub, suggests a pseudoblack and even pimpish character. Were the animators using *Mack* and *Superfly* to model their monster after?

According to Freud, as examined in David Eng's *Racial Castration*, one creates a fetish that disavows the lack of something and thus circumvents a

---

    [7] Richard Fung, "Looking for My Penis," in *Queer in Asian America*, ed. David Eng and Alice Y. Hom (Philadelphia: Temple University Press, 1998), p. 115.

paternal threat. One finds a substitute that is projected in place of that which is absent. The existence of such both denies and attests.[8]

Non-Asian men love to maintain the myth of Asian men in the genital area. They pass it on to non-Asian women. Confessing my interest in Asian dick to my girlfriends provokes comments like "Girrrlll, now you know they ain't got no dick!" The peer pressure repels me from seeking out the truth. Thus, I am back at reexamining Eng's psychoanalysis of repressed Asian-American sexuality and homosexuality, I substitute the mystery dick with Anime flicks, Hong Kong flicks, Japanese-as-a-second language books.

Though the Asian man may be clinically defined by the "striking absence" of a penis, Bruce Lee had other means of projecting sex than waving his dick around. He was erotic by way of sexualizing his craft and his persona. Those fight scenes where his latissimus dorsi was spread wide and glistening with sweat. That sharp flick of the nose with his thumb implied that he'd be perfectly able to perform if the opportunity arose. He never had to grab his testicles to make sure they were still there.

GAME FIVE: WHY I HATED ROMEO MUST DIE

"Your wife's a nigger huh? You're very liberal. Blacks are beautiful. Color doesn't matter, does it? You really look like a couple."
—HOI, from the movie *FALLEN ANGELS*

Upon seeing the previews and ads for *Romeo Must Die* (2000), I expected some incredible magic to be happening on screen between the cast members. I was given the impression that my fantasy of Asian penetration was going to be executed by Jet Li (who's far more cute bald in *Once Upon a Time in China* and *The Legend*) via the late Aaliyah. I had my doubts about her acting ability, but beggars can't be choosy. What I didn't expect was the complete idiocy

---

[8] David Eng, *Racial Castration: Managing Masculinity in Asian Americ* (Durham,96 N.C.: Duke University Press, 2001), p. 146.

of the project. Maybe I'm being harsh, but needless to say I take Asian and black intermingling on screen pretty damn seriously. Romeo was a bad joke. Blacks fighting Asians over the right to sell property being sold to junior Mafioso. The film's moral was that the Chinese are smarter than African Americans but Whitey will watch both of you kill each other and pay for the privilege. Almost every black man in the movie is a fool, some repeatedly referring to Jet's character as "dim sum" to make the audience laugh (they wish!) before he symbolically castrates them. Worst of all, what I wanted most from Aaliyah and Jet never went down. They were obviously attracted to each other but things stayed dry. I wanted a kiss. I wanted the dream.

Journalist Hyun Kim suggested that "audiences weren't ready to see one of hip-hop's prized young kittens getting it on with an Asian kung-fu master sixteen years her senior." But where he sees a Dorothy Dandridge–like prized kitten I see a slight hint of Xica, the oversexed African slave girl any virtuous man needs to be wary of. In this scenario, it is Jet Li who must be protected from the evils of miscegenation, not Aaliyah. (Small wonder that her next and last role was as an Egyptian vampire so blood-lusty all the white vampires became appalled and destroyed her for it.)

Perhaps Aaliyah kissing or having a nipple in Li's mouth would have disturbed a number of black penises. Perhaps these would be the same brothers we see sporting a fetish for Asian women in current hip-hop videos. Perhaps Aaliyah and Jet embracing would have disturbed Asians, blacks, and whites.

GAME SIX: WHO'S KISSING WHO?

"Race cannot be narrowly defined in terms of race hatred. Race is a factor in even our most intimate relationships."—RICHARD FUNG, "LOOKING FOR MY PENIS"

From Eng's analysis of Kaijou Silverman's *Threshold of the Visible World:*

Silverman delineates a social structure in which the black penis works to disturb the sexual relations between white man and white woman. The differentiation of the white man from the black man, on the basis of the black man's hyperbolic penis, consequently reverberates in disturbing ways within the domain of gender. It places the white man on the side of the "less" rather than "more," and so threatens to erase the distinction between him and the white woman. The hyperbolic black male penis threatens the unity of the white male ego by placing him in the position of being less masculine, thereby endangering the structural distinction between him and the white woman.[9]

If Asians are thought of as being sexually lesser, they cannot disturb white superiority. This may explain why Japanese-Taiwanese pop star and actor Takeshi Kaneshiro (*Fallen Angels*, 1995; *Chunking Express*, 1994) was allowed to play opposite Mira Sorvino in *Too Tired to Die* (1998) and why Tony Leung Ka Fai's (not to be confused with Tony Leung Chiu-Wai from *Bullet in the Head*) thirty-two-year-old character could make continuous love to an eighteen-year-old English girl in the movie adaptation of Marguerite Duras's *The Lover* (1992)[10] and why Jodie Foster could befriend Chow Yun-Fat in *Anna and the King* (1999) or Jet Li could be heroin-addicted screen prostitute Bridget Fonda's white knight in *Kiss of the Dragon* (2001). The Asian superheroes are presumed to be no threat to either white or black men.

Quoting Earl Jackson, Jr.—as quoted from Eng's book—white men occupy a peculiar position in a heterosexist society. I would argue that white women hold a fair share of this society also. They too contain an adequate (but not equal to gay white men) amount of access to the very power mech-

---

[9] Eng, *Racial Castration*, p. 150.

[10] In the movie *The Lover*, actor Tony Leung has one of the most amazing lines. When his character is confronted by the girl's older brother—who sees him as dirt despite his wealth—he replies, "You have no idea how weak I am." Having not read the book, I perceived it as an acknowledgment and reversal of what the Western mind assumes, making it sexual and dominant. However, I can't be held fully to this statement ten years from now. Marguerite Duras did write the book and I need to read it.

anisms that bridle them. More important, the white male mind believes she will come back because the Asian dick is not a black dick.

Her gender counterpart who cannot pass is the black woman. Because black women are also framed in the hyperbolic sex category, Aaliyah, the kitten, may have no chance with an Asian dude because she, like Zeze Motta in the movie *Xica* (1976), is "in heat." She will be the one who will disturb the equilibrium of ethnicity. Black people, as Fung suggests, "are endowed with a threatening hypersexuality" while Asians are "collectively seen as undersexed."[11] Jet Li, in keeping within the stereotype of "sexless" (he the "oriental" is not perceived as being completely masculine), may have not returned home if he got a taste. Then again, Jet Li, in keeping within "honor," may have dumped her after the first night for fear of being excommunicated from Beijing and Hong Kong.

GAME SEVEN: EXIT

I sit in a Korean restaurant dining on *bi bim bab*. Eggs and rice and vegetables and a taste of tofu. There's this man sitting at a table beside me. Asian. Older. Handsome. He groans sensually from his meal of pork and things I can't recognize. The groaning is causing me to sneak at his facial details. I hesitate to look directly. I fumble with the chopsticks. I am consumed with placing them down the correct way. Never have them sticking out of your rice like totem poles. Honestly, I want to impress him with these sticks; with the usual stupidity I've come to admit is Western fascination. Keep my eyes lowered, use my sticks the right way. Maintain a type of submissive, subordinate presence that is part Asian woman, part lily Southern-belle white girl. Eat slowly and neatly. Maybe get his attention.

Flashback. A cute Japanese boy tries to grind me on the dance floor with

---

[11] Fung, "Looking for My Penis," p. 116.

his processed locks. Why is he trying to grab my hips? He's being too ag-gressive. I've seen the MTV specials of tanning salons, the nappy hair ma-chines, the many efforts to look "black." Who told him he could put on a Rasta tam, some baggy jeans, take some hip-hop house dance lessons from Ejoe, Stretch, Voodoo Ray, and Majorie, and get some black ass?[12] I would like him to be one of those men I served at the coffee bar while working at the World Trade Center back in '96. I want him to be that A-typical Japan-ese male—the one who does not look directly at me, attempts to traffic in sneaks, knows no English, wears a tight black suit (sometimes Banana Re-public khaki), and orders a medium black with a raisin bun. He's the one. Not this kid.

Reading the late Joe Wood's essay "The Yellow Negro" in *Transition,* I be-come annoyed all over again with the recent obsession to go blackface in Japan. I am bored of the yellow fever trend among black boys. Especially with so many Japanese girls in New York trying to look like Britney Spears and breaking their ankles with ten-foot-high platform boots. I'm even more annoyed that Mr. Wood was able to see what I've only read about. I am im-potent for lack of Wood's journey.

I continue renting videos. I continue reading and mumbling small phrases I've remembered since befriending a handful of Japanese folks. I continue to watch Janet's "If" video; not for the dancing but for the Asian boys reclining in the background. I'll get there, I suppose.

---

[12] The four individuals are some of the top hip-house dancers for the past fifteen years. Since the rise of gangsta rap, dancers were—at one point—considered unneces-sary for the stage. Since being resurfaced, dancing has morphed into modern Frank Hatchett theater jazz, Janet-esque house, and Back Street Boys/P. Diddy/burlesque hip-hop choreography. I mention these people because while dancing was viewed for a mo-ment as "wack," Japan continued to employ them as instructors, seeing them as an important asset to hip-hop culture and black culture.

15. Afro-Kinky Human Hair

by Meri Nana-Ama Danquah

AFTER TWENTY-SEVEN YEARS OF LIVING in the United States, I decided to pack up my life and return to Ghana, my native country. It was a move that was probably long overdue. When my family emigrated to America, I was six years old and it was the early 1970s, a time when black was being regarded as beautiful and Africa was being celebrated not merely as a continent, but as a state of mind. It was the decade of dashikis, of Black Power fists and blaxploitation films, of afros, Alex Haley's *Roots* and Bob Marley's righteous reggae music. But not everybody black was feeling that kinship. Some folks weren't keen on having their consciousness shifted in the direction of racial pride; there were a number of black people who had no love for Africa and no use for the likes of me. If I had a dollar for every time, during those first few years after my arrival, that I was told (by both blacks and whites) to "go back to Africa," I might certainly have raised enough money to buy a plane ticket and make the attempt.

I didn't know much about Africa, only what had been told to me by family and friends, what little I had read in books or seen on television or at the movies. I definitely couldn't rely on the veracity of my own memory. The tiny bit that I could recall of the time I had spent there, in Ghana, was as vague and undecipherable as a dream. And sometimes I wasn't even sure whether those memories were real or whether they were recycled, faces from photographs that had found their way into my rather fertile imagination.

Whatever the case, I became fascinated with Africa, with the magic and the mythology of it, with the way it invoked such passion from both its supporters and its enemies, the way that it was used as a symbol of all that was either right and attractive, or wrong and utterly repulsive, with blackness. The people who romanticized Africa, the ones who chose to believe that it was pure and good would make statements like "We can't ever forget where we come from" or "Back in the motherland, they like their women dark and plump." The others were not as beholden to our shared history. "I'm not from no damn Africa," they would say. "I'm from Chicago." For them, Africa, and all that it represented, was a source of shame, something from which they wanted to be distanced.

The older I got, the more I wondered what it would be like to live in Africa, to actually exist in a place where people who looked like me were the majority, the mainstream, the citizens empowered to shape language, set standards of beauty, define societal canons. I was tired of living in America; I was tired of being black in a predominantly white country. It was just too much like hard work, a constant uphill climb. I wanted to know how my spirit would feel living someplace where self-love did not always seem to be an act of self-defense, an emotionally exhausting effort to cancel out the effects of all the pervasive lies, stereotypes, and negative images of blackness. I wanted to be done with the intrusion of white supremacy and the internalization of my supposed inferiority.

I applied, and was selected, for a visiting scholar appointment at the School of Communication Studies, University of Ghana. So I decided to take myself and my nine-year-old daughter, Korama, back to the land and the freedom that was my birthright.

Just before the move, I went to get my hair done. For several years, I'd been wearing it short, close to the scalp. I hadn't cut it in weeks, so it had grown out enough for me to try a new style. Anything that involved chemicals was out of the question. The last time I'd had it permed, I was pregnant. Maybe it was because of the excessive hormones; but every time my hair was combed, brushed, or washed, it would fall out in huge clumps.

Not being a big fan of braids, I opted to go the rasta route. The problem was that I didn't want to be bothered with all the work that went into locking. All the twisting, re-twisting, waiting, worrying about whether or not it was actually ever going to happen, if those kinks were actually ever going to mat. I'd been there and done that, and would've just as soon preferred to skip that arduous, albeit necessary, part of the whole process. But I didn't know if that was even possible.

"Sure," Bee-be, an actress-cum-hairdresser friend of mine, told me. "They're called Nu-Locks. I can do them for you if you want."

Days later, she and I went to a huge store—a factory, really—that was owned and run by what appeared to be a family of Koreans. There, we bought several "loaves," as I learned they were called, of "Afro-kinky" human hair. They were small, neatly netted squares, each one about the size of a thick bar of soap. They were full of pure, grade A, 100 percent nappy Negro hair. This store was no mom-and-pop corner shop. It was a major operation, with a toll-free order number and clients all over the country. I had no idea that there was a market for such a thing. All those years I'd been shaving off my fast-growing 'fro and simply tossing it in the trash without even considering that it might actually be worth something to somebody!

Bee-be first braided and then extended the length of my natural hair with yarn. Starting from the scalp, she tightly wrapped strand after strand of the store-bought hair around the braids and the yarn, in much the same way one would wrap an Ace bandage around a sprained ankle. She then took each newly wrapped tress and rolled it smoothly between her palms. Twelve hours later, I had some very legitimate-looking dreadlocks.

The plan was to keep the Nu-Locks in as long as possible so that my natural hair would have a chance to lock. Once my own hair had locked and reached a desirable length, I could take off the fake-me-out hair and no one would be the wiser. After teaching me how to maintain my do and apply the wraps to my new growth every few months, Bee-be sent me on my way. Before going home to finish packing, I stopped at the grocery to pick up a few food items—and wouldn't you know it? The customer who was behind me in line paid me my first compliment.

"Girl, your dreads are nice." She looked as if she was forcing herself to resist the temptation to touch them. "How long have you been locking?" Her question caught me off guard. Not sure what to say, I hesitated. If someone would have asked me that the first time I'd had dreads, I could have easily told them how long it had been, right down to the day, the hour probably. Back then, it wasn't about sporting a new hairstyle, it was about creating a new lifestyle, one that revolved around an acceptance of myself, without any additions or enhancements. Suddenly, I felt like a fraud.

I looked at the woman and wondered whether or not to tell her the truth. She wore her hair in a permed, asymmetrical bob. I briefly studied her face—wide-eyed, thick-lipped, high-cheekboned, chestnut-skinned— and immediately decided that she would look better in locks. This, of course, made me want to laugh. Me with a string of lies in my hair stand-ing there trying to picture her without the lye in hers. "Oh, it's been about twelve hours." I laughed. "They're not real. They're extensions." Her smile shrank into a smirk. "Thanks, anyway," I quickly added, embarrassed. Then off I rushed to prepare for my move to Africa, my search for an authentic black experience.

. . .

At first, Ghana seemed to be exactly what I'd imagined it would be: no spaghetti and marinara sauce, hot dogs, or apple pie à la mode. No half-naked blonds trying to scat like Ella or dance like Debbie. No Banana Republic, Pier 1 Imports, or other "ethnic fantasy" stores selling wicker, sa-fari clothing, overpriced wood carvings, and faux kente cloth manufac-tured in Taiwan. At first, Ghana seemed to be a far cry from the Western world, with all its pretensions and appropriations. The airwaves were full of multilingual programs; the food was heavy and spicy, meant to be eaten with freshly washed fingers, not metal utensils. Everywhere I went, there

were people wearing traditional attire, women walking around in beauti-
fully dyed cloths with deep, rich colors: indigo, olive, emerald, plum, lilac.
And the men, the men, the men; damn, they were fine. A nation of Denzel, Wesley, and Don Cheadle look-alikes multiplied a million times over.

Often, we see only those things that we want to see, be they good or
bad, those things that affirm whatever notions we have about ourselves,
about the world around us. I suppose that's what happened when I arrived
in Ghana. It was like stumbling into a dark room: you train your eyes to focus on one thing until you can find your bearings, but eventually your vision adjusts and you see everything as it is.

After a short period of time, I began conducting my daily negotiations
not as a tourist or a newcomer, but as a full-fledged resident. I rented a
house, opened a bank account, registered Korama in school, made a few
friends, and figured out where I would shop, eat out, and go for drinks on
a Friday night. And it was through those mundane activities, those tedious
interactions with the banker, the market women, the neighbors on the
block, that I came to realize that Africa wasn't actually all that Afrocentric,
after all.

There is, certainly, a wealth of indigenous tradition and history that has
remained intact, despite the many decades of colonization. But there is
also a great deal of emphasis on, and admiration of, the ways and the won-
ders of the Europeans. A lot of the damaging effects of colonization are yet
to be undone.

Like language. There are hundreds of languages spoken in Ghana;
however, English is still the country's official tongue. Be that as it may, it
is not enough to merely speak English, one must also sound like an Eng-
lishman, use words like "bloody" and "jolly." (So I should probably add that
the Denzel, Wesley, and Don Cheadle look-alikes sometimes sound a
whole lot like Tony Blair and Michael Caine.)

There was this man—I will call him Kwame—who lived in my neighborhood. Kwame was a journalist, a liberal-minded fellow who had been

educated abroad but immediately returned to Ghana upon his graduation so as to not contribute to what he called the "brain drain," the permanent loss of the country's brightest and most promising minds. Kwame took it upon himself to ease my transition, to help me navigate my way through the system. If I needed to get directions, I called Kwame; if I had a question about proper cultural etiquette, I asked Kwame; if I wanted someone to accompany me somewhere, I invited Kwame.

On one of our regular trips to Makola, the huge open-air marketplace in downtown Accra, I came across a merchant who was selling jars full of an ivory-colored cream that resembled mayonnaise. I was curious about the cream, curious about the ingredients used to make it, about what the benefits of using it were. Since I'd been in Ghana, I'd been learning quite a lot about local herbal remedies. Earlier that week, I had come to Makola and purchased—for next to nothing—a vat of shea butter, which comes from the nut inside the fruit of the karite, a tree that is native to West Africa.

Shea butter is similar to cocoa butter in that it nourishes the skin and hair, protecting them from the sun and other harsh elements; it reduces scarring after childbirth and surgery; it has even been said to alleviate dermatological ailments, like eczema. When I went home, I saw that the oh-so-expensive lotion I had brought from the States with me contained shea butter—as did the majority of the "upscale" skin care products that I owned. I thought perhaps this ivory-colored cream was another natural, "old world" treatment that some huge North American cosmetics company was probably bottling up and selling for goo-gobs of money.

"What does it do?" I asked the woman.

"It brightens the skin," she said. "Makes it pretty."

"Like, it brings out its natural glow?" I asked, repeating a marketing slogan I had heard countless times on television commercials.

"Yes, yes," she confirmed. "It will make the skin glow. It will make it light."

"Oh, okay. I'll take one. What's in it? How does it work?" While I was waiting for her response, I pulled out some crumpled bills from my purse to give to her. Just then, Kwame walked up. He'd been buying smoked fish from another merchant nearby. He watched me hand the money to the cream-woman.

"Oh hey," I said to him. "I just bought . . . um . . . what's it called again?" I asked the cream-woman.

"Skin bleach," Kwame said, before she could reply.

Skin bleach? "What? Did you say skin bleach? As in—"

"Yes, skin bleach," he repeated. "As in one application a day helps to rub the dark skin away." I was totally speechless. I turned to the cream-woman, shot her a look that said *Please, help me out here.* I guess I was hoping that she would tell Kwame he was mistaken. Instead, she offered this: "It brightens the skin. Makes it pretty."

Skin-bleaching creams—which are sometimes referred to as skin toners, fade creams, blemish/spot removers, lightening lotions—are solutions that usually contain a very small percentage of hydroquinone, a potent chemical agent that reduces the skin's pigmentation by inhibiting its production of melanin. The creams (which are used worldwide by people of all races) are intended to combat acne scars, liver spots, freckles, melasma, and other conditions that cause discoloration. But in Africa, these bleaching creams are popular for their ability to combat a condition that is, apparently, even more undesirable: being black.

"So even here," I said, "in the middle of Africa. Even here, the women want to get as close as they can to being white?"

"Yes, but it's not just the women," said Kwame. "The men bleach themselves, too. And it's not just us. Even the half-caste people do it. And the Indians that are here bleach themselves, and so do some of the darker Lebanese. They all want to be lighter."

"Even here," I muttered again, to no one in particular. This is sick, I thought, this plight to be white. It is a sick, sick joke.

"All except the white people," Kwame continued. "Like them." He nodded his head toward a trio of white women who were walking by us. They were wearing sandals, dresses sewn from batiks with matching head wraps and beaded bangles. "They," Kwame announced, with a mischievous smile slowly spreading itself across his face, "they want to be black, like us. They know what it's worth."

. . .

When I was growing up, I used to love seeing the photographs in magazines like *Life* and *National Geographic* of tall, radiant dark-skinned beauties wearing those intricately braided crowns on their heads. I assumed that the women I'd meet in Ghana would look as if they had just stepped right off those pages. Sure, a lot of them wore braids, but a lot more of them had weaves and relaxers.

Even the dusty, rail-thin homeless girls who sold PK gum (Wrigley's equivalent of Chicklets) by the side of the road wore their hair permed. Not styled, mind you, because it was too hot and humid. Only people who could afford air-conditioning could manage to hold crimps or any other type of curl. The less fortunate had to just settle for it being sun-dried and straight, which appeared to be good enough for them. Very few people had dreads. The people who did were almost always the blacks from the Diaspora who were there on holiday, the fetish priests, the musicians, and the madmen who had wandered off from the mental asylum.

The students wore their hair in short naturals. Boys and girls. It was a requirement at all the schools except the international ones, which were attended by the privileged offspring of expatriates and upper-crust citizens. I had wanted Korama to go to a regular school, but I didn't understand why she had to sacrifice her hair to do so.

"Give me one good reason," I told the administrators at the prospective schools.

"That is the rule" was the sole reason that I was given again and again.

"But why?" I pushed. "What is the point of that rule?" For weeks, I got the same stock answer again and again. Finally, just when it seemed like nobody was gonna 'fess up, an honest answer.

"Because our hair is too troublesome and time-consuming," the headmistress at one of the schools informed me. Needless to say, I ended up enrolling Korama in the American international school, where she, like all the other students, was able to wear her hair any way she wanted.

So, now that I had come to a decision about the fate of Korama's hair, I had to come to one about the fate of my own. By the time the school year started, we were three months into our stay. My roots had grown out and it was time to re-wrap them. But I had been so anxious to leave the States that I hadn't thought ahead. I hadn't brought along any extra loaves of the Afro-kinky human hair. I phoned one of my aunts and asked her if she knew where I could get my hands on some.

"Afro-kinky human hair." She said each word slowly, deliberately, as if it were its own sentence. My aunt suggested a wig shop, the largest in the city, and assured me that if it was being sold anyplace in Accra, it was being sold there. The next morning, I went to the shop.

"What?" the Lebanese woman behind the counter asked. "What is that, Afro-kinky?"

"It's kinky hair," I said, realizing that I wasn't providing her with any new information. "It's nappy hair like . . ." I glanced at all the Caucasian-flesh-colored mannequin heads displayed in the shop to see if any of them was fitted with an afro wig, but I couldn't find a single one. "It's like, um, um, that." I pointed to a man who was walking by the shop's front window. "That kind of hair. Kinky, I mean, nappy hair. Black people's hair. Do you sell any?"

"Oh," she snickered. "No, nothing coarse. We carry only silky hair. Why don't you try that? It would look very nice on you." When I declined, she suggested that I try to find it at another wig shop across town that catered more to "those kinds of things."

The next morning I went to the second shop (which was a stone's throw from the Ikea—yes, Ikea—outlet), where I was attended to by a rather hostile clerk who couldn't fathom why anybody would want to buy black hair in its original state.

"But I do not understand. Is it not the very same hair that grows from your head?" she wanted to know. "If it is that kind of hair you like, then why must you buy it? Why not simply grow it yourself?" That is when the brilliant idea of pilfering came to mind.

"You're right," I shouted, jumping up and down excitedly. It was the perfect solution. I was so thrilled I could hardly contain myself. "You are absolutely right." The clerk grinned and cautiously stepped away from me. Looking back on the whole scene, what with my dreads, my seemingly nonsensical request to purchase hair that I was quite capable of producing myself, and my joyful outburst, I wouldn't be surprised if she thought I was a recently released asylum patient.

But right then, I couldn't have cared less. She had placed the answer to my problem directly into my lap. Korama. Why hadn't I thought of that before? Korama had a head full of thick, gorgeous, unprocessed hair. Starting that day, whenever I did my daughter's hair, instead of throwing the loose strands that she had shed away, I would pull them from the brush or comb, untangle them, and then put them away for safekeeping. Within a month, I had gathered enough to successfully complete my re-wrap.

It seemed like no time at all before I was due for another re-wrap. But there was no hair. While cleaning, the housegirl had discovered my hidden stash and dumped it in the garbage. Most households, mine included, had domestic help—housegirls/boys. Even the poor had help because there was always someone poorer, someone—usually a distant relative from the village—who was willing to do the menial chores in exchange for food, shelter, and the slightest chance of a better life. In a country that idealizes long, blow-in-the-nonexistent-breeze hair, I can only imagine what my housegirl thought when she found that bag full of gently organized naps. What else could she, or anyone, do with hair like that except throw it away?

Without the hair that I had been saving, I was back at square one. It was an utterly ridiculous dilemma. How is it possible, I wondered, that shelves upon shelves in a Koreatown store in Los Angeles could be stocked with Negro hair, but the shelves in all the beauty supply stores in

Accra, a city with Negroes by the numbers, were only stocked with what resembled Asian hair?

For almost a year, I had been living in Africa. Africa, the dark continent, the motherland, the one place I had imagined that I could be black—I mean *really* Black, Negritized—without explanation or envy, without penalty or apology. I had moved there because I figured that there *had* to be one place that was there for us, governed by us, and all about us. If Africa wasn't that place, then where was it? I was completely disillusioned, confused, downright bitter.

Tired of the charade, I had the Nu-Locks removed and, ultimately, I caved in and allowed my hairdresser, a local woman named Peace, to give me a perm. She had been pressing me to do it since the first time she laid eyes on me. "If you permed all of that, it'd be flowing down your back," she'd once told me. The saddest part of the situation is that when Peace was done, when she turned the chair around and let me look in the mirror, I actually recognized the person that I saw. Peace was right. Chemically relaxed, my hair was long, almost as long as the Nu-Locks had been. It was exactly the way I used to wear it when I was a teenager, one of a handful of black girls in a predominantly white school.

Those were the days I used to dream of Africa, the days I used to sit in the library flipping through the pages of *National Geographic*, wanting so much to be there, in those pictures, with those women, those regal-looking ebony-skinned, corn-rowed women, whom I thought were far more stylish and sophisticated and breathtaking than any of the models I had ever seen on the covers of *Vogue*.

Seeing myself in the mirror like that, remembering the misery and self-hatred I felt during those years in boarding school, made me think of a story that Kwame told me. He had also attended a boarding school, an exclusive all-boys academy in Europe. His family lived on the outskirts of Accra, but he rarely spent time there, only when he was home on holiday.

"No matter how long I had been gone, being in that house used to always bring me back to myself," he confided. "My grandfather built that house. He built everything inside of it, too. The cabinets, the furniture, everything. That house had been the same since the day I was born."

One Christmas vacation Kwame came home from school to find that his father had redecorated, taken all the mahogany furniture pieces and replaced them with Formica tables and Italian-style leather sofas. "It's not as if I minded the new things," he said. "It was a change. It was a different experience. What I believe truly hurt my heart was that—"

"—he sold the things your grandfather made?" I asked.

"You know, there is a saying that if there was a sea in Kumasi, the Asantes would have sold it by now. We Africans do sell a lot of things that should be kept in our family, in our culture. That is a source of anger and frustration, yes. But when we sell our belongings, we at least make it known that they are of some value to us. We at least give them a price. My father did not sell those things. He gave them away to some missionaries. And that is what hurt most of all. I have come to believe, Nana-Ama, that we are the enemies of our own progress. Who can complain about the taking? Who can say what white people are taking from us? It is not theft. It is not a crime to take what is being given freely. And we give so much of ourselves of our history away. Too much. What will there be left, Nana-Ama, once we have given it all away? What will there be left of us?"

"I don't know" was my immediate response to his statement. And that day, after hearing that story, I really didn't know. I couldn't fully grasp what he was saying. What I can remember, though, is how comfortable and free I had felt just hearing my name, my proper and preferred name being spoken, being pronounced correctly. No one in Ghana ever called me Meri, the Christian name that had been given to me at birth, which I'd insisted upon using in the States because so few people ever attempted to say Nana-Ama properly. It was so freeing to be called by my true name. It was the sort of freedom I had wanted to experience in every other aspect of my life there in Ghana. I just wanted to be whole. Not in spite of my history, but because of it.

Sitting in front of the mirror at the salon, staring at myself—curled bangs and all—I realized that I did know. I did know the answer to what Kwame had been asking. I looked around the salon at the other clients, their permed hair and bleached-bright skin, their fancy mobile phones bleeping and ringing every two minutes. I might as well have been in America, in some 'round-the-way beauty shop. Disgusted, I turned my gaze to the milk-chocolate flesh of my hands, which had been resting on my lap, clasped together, as if in prayer. I held one hand up, spread the fingers apart, and then ran them, like a comb, through my newly straightened hair. "This, Kwame," I said softly to myself. "If we're not careful, *this* is what will be left."

16. Captive Herstories

BY DANZY SENNA

CAMBRIDGE, MASSACHUSETTS, 2036

There is an auction held every September at Hammerschmidt's, a literary auction house in New York City. I make the trip down each year, hoping to find some lost diamond-in-the-rough of African-American letters. I feel it is my duty—as a scholar of some distinction—to preserve and promote the lost writings of people of color.

In years past, I've come back from Hammerschmidt's with some amusing but not entirely academy-shattering purchases: a poem scribbled on a bar napkin by a certain spoken-word poet now famous for his televised "hip-hopera"; a letter from a young multiracial writer to her publisher imploring at the last minute that they change the title of her memoir from *Everyday People, Together Everyday* to *Why I Hate Everybody*. About four years ago, I brought home a casino matchbook on which a larger-than-life dreadlocked Pittsburgh poet had written, in Magic Marker, FUCK WHITEY over his confirmed signature.

These were all, of course, precious additions to my private collection, but I—and let's face it, my wife—knew that these finds would not pay the mortgage.

So this year, it was with some degree of trepidation and world-weariness that I flew to New York and lumbered up Madison Avenue to the Hammerschmidt Auction House. I did not expect to find anything of much value, and my wife had forbidden me to shell out "another eight hundred dollars for a piece of certified afro-garbage." I even at one point dozed off during the auction.

But somehow, by the grace of God, I was awake when the auctioneer announced a recently discovered manuscript by an unknown poet named Wilona Wilkerson, said to be dated in or around the turn of the century.

Never heard of a Wilona Wilkerson? You will. Mark my words. You will.

Add her name to the pantheon of late-twentieth-century black female poets. June Jordan. Audre Lorde. Maya Angelou. This is, as they say, "the real deal" you are about to witness.

Wilona Wilkerson. The fact that we know her name at all is a kind of miracle. Her tattered and stained manuscript was found four years ago in an abandoned car on the outskirts of Watts by an old junkman by the name of Red Sandford. He—for reasons we will never know—took the manuscript home with him and kept it safely tucked under his mattress for over two years. When he died and his apartment became vacant, the next miracle occurred: the landlady, a literary buff named Judy Grinch, rather than throwing the pile of pages into the trash, sat down at his kitchen table to read them and, as she put it, "felt a chill go up my spine." She immediately brought the manuscript to the attention of a Santa Monica used bookstore, which brought it to the attention of Hammerschmidt's.

The manuscript is not in great shape. From the looks of things, Wilona Wilkerson was a chain-smoker and an alcoholic and a coffee addict extraordinaire. The pages came to my hands burned, gin-soaked, and coffee-splattered. Several pages appear to be missing, and her final poem, as you will see, ominously stops in mid sentence. But none of that deterred me from my

mission—to bring the vibrant, eccentric genius of Wilona Wilkerson to the world.

Why should we care? At their most basic level, these poems
are anthropological gems, giving us an intimate peek at a world
previously believed lost to us for good. They are a direct life-
line to the past—offering, as they do, the details of everyday
life for a subjugated black woman living in a late-capitalist patriarchal hegemonic wasteland.

Ultimately, though, it was the literary rather than historical
merit of this work that will ensure Wilkerson's place in the
canon of African-American letters in the decades yet to come.
Her language itself is both unadorned and complex, stream-of-
consciousness and yet somehow strictly formal, enraged and yet
somehow, simultaneously, buoyant.

In the end, I paid a total of $125,000 for the work, and I
have never regretted the purchase for a moment, no matter
how Daryl Doggett tries to discredit its value.[1] This is the voice
of an authentic turn-of-the-century black woman. And no price
tag can be placed on such a discovery. So here with great pride,
I bring to you Wilona Wilkerson's manuscript, which I have

---

[1] Daryl Doggett is an associate professor and sore loser from a state college in
the Bronx who dropped out of the Wilona Wilkerson bidding at $15,000. Later, on
the sidewalk outside of Hammerschmidt's, Mr. Doggett approached me in an ag-
gressive manner and claimed that he had never really wanted "that piece of baloney"
anyway. When I asked him why he'd been bidding on the work if he thought it was
so awful, Mr. Doggett insisted that he had just been trying to inflate the price so he
could watch with pleasure as I shelled out more of my "crimson blood money."
When I tried to ignore him, Mr. Doggett announced in a loud, obnoxious voice to
the pedestrians trying to go about their business that the work of Wilona Wilkerson
was a fraud. He proceeded to say that it was written by a "white trash transvestite"
who went by the name of Terry Cloth Jones—and the poems had been widely read
by Jones in the gay stand-up comedy clubs of Los Angeles as part of his "angry sis-
tah outsider" persona. Alfred Knopf, the publisher of Captive Herstories, have since
looked into the claim, and have found no evidence of a Terry Cloth Jones ever having perfomed such an act on the Strip. I will state on the record, here and now, that
I believe Terry Cloth Jones is a figment of Daryl Doggett's paranoid, untenured
imagination.

taken the liberty of naming *Captive Herstories*. It is, I'm sure
you will agree, evidence of a brilliant, disturbed, and ultimately
doomed black woman, whose lone subaltern voice cries out to
us from that moment we have all come to know as "the Cusp
of Hell."[2]

—CHARLES "CHIP" DEWEY
PROFESSOR OF HERSTORY
HARVARD UNIVERSITY

---

[2] Fun Fact: A major motion picture based on the imagined life of Ms. Wilona
Wilkerson is currently in production at Disney, and will be released in the summer
of 2038, introducing Ruby Taylor as the young Wilona Wilkerson, and starring Tangi
Miller as the elder Ms. Wilkerson.

Captive Herstories

BY WILONA WILKERSON

YO CHANDRA!

you goin to the store?
get me a pack of benson & hedges
menthol.
some preparation h
and a super sized bag
of cool ranch doritos.

oh yeah
and some
primotene mist
this fuckin heat got me
wheezing.

SHOWTIME

i just gotta know
i mean
i just GOT to know
why trifling
motherfuckers like
you are all alike?
i mean,

why you
gotta
run out on my
ass
just when they're about
to turn off the
motherfucking
cable?

DEAR MARIAH

you think you look
so cute
with your hinkety
high yella ass

but just this morning
i seen you dancing around
on mtv spring break
your titties hanging out
your ass kind of chunky
and your frown
lines were deep
even as you smiled.

better botox your ass
before i do it for you.

CRACK

woke up this morning
feeling real nasty
inside and out.

temp agency didn't call
and my man gone off and
left me for some heifer called
toni.

went to the center
where my counselor
that cute little faggot with
the side winder in his pocket
told me to cheer up!
see the bright side of life!

later walking home
through the park
a pit bull tried to hump
my leg while his owner
looked on and laughed.

and this evening
after C.O.P.S.
i looked out my window
and saw a crack running down
the middle of the sky.

one of these days

it's all gonna fall down.

don't say I didn't warn you.

BUSTED

so i got my ass
evicted.
and i failed
the last urine test
i'm livin in a burned
out plymouth reliant
here on the edge of
watts.
yesterday, pushing my cart down
sunset blvd.
i seen a poster of kwame cohen
his grinning dreadlocked ass
over the words
"discover the power within!"
i hate that light skinneded
think-he-so-cute motherfucking guru
i really would like to see him
busted, evicted,
livin in a car
with me.

PRIME TIME

saw Kwame Cohen again
today

on the t.v. we all hooked up
down by the freeway.
he said we needed to
"awaken the queens and
kings within."
he said we were "the rulers
of our own inner kingdom."
i sent him a present
afterward.
something special
i picked up that made me
think of him.
a piece of petrified dog shit
from sanford's mutt
willy
wrapped in tin foil
and tied
with a
terry cloth
sash.

hope he likes it.

i do.

DEAR KWAME COHEN

can I tell you
a secret?

i'd like to give it
to you

real good
up there
where the sun don't shine.

APOCALYPSE NOW

the army tanks rolled in
this morning
telling us we got to
pack up
and go.
they crushed
my pump jemsons
and a box of records,
patti labelle, sylvester
and diana ross
among them.
damn!
they say the world's gonna
end. say the queers and the gimps
and the nigras all gots to move
underground before we get
nuked.
i ain't scared.
nobody gonna take out
no wilona wilkerson
i'm here to stay.
i'm here to say,
"yo

17. Affection Afflictions: My Alien/My Self or More "Reading at Work"

"Utopia's description of the social space provides an opportunity to 'visualize' the relation between the experience of oppression and the vision of a transformed society, and to visualize the problematics of moving back and forth between them . . . In examining the relation between the utopian and critical impulses, I have therefore also focused on this temporal pole by recognizing the fact that utopia is not finally a space, but rather the narration of a space."[1]

"Again something is missing. That is to say, the lived experiences of women and men all around us are again and again in excess of the theory."[2]

INTRODUCTION STORIES

"Loving the Alien," a provocative phrase and also a conference held in Berlin in 1997, spurred the writing of this essay.[3]

---

[1] Jennifer Burwell, *Notes on Nowhere: Feminism. Utopian Logic, and Social Transformation* (Minneapolis: University of Minnesota Press, 1997), p. 203.

[2] Samuel Delany, "Reading at Work, and Other Activities Frowned on by Authority," in *Longer Views: Extended Essays* (Hanover, N.H.: University Press of New England, 1996), p. 104.

[3] I'd like to thank Diedrich Diederichsen for inviting me along with Kodwo Eshun,

At the time I let the words "Loving the Alien" slip around in my mind. A hodgepodge of associations began to multiply, gaining memory fuel and associative momentum as I pondered what the possibilities of the combined terms "Loving the Alien: Diaspora, Science Fiction, and Multikultur" could mean.

Music memory links made me think back to some seventies album covers, which included one of Herbie Hancock in a spaceship bubble flying over a purple spacescape on the album called *Thrust*. Other suggestive fragments passed through my brain like Stanley Clarke's staticky and digital-sounding electric guitar played solo or with the group Return to Forever and Rahsaan Roland Kirk's "Theme for Eulupions," which I for some reason associated with Sun Ra's "Space is the Place," maybe because my friend Book had cracked my Sun Ra album and in his guilt gave me the Rahsaan as a kind of related compensation. At any rate my thoughts spun around to the seventies, which also included first hearing George Clinton records in junior high school and being introduced to P-funk and the Mothership Connection in a public library record section in Cleveland, Kinsman Avenue to be exact. Strange. Why the seventies now? There were other thoughts and sensations piling up having to do with LTJ Bukem & friends' ethereal drum and bass sounds with fragments of funk, images of silver clothes and nonstop techno beats, but . . . It seemed as if these early impressions really stuck and melded with the present. I was curious about this phenomenon in myself and I also began to detect it elsewhere in varying permutations.

During the mid-1990s it was no news that the seventies had been back in the media and in fashion for a while then. We're used to these cyclical returns or part of what was so frenetically hailed awhile back as the bricolage of postmodernism. Predictably enough, in 2000 the eighties again reared its disco-balled head. In the seventies it was the fifties, and so on.

Maybe these seventies links were fresh in my mind because I too have

---

Greg Tate, John Szwed, Mark Dery, The Sun Ra Arkestra, and others to participate in the stimulating and unusual conference "Loving the Alien: Diaspora, Science Fiction and Multikultur" held at the Volkstheater in Berlin in November of 1997. The book version was published in German under the same title by ID-Archiv, Berlin, 1998.

been interested in the seventies, and most interested in the interest in the seventies—including my own. Might it be imagined as some postutopian moment (although things get sticky when one tries to periodize a decade and its many modes)? I'd been collecting as many seventies albums as I could get my hands on to listen to and look at. These showed some of the eclecticism of the decade. I saw them as some sort of index to a childhood past. Nostalgia wasn't what I was seeking, yet what was I searching for? I'd also been thinking a lot about art and technology and how these had been thought of in the recent past, as well as the artist Robert Smithson's interpretation of entropy. (His writings from the seventies were reprinted in 1996.)

Apollo space missions fascinated me in the seventies also. I remember these seeming very personally important when I was around ten and I would watch with anticipation every move of the TV camera no matter how static the image on the screen appeared. In retrospect I don't know why I cared so much, maybe it was one of those kid attachments, the idea of walking on the moon, which now seems very far away since the *Challenger,* among other things, exploded. Many of the films which I recently watched on video in preparation for this essay I'd had a vague recollection of having watched on TV in the seventies. The names seemed familiar, like *Soylent Green,* although I couldn't remember the plots. These films had in common a kind of doom which seemed to be immanent and linked to technological "man."

I don't remember having had any role models of women in space besides Uhura in *Star Trek.* It would not be until years later when I was in college that I would learn that Uhuru meant "freedom" in Swahili and that Gene Roddenberry had produced progressive SF parables.

The metaphoric expression which could flip to a literal expression intrigued me: "loving the alien." Again the question nagged, What many things could that mean, especially when combined with thoughts about Diaspora, science fiction, and multiculturalism? And behind that lurked another question: How was I to approach this combination and deal with the possible profundity of the tangle?

THE SEVENTIES AS PRIMAL-SCENE FANTASY AND UTOPIAN IMPULSE/DYSTOPIAN ROMANCE, REPEATING RETURNS AND TIME-LOOP PARADOX

"It was twenty years ago today" is how the essay "Culture is a metaphor for 'it's their problem' " by Diedrich Diedrichsen begins. That was written in 1994 for the "Contact Zone" symposium.[4] So the date referred to was 1974. "The German left and its revolutionary allies" is the title of the section heading and the moment described is that in which Portugal's dictatorship was overthrown by the Movement of the Armed Forces. The text continues:

> It looked like your classical socialist revolution. The one you knew from
> textbooks you were studying in your after school maoist-high-school
> groups and right about that time nearly ceased to believe in. But then it
> wouldn't have been possible without the anticolonial fight in Angola
> and Mozambique. In 1974 Portugal also became the favorite holiday
> destination for the radical German left. The German New Left, the
> revolutionaries from the '67 and '68 student riots, were always the most
> internationalist leftists in the world. They always felt closest to Ho Chi
> Minh, the revolutionary fight of the oppressed of the Third World,
> especially in Africa and South America. And of course in South East
> Asia and the Middle East.

In the mid-1990s, especially in the media, the 1970s were ripe for returns. But which returns exactly? The description just excerpted relies on historical markers to interweave some of the then-popular counterculture sentiments. A jaundiced eye is cast on the enthusiams involved in adopted revolutionary struggles of other countries. Yet, what has been offered in the cinema regarding these returns?

---

[4] Renée Green, ed., *Negotiations in the "Contact Zone"* (Lisbon: Centro Cultural de Belém; Free Agent Media, 2002).

The movies *Crooklyn* (1994), *Dazed and Confused* (1993), and most recently *Boogie Nights* (1997) immediately come to mind. All three rely on the experiential memoir form, yet this floats outside of any politically inflected historical context. While all are absorbing and draw viewers back in time, using the devices of period music, period slang, and fashion rehashes, they beg a question: What would a reading of past narratives or refashioned narratives of the past be like if they were more complexly and historically situated? Where do these and other narratives resist the apparent seamless reception of the return as one more product? What is repressed in the narratives and where do the clues to these more uneasy moments reside?[5]

The 1970s could be viewed, for some, as a version of a primal-scene fantasy as described by Constance Penley:

> . . . the name Freud gave to the fantasy of overhearing or observing parental intercourse, of being on the scene, so to speak, of one's own conception. The desire represented in the time travel story, of both witnessing one's own conception and being one's own mother and father, is similar to the primal scene fantasy, in which one can be both observer or one of the participants . . . A patient can consciously fabricate such a scene only because it has been operative in his or her unconscious, and this construction has nothing to do with its actual occurrence or nonoccurrence. The idea of returning to the past to generate an event that has already made an impact on one's identity lies at the core of the time-loop paradox story.[6]

---

[5] This is not to say that style as a representation of cultural moments isn't historically inflected. *The Ice Storm* (1997) provides an example of a film which shares the fascination with the modes of seventies "lifestyles," but which also situates the angst and silliness it presents within a context of political, social, and economic circumstances in an eerily thought-provoking way, even though the focus is on families in a suburban American milieu.

[6] Constance Penley, "Time Travel, Primal Scene and the Critical Dystopia," in *Alien Zone: Cultural Theory and Contemporary Science Fiction Cinema*, ed. Annette Kuhn (London; New York: Verso, 1990), pp. 120–21.

The repetition involved in revisiting the seventies, which for me represents childhood and its multiple associations, is something I probed in a work called *Partially Buried in Three Parts*. The work combines a fascination for a time before one was able to articulate the observations which have since been supplied in retrospect by reading histories of those times.[7]

The American New Left's process of imagining others is a means to identify desired identities which they can attempt to claim for their own uses. This desire echoes the previous description of the German New Left's enthrallment with other models of struggle and suggests the media's role in the process:

> Images, illusions, and icons of revolution, packaged in film, voice, and videotape in Moscow, Peking, Algiers, Havana, Cairo, New Delhi, Accra, Hanoi, Leopoldville, Djakarta, Nairobi, Belgrade, and Conakry, incessantly were broadcast and rebroadcast in the American mass media as a spectacle of global revolution. From these prepackaged metatexts of transformation, 1960s radicals—black, white, brown, male, female, young, and old—borrowed the names, battle cries, and costumes of their revolutions. As a result, Marxism-Leninism and Pan-Africanism, which had virtually no groundedness in the lived history of advanced industrial America, were adopted as schemas of "wholesale theoretical clarity" into the countercultures of the 1960s. . . . The New Left intended to create a revolution, but in the process, it unintentionally revolutionized the workings of corporate America.[8]

---

[7] See my books *Shadows and Signals* (Barcelona: Fundació Antoni Tàpies, 2000) and *Between and Including* (Cologne: DuMont; Vienna: Secession, 2001).

[8] Timothy W. Luke, "The Modern Service State: Public Power in America from the New Deal to the New Beginning," in *Race, Politics, and Culture: Critical Essays on the Radicalism of the 1960's*, ed. Adolph Reed (Westport, Conn.: Greenwood Press, 1986), p. 247.

Cultural forms are always barometers in some way of the ideologies which are enacted in our societies. The repressed aspects and the ways to critically read these provide a repetitive interest, at least for those engaged with how cultural forms function and continue, and also provide a benefit which, ideally imagined, can be transmitted into how we live and into what we produce. With this incentive in mind, consider the questions Samuel Delany asks in his essay "Reading at Work":

What is this "work"?
What is "reading"?
What is "metaphor" and how do we "read" it?
How does "metaphor" "work"?

Frankly, I do not see how reading can be other than a violent process. The violence of the letter is the violence of the reader—a reader involved in an unclear, cloudy, struggling, masochistic relationship with a text that, at any moment, would produce joy, must do so violently.

For without violence, all ideology—radical or conservative—is incomplete and blind to itself.[9]

And what about the metaphors: eating the other, loving the alien, and the violence of reading? Being ingested by the mothership?
Again to quote Delany:

Nevertheless and once again: metaphors are not radical in themselves, whether they are delivered by TV soap operas, science education programs, science fiction tales, or socialist feminist manifestoes. Critique—critical work—is created and constituted by people, by individuals, by individuals speaking and writing to others, by people

---

[9] Ibid., p. 98.

who are always in specific situations that are tensional as well as technological.[10]

The stories I've presented so far could be thought of in relation to the above-mentioned primal-scene fantasies which could inconclusively situate them in relationship to some unconscious operations. But as examples of "experience" they can be historicized and thus more questions are raised. As Joan W. Scott points out:

> And yet it is precisely the questions precluded—questions about discourse, difference, and subjectivity, as well as about what counts as experience and who gets to make that determination—that would enable us to historicize experience, to reflect critically on the history we write about it, rather than to premise our history upon it.[11]

KINDRED AND THE OMEGA MAN WITH BLADE RUNNER HIGHLIGHTS

An initial point of interest I had in the three titles I'd like to discuss is that they are all set in Los Angeles, which seems to be the capital of science fiction dystopias, a world overrun by technology and multifarious forms of transportation. *Kindred,* a novel by Octavia Butler,[12] and the film *The Omega Man* (1971) both take place in the 1970s—a post-Watts riot and pre-L.A. rebellion/Rodney King time, while the film *Blade Runner* (1982) is set in a future in which other planets have become colonies of the earth's military-technological-corporate complex.

Beyond these initial observations other aspects of these stories became

---

[10] Ibid., p. 114.

[11] Joan W. Scott, "Experience," in *Feminists Theorize the Political,* eds. Judith Butler and Joan W. Scott (New York: Routledge, 1992), p. 33.

[12] Octavia Butle, *Kindred* (Garden City, N.Y.: Doubleday, 1979).

of interest. The functions which the body plays in these narratives is one aspect. Questions in each story arise in differently inflected ways about what an acceptable body is and what the terms to judge this designation might be. Is there a link between humanness and what becomes societally deemed an acceptable body? How are "humanity" and "civilization" conflated? How are these distinctions between acceptable or appropriate bodies being made and how is the equation of such a body with qualities of the human configured once a deteriorization sets in, which makes clear designations of these distinctions difficult? What happens when a body changes into a diseased form? Does the person also change and become less human? Another question which arises in each of these narratives is what does civilization mean when those who are assigned the role of humanness (and by implication civility) act with barbarity? Last, how does memory function in relation to being human? What might it mean that memories might be retained by man-made creations? How and by whom is subjectivity determined? Is it solely a human characteristic? What's so great about human subjectivity or humans anyway?

In *Kindred* the protagonist, Dana, is pulled back in time. Rather than present an imaginary utopian, dystopian, or heterotopian future, *Kindred,* set in 1976 (America's bicentennial year), refers to a past time, nineteenth-century antebellum Maryland, i.e., the Old South, and to events which are recognizable from slave narratives. *Kindred* has been described by Jennifer Burwell as a "grim fantasy" which "moves between the present and a dystopian period in American history." Yet elements recognizable from the science fiction genre are still apparent. In particular the "time-travel paradox," which while not technically explained occurs repeatedly. The novel encompasses a personal search, which begins involuntarily, as well as historical and social commentary encoded in fiction.

Kindred provides an example of a way of imagining the contradictions involved in negotiating one's relationship to history and the present, which extend to family relations. It also approaches the scariness of what a return could entail, as well as the traces that persist in the present which are shades of the past. Slavery exists in a way as a primal scene fantasy/fact for African diasporic peoples and always somehow never quite goes away.

PLAYED OUT IN THE BODY

The central paradox which Dana is forced to accept is that the ancestor who calls her back is a white male named Rufus. Six incidents of return occur within the space of the novel. Each one is progressively more lengthy and dangerous. Rufus calls Dana when he is in trouble during different times in his life. On each return Rufus is older, so she is a presence during Rufus's boyhood, adolescence, and early manhood. It is her hope to influence him in some way not to be a typical slave master, but to learn compassion and perhaps influence him to realize the horrific aspects of slavery so that he might act in another way. She doesn't expect miracles, but attempts to influence him at least in terms of daily encounters. She literally becomes his private tutor, to everyone's amazement—how does a black woman know how to read, since knowledge of reading was illegal for slaves? And she also develops an affection for him, which is constantly thrown into conflict by his actions.

Dana gradually discovers that she can only return to her home in contemporary Los Angeles when her life is threatened. To return she is forced to take greater risks, yet she must continue to live to protect Rufus, because she doesn't want to test what would happen if she interfered with the birth of her great-grandmother, who is the daughter of Rufus and a slave woman named Alice.

Other aspects of Dana's learned negotiations with the past involve her encounters with slaves. Her knowledge of slavery is only from books she's read, but living in the past forces her to acknowledge and feel through her body the force of that oppression. Nothing she had experienced in the twentieth century had prepared her to survive slavery, and her tactics for survival extend to a suicide attempt, slashing her wrists to force a return to Los

Angeles. As is stated in the Prologue of the novel: "I lost arm on my last trip home. My left arm."

Butler's novel presents the tension felt by some contemporary people who are black and middle class and artists (for example) and who think (and wish) they can live their lives focusing on their interests as Dana tries to do, yet are called upon to consider social conditions and the past. Some Gil Scott-Heron lyrics from Dana's contemporary period come to mind and suggest the tension between a past and a present which Dana finds herself inadvertently grappling with: "Gotta move on I gotta see tomorrow . . . can't look back there's nothing there but sorrow." The pull back is graphically depicted as an abduction by a relative that Dana didn't even want to acknowledge, because of the so-called impure mixing of the blood.

The violence of the act and the associations with bastardy as a negatively configured event ("bastard" being defined in the *Oxford English Dictionary* as "illegitimate by birth, unauthorized, counterfeit, hybrid," but also meaning a person of specified kind, like you "lucky bastard"). At any rate, what Dana is forced to face is that the violence demonstrated by Rufus toward Alice is mixed with love. The impossibility of a reciprocal relationship due to the imbalance of power between them distorts any feelings they have for each other. They were childhood friends, he fell in love with her, he was legally her master, he thought he could control her. She fell in love with another slave named Isaac. They tried to run away. Upon their capture her "master" ordered Isaac's ears cut off and Alice devoured by dogs. Isaac was sent away and Alice remained in Master Rufus's bedroom as a patient nursed by Dana. So by playing his trump card as the master he got her back and eliminated the competition physically, but not in her mind. When she was well she could either deal with his "love," which meant to be his mistress, or she could die. Eventually, after she bore two babies, she hung herself.

One of the most interesting tensions set up in the novel is between parallel stories of Dana and Kevin, her white husband, who like Dana is a writer, and Rufus and Alice. This forces one to examine the tensions involved in the contemporary relationship, which is one of voluntary love and supposed equality, but exists within a country with a past history of slavery, to which eventually both Kevin and Dana are transported. The way slavery could shape the kinds of relationships individuals could legally have is made manifest when it is assumed that Kevin is Dana's master: they are forced to play the master-slave roles to survive.

HOME AND BOUNDARY LOSS/INVOLUNTARY FLASHBACKS; THE CALL OF THE FAMILY; ALIEN WITHIN/BLOOD RELATIONS/GERM WARFARE/ BECOMING ALIEN, LOSS OF CONTROL; INNER-CITY DISSOLUTION AS METAPHOR AND FACT

In *The Omega Man* another view of family is presented: a lone male individual urban commando staves off possible invasion/absorption by The Family—diseased remains of the human population who have been infected by germ warfare. In this narrative the future is the 1970s, and military scientist Robert Neville, played by Charlton Heston, is the last man on earth.

Before elaborating on *The Omega Man* I'd like to remind the reader of the title, "Affection Afflictions: My Alien/My Self or More Reading at Work." The definition of "affection," again from the *OED*, is: "1. goodwill, fond feeling; 2. disease; diseased condition." Affection is associated with love, yet this definition encompasses disease, infection, invasion, and implies a loss of boundaries, something beyond one's control. In relation to *The Omega Man* and to *Kindred*, the notion of the loss of boundaries and of bodily, as well as spatial invasion, are recurrent references. "Alien," when defined as an adjective, means "unfamiliar; unacceptable or repugnant; 2. foreign; 3. of beings from other worlds." As a noun it is defined as "1. foreign-born resident who is not naturalized; 2. a being from another world."

. . .

Dutch: "Everybody has it."

Neville: "Everybody, but me."

Neville is supposedly the last man on earth in the wake of germ warfare, which has invaded everyone's body except his, because he possesses the test serum which worked. *The Omega Man* can be seen as a Hollywood parable for the times just survived, the 1960s and early seventies. The ways in which gender, race, and youth are woven into this narrative raises questions concerning the humanity/civilization conflation as an aspiration. The infected "aliens" are humans. The physical change they've undergone is signaled by their hair becoming an albino white and their eyes an otherworldly green. The Family resembles a medieval Charles Manson cult who've taken to the streets with wooden flamethrowers.

As the lone survivor and upholder of the best of civilization, Neville is still lonely. With no "people" around the city is by day his playground. Like vampires The Family can't bear the daylight. By night Neville is hunted and taunted by them. During his daily jaunts jogging and searching for The Family's lair he also scavenges from department stores. Instead of riots in which inner-city stores were stormed for consumer goods, he does this alone and in a casual manner. It is in a department store that he first gets a glimpse of Lisa (Rosalind Cash) among the female shop dummies he'd tentatively appeared to be lusting after.

When Neville is abducted by The Family and on the verge of being executed after an exchange about who the real barbarians are, technological man or the new Luddites, he is saved by Lisa and Dutch, who then kidnap him. It is revealed that there are two families existing—Mathias's (former TV announcer turned cult patriarch) family (The Family)—and another alternative family of not yet visibly infected youth and children. Their surrogate parents are Lisa, a young black, supposedly streetwise woman, and Dutch, a former med-student-hippie-utopian whose studies were halted when "they scratched the world." This family includes Lisa's sick brother Richie, who is on the verge of albinoization ("the tertiary stage"). The assortment seems to represent the promise of a rainbow family of the future. Neville discovers he was kidnapped by Lisa and Dutch's family because they want the serum which has helped him remain healthy. He then immediately becomes a patriarch, who makes decisions and carries out actions. Dutch is reduced to a desexualized dreamy boy and Lisa, who originally had threatened Neville at gunpoint, becomes his lover and helpmate, as she's meant to be the last woman on earth and he the last man—"The Man." Lisa introduces him as such, also referring to the African-American slang-inflected meaning, widely used by the counterculture and their Hollywood counterparts, to connote The Establishment and The System, terms which crop up repeatedly in films of that time which depict transgressive yet lovable black and/or youthful revolutionary elements. The lovable aspects usually have to do with these elements' closeness to nature and their raw emotions—sometimes destructive, but also naively hopeful and desirous of harmony and freedom. This impression is highlighted in the opening scenes of the movie when Neville watches *Woodstock* in an empty theater. After he's mouthed the words of the movie he says, "They sure don't make pictures like that anymore," implying that *Woodstock* was only a piece of film left over from a past time which can't be reclaimed, a memory stimulant, ephemeral as the light which allows us to see these moving projections—the media as the location of utopian revolution, as previously mentioned.

As Richie, Lisa's infected brother, responds to the serum made from Neville's blood ("100 percent Anglo-Saxon, baby," he tells Lisa), he asks Neville why The Family, as fellow human beings, don't also deserve a chance to be saved from their disease. By this time Neville imagines the future existing with his newfound family and wants nothing but to escape to the hills upon Richie's recovery. Despite Neville's desire to maintain a disease-free family, the two families merge after Richie's attempt to convert Mathias fails and he is killed. Mathias echoes a sentiment expressed about those rioting ghetto dwellers of the recent past in saying that The Family didn't want or need to be saved. Soon after Richie's murder Lisa emerges from a store "actively infected" and somehow becomes a zombified devotee of Mathias's. She's been alienized. Everything is invaded, Neville's house and his woman. Neville becomes an avenger.

The death of the father seems to be required for the new contingent family to exist. Neville is ultimately "sacrificed" by Mathias and The Family amid symbolic crucifixion imagery. Lisa is feebly sorry and out of it, seeming about to nod off. Dutch comes with a van and the kids, scoops her up, leaving Neville in a pool of blood, but salvaging the serum, and off they drive into the sunset.

WHO MADE YOU? WHO OWNS YOU?/WHO'S HUMAN AND WHY DOES IT MATTER AFTER THE END OF CIVILIZATION?

Vivian Sobchack refers to two different logics which have appeared in science fiction films of the last decades. One involves the embrace of the alien and the other suggests the erasure of alienation. In this distinction she references Foucault's distinction between resemblance and similitude:

> [T]he most postmodern SF does not "embrace the alien" in a celebra-
> tion of resemblance, but "erases alienation" in a celebration of simili-
> tude. Thus, it is not critical of alienation. Indeed, the postmodern SF
> film maintains only enough signs of "alien-ness" to dramatize it not as
> "the difference that makes a difference" but as the "difference that
> makes a sameness." The "alien" posited by marginal and postmodern
> SF enables the representation of alienation as "human" and constitutes
> the reversible and nonhierarchical relations of similitude into a myth of
> homogenized heterogeneity. That is, nationalism no longer exists as a
> difference in the culture of multinational capital.[13]

---

[13] Vivian Carol Sobchack, *Screening Space: The American Science Fiction Film* (New York: Ungar, 1987), p. 297.

CONTINGENT NEW WORLD?: FAMILIES, NATIONS,
CORPORATIONS/WHAT DO FORMS OF LOVE HAVE TO
DO WITH THE "NEW WORLD ORDER"?

What sorts of ethical responsibilities do we have to others? What could one's relationship be to a replicant who is made and owned by a corporation, but who has organic parts and whose body is linked to a mind which can interpret, analyze, and express emotion? Memory and the desire for it are key aspects of the struggle of the replicants in *Blade Runner*. Life and memory are connected. But the replicants have four-year life spans, a built-in "fail-safe." The replicants are man-made and partly organic. They look like perfect human specimens. What characteristics separate the replicants from a definition of humanness, beyond not having a long-term memory which would accompany a life lived in stages from childhood over a longer duration of time? The question is asked by Rachel, a replicant, whether Decker, another lone survivalist, has ever accidentally "retired" (killed) a human. Who is the brute? The replicants were made to serve humans, in a way similar to how slaves were designated as nonhumans and made to serve. They become hunted on earth after they've mounted a rebellion in the colonial "off world."

POSTSCRIPT: HOME: WHAT CAN WE DO HERE?
DIFFICULTY IN IMAGINING OTHERS/SENTIMENT VS.
CONSTITUTIONAL CHANGE: EMOTIONAL KNOTS AND
IRRATIONAL LOVES

What ethical responsibility do we have to others whether they be other animals or whether they be instruments for labor, war and sex, made from flesh and blood (organic life forms) of interpretive mind, lived emotion and perception, having eyes which see and transmit images which are felt? Can humans be equated with aliens when becoming diseased? When becoming rebellious? Are these creatures discardable like barbarians and vermin (the conflation Neville makes), like replicants?

To bring this rumination "home," which I hope is a concept now thrown into question, I'd like to close by thinking about Elaine Scarry's essay "The Difficulty of Imagining Other People," which is excerpted from a longer essay of the same title which she gave as a lecture for a public meeting in Frankfurt about injuries to Turkish residents in Germany.[14]

One of the main points of Scarry's essay is this:

> The problem with discussions of "the other" is that they characteristically emphasize generous imaginings, and thus allow the fate of another person to be contingent on the generosity and wisdom of the imaginer. But solutions ought not to give one group the power to regulate the welfare of another group in this way.[15]

What she calls for instead are legal and constitutional safeguards which can protect people's rights rather than depend on the messy emotions involved in imagining others. She says: "The work accomplished by a structure of laws cannot be accomplished by a structure of sentiment. Constitutions are needed to uphold cosmopolitan values."[16]

---

[14] Elaine Scarry, "Das scwierige Bild der Anderen," in *Scwierige Fremdheit: über Integration und Ausgrenzung in Einwanderungländern* (Frankfurt: Fischer Verlag, 1993).

[15] Elaine Scarry "The Difficulty of Imagining Other People," in *For Love of Country: Debating the Limits of Patriotism,* ed. Martha Craven Nussbaum (Boston: Beacon Press, 1996), p. 110.

[16] Ibid.

18. My Black Death

BY ARTHUR JAFA

THERE WERE TWO MAJOR INSTANCES IN which black aesthetics radically redirected Western art practice in the twentieth century. The first is the advent of African "art" in Europe. Europeans were confronted with artifacts that were essentially alien, i.e., they were the products of radically different assumptions about how one apprehends and responds to the world. There was little understanding of the cultural context that generated these artifacts, how their forms were arrived at or how their structures of meaning operated, what they might mean to their makers.

The second instance occurred with the emergence of jazz, yet another alien artifact but one decidedly more familiar (due to its domestic origins). In the first instance—the arrival of African sculptural artifacts in Europe— you get the artifact without its creators in tow. But with the arrival of jazz, the impact isn't solely the result of the music, the artifact in this instance, but it also results from the manifest being of its creators, the way they spoke and behaved, the way they dressed, their idiomatic manner of occupying (and penetrating) space, their individual styles and philosophies, and the consensual articulations of the aesthetic and generative processes of the music. The repercussions of these two instances of cultural insurgency are near unquantifiable in magnitude, but a few things seem clear.

Picasso's *Demoiselles d'Avigon* (and hence modernism) is the direct result of his confrontation with African artifacts. His invention of Cubism was provoked by his inquiry into the spacial implications of these artifacts. This is a commonly accepted line. To be more precise, Cubism is the direct transposition of these spacial implications onto the practice of Western painting. At the time Western painting (despite Cézanne's violent cage rattling) had become trapped by the limitations (and distortions) of Western Renaissance perspective (single "fixed" vantage/vanishing point), itself a conflation of the logic of Western egocentricism (the sun revolves around the Earth) into a system of ordering space and time. African artifacts provided an alternative system with which to order space and time.

Cubism's utilization of multiple "fixed" vantages, rather than the single "fixed" vantage of Western Renaissance perspective, betrays a limited comprehension of the logic of multiple "dynamic" vantages apparent in the forms of African artifacts, a logic shared by post-Einsteinian views of space/time. Robert Farris Thompson has described in *African Art in Motion* how many of the artifacts in the possession of European artists like Picasso were never intended to be (i.e., were not designed to be) seen on a pedestal, in a fixed position. These sculptural artifacts moved around the viewer, as much as, if not more than, the viewer moved around the artifact. This is a radical alternative to the Western paradigm in which the subject has agency while the object has none.

Picasso, as quoted by André Malraux, said:

"People are always talking about the influence the Negroes had on me. What about it? We all loved the fetishes. Van Gogh said his generation had Japanese art—we have the Negroes. Their forms have no more influence on me than on Matisse, or on Derain. But for Matisse and Derain, the masks were sculpture—no more than that. When Matisse showed me his first Negro head, he talked about Egyptian art. But when I went to the Musée de l'Homme, the masks were not just sculpture. They were magical objects. . . . I understand what their sculptures did for the Negroes. . . . They were weapons—to keep people from being ruled by spirits, to help them free themselves. Tools. *Les Demoiselles d'Avignon* must have come that day, not because of the forms, but because it was my first canvas of exorcism!"

Another crucial aspect of Picasso's confrontation with black aesthetics has only recently come to light. Ostensibly an investigation of Picasso's utilization of photography, one can only smile in wonder at the publication of *Picasso and Photography: The Dark Mirror* (Baldasari, 1998). The book reveals that Picasso possessed some forty photographs taken by Edmond Fortier, a Dakar-based photographer who was the most prolific publisher of postcards from French West Africa beginning in 1900–01. The photographs, supposedly "studies," are of African women, generally bare-breasted and often with arms raised over the head or folded behind the back. (I suspect the appearance of these clearly suppressed materials is a result of the Picasso Museum's desperate need to feed its publishing wing.)

This book reveals, in rather explicit comparative detail, how Picasso used these photographs as the basis for the development of *Les Demoiselles d'Avignon*. The standard argument is that *Demoiselles* represented "the invention of colored forms that no longer intended to imitate the external world but only to signify it. The canvas ceased to be a mirror—however deforming—of the visible, in order to become a plastic language (*écriture*)." In fact, as these materials make evident, Picasso's work imitates not only the African artifacts to which he had access, but the very bodies, by way of Fortier's "objective" representations, from which these embodiments of black being were derived. Picasso's combined access to African artifacts and Fortier's photographs made explicit the presence of the highly conceptual formal system employed by these artifacts. The implications of this would seem to demand some major reconsiderations of the conceptual origins and parameters of modernism: how black bodies activate space, or the volumetric intensity of black bodies, of cities; and the attraction of the entropic; modernism as a substrand of black aesthetics; the black body as the premier anti-entropic figure of the twentieth century. The trauma provoked by the introduction of the black body into white space is profound).

Our notion of the "abstract" arises from a simple refusal of, or resistance to, the ontological fact of black being (and its material dimension, the black body), what I've described as "the inconceivability of the black body to the white imagination." Simply put, representations of the black body, as rendered by traditional African artifacts, were rejected (by whites) as instances of verisimilitude and instead received as "highly stylized" or "abstract." Europeans preferred to understand these artifacts as creative distortions rather than accept the existence of human beings that looked so radically different in appearance from them. This radical difference of appearance functions, in the Western mind-set, as the sign of a radically different (alien) ontology, which of course threatened the Eurocentric belief in itself as the defining model of humanity. This, in turn, has provoked the ongoing struggle against the acceptance of the "other," and its full humanity.

Duchamp was initially as content as Picasso, and others, to explore the space/time implications of African artifacts. But inevitably, Duchamp, smarter than anyone else around, became deeply interested in how African artifacts *behaved* rather than simply how they looked (their gaze). Duchamp peeped that these artifacts were, in fact, not art but instruments whose functionality had been arrested, and that much of their power was derived from their radically alienated, and de facto transgressive, relationship to the context in which they found themselves. Consequently, Duchamp's urinal was engendered by his desire to model a work after the contextual dissonance provoked by the placement of these (black) artifacts in (white) museums. And it's no accident that Duchamp chose the urinal, a white artifact which contains and channels dark matter, or shit, the stuff of black being. Surrealism can be understood as an investigation of the psychic frisson produced by the juxtaposition of incongruent objects (a cow and an ironing board), the paradigmatic example being "the black body in white space."

In similar fashion, Jackson Pollock ('s practice) couldn't have been without jazz. It's indisputable that Pollock was very good at what he did, but the problem arose, inevitably, because he didn't know what he was doing. His genius, and I think it was genius, resided in his ability to transpose jazz's improvisational flow and trajection, an essentially alien aesthetic methodology, onto the practice of painting. Western painting, which up until the twentieth century had been primarily mimetic, i.e., primarily preoccupied with capturing the appearance of the physical universe, realized with Pollock a radically new, and fully implemented, paradigm. This new paradigm privileged the performance of processional formations, and constituent significations, at the expense of the mimetic impulse.

Pollock's method, often spoken of in terms of gesture and choreography, consists largely of improvised dance as a means of getting paint down onto the canvas. Lee Krasner has related that Pollock would listen to jazz continually, and obsessively, while he painted. This is particularly significant given the absence of a mimetic subject in Pollock's work. (The works to which I am referring, clearly those on which his reputation lies, are those which dispense with even the vestiges of, generally psychoanalytically read, iconographies.) Were Pollock painting a mountain or an apple, the music to which he painted would be of questionable relevance or significance, but because Pollock's paintings are pictures of his process of getting the paint onto the canvas, of the physically located rhythmic perturbations of the paint's application, the music which animated his movements while simultaneously providing the aesthetic model for his action becomes extremely significant.

Why black music? It's clear that one of the defining factors which contributed to the development and power of black American music, and other musics of the Diafra (the black Diaspora), was a sort of contextual displacement equivalent to HIV's leap of the species barrier. By this I'm suggesting that with the Middle Passage, African music, like HIV (which hypothetically existed for some time in a species of monkey found in Central Africa), found itself freed from its natal ecology—with its attendant checks and balances, its natural predation—and thus freed, expanded exponentially, in the process mutating from African music(s) into black music(s).

(In the 1930s the USDA, in an effort to combat soil erosion, introduced kudzu, a Japanese vine, to Mississippi. By 1955, having escaped its original planting, kudzu had become "the vine that ate the South." Today, it infests over 250,000 acres of land in Mississippi, costing over $20 million a year to combat. Similarly, "Plague of Europeans" David Killingray '73)

It's somewhat paradoxical that in a context which radically circumscribed the mobility of the black body, black musical expressivity found itself both formally unbound and pressed into service in a manner which, classically, it would not have had to serve. Black musical expressivity not only survived the Middle Passage but, free of the class strictures of its natal context (which had limited its avenues of articulation and calcified its content) and unconstrained by a need to speak the experiences of a ruling class, evolved new forms with which to embody new experiences. A black music evolved equal to the unprecedented existential drama and complexity of the circumstance in which black people (Africans) found themselves.

Is it an accident that Mondrian was the first major European artist to recognize Pollock's work as some new shit?

(Vinyl recordings became black in sublimated response to the separation of the black voice from the black body, a separation which solved the conundrum of how to bring black music into white spaces minus the black bodies, i.e, black beings, which, by their very nature as musically productive entities, were assertive and thus troubling to whites.)

Pollock's crisis was precipitated by his inability to access the signification inherent in the methodology (jazz improvisational flow and trajection) he had so powerfully appropriated and implemented in his work. Classically, jazz improvisation is first and foremost signified self-determination. This actually precedes its function as musical gesture. For the black artist to stand before an audience, often white, and to publicly demonstrate her decision-making capacity, her agency, rather than the replication of another's agency, i.e., the composers, was a profoundly radical and dissonant gesture (akin in contemporary terms to the catalytic effect of hip-hop sampling and/or Sherrie Levine's practice in their respective discourses). This signification of one's "self-determination" is in turn premised on one's "self-possession." There is no "self-determination" without "self-possession." And, "self-possession" is *the* existential issue for black Americans.

For Pollock—a white man and as such assumed to be self-determined and self-possessed—the demonstration of such reads as little more than ubiquitous white masculinist privilege (jacking off, the primary critique of the following generations of abstract expressists). Pollock, unable to access his work's signification, its structures of meaning, found himself vulnerable to critiques that the work was essentially without meaning. It's significant that Pollock's last productive period, and certainly his healthiest, ends, so the story goes, with the first viewing of Hans Namuth's famous film of

Pollock painting, projected in the kitchen for Pollock and his friends. Apparently Pollock got up when the film ended, walked over to the liquor cabinet, and proceeded to drink himself into a violent stupor, thus ending over two years of sobriety, a sobriety which he never recovered.

"When I am painting, I'm not aware of what I'm doing." Pollock saw himself dancing around, a white being behaving, embarrassingly, like a black being (like a nigger), thus destroying the fragile state of grace, of disembodied (white) being, under which he'd created his most powerful works.

(The classic cartoons showing monkeys making abstract paintings spoke to the sublimated realization that Pollock's practice was in large measure black.)

Pollock, feeling like a charlatan, reintroduces figuration in his late works. This pathetic attempt to inject the work with meaning, a meaning which he himself could access, signals a total aesthetic collapse. So tragically, having failed at legitimately investing the work with meaning, Pollock kills himself.

Was Jackson Pollock white trash? Pollock's particular genius was possible precisely because of his alienation. In that his alienation allowed him an atypical relationship to the culture of black America. This is similar to the relationship which Elvis had to black American music, and which Picasso, in a much more covert fashion, had to African art. (Elvis's black saturation and white trash status is mirrored by Picasso's status as a Spaniard, un/moored, in Paris.) In each of these instances, and despite the seemingly inevitable denial that occurred once influence became an issue, the breakthrough nature of the work achieved was made possible by an initially humble, and thus by definition nonsupremacist, relationship to the catalytic artifact at hand. Just as Beethoven was humble in the face of the body of work that had preceded him, these artists were each students of the work under whose influence they had fallen, students in a fashion which white supremacy would typically make unlikely.

(John Cage spent his entire career avoiding the term "improvisation," saturated as it was with black meaning.)

This is a story I've told a number of times. I worked on Stanley Kubrick's *Eyes Wide Shut* as second unit director of photography for approximately a year and a half. We'd occasionally receive calls from Stanley while we were shooting. Lisa, the second unit director, would relay his instructions and add, typically, that Stanley said to "keep up the good work." A couple of times Lisa tried to hand me the phone so that Stanley could speak to me. Each time I waved her away, saying I'd speak to him later, ostensibly because I was too involved in shooting.

A little before the film was set for release, I'm hanging out in Germany and I get a call from Lisa. She asks if I'm available to shoot in New York the following week. We agree on a date and I make arrangements to return to New York. A few days later, I'm boarding a plane for New York, I look over and see the cover of *USA Today:* "Filmmaker Stanley Kubrick dead at 70." I'd spoken to Lisa not five hours earlier. I figure it to be a hoax, but I get to New York and it's confirmed: Stanley had passed suddenly and the shoot was canceled.

Over the next several days, I got extremely depressed. I'd never spoken to Kubrick. I wondered why, in over a year of working on the film, I'd never been available to speak to him. I realized that there'd been too much that I'd wanted to say. I'd, unconsciously, been waiting for the film's completion in the hope that I'd be able to have a real conversation with him. I'd wanted to tell him that he'd changed my life, and that I'd surely been, as a black, preadolescent inhabitant of the Mississippi Delta, the farthest thing imagined when he'd envisioned who the audience for *2001: A Space Odyssey* might be.

Two years after its initial release in '68, the film finally reached my hometown, Clarksdale, Mississippi. It played a drive-in theater on the outskirts of town, three nights only, Friday, Saturday, and Sunday. I barely slept that week. My father had promised to take me but by Sunday something had come up. So, a year later, I'm ten, the film finally plays at a movie theater proper. Recently opened, the West End Cinema is located in a part of town that's exclusively white. Clarksdale was essentially segregated at this point.

That Saturday my parents dropped me off at the twelve-thirty matinee. There's clearly no big demand, over two years after its release, for *2001: A Space Odyssey* in Clarksdale, Mississippi. The theater's empty except for me and two couples, both white. The lights go down, the movie begins, and it's like being buried alive. I'd never experienced anything like it before. It quite literally blew my mind. And to say that I couldn't make heads or tails of the movie is an understatement. (And even now, I'm still searching for an art experience capable of matching the effect this film had on me, its ability to simultaneously alienate and ravish. And in this fashion, the film had provided me with a model for how powerful art could be.)

There's no dialogue for the first twenty-five minutes of the film. There's little exposition. When people finally speak, they speak in hypnotic, sedated tones. And dramatically speaking, very little seems to happen during the first two thirds of the movie. The disembodied computer, HAL, displays decidedly more emotion than any of the flesh-and-blood characters. The few dispassionate exchanges between characters are punctuated by extended sequences containing little or no additional dialogue.

By the time the film reaches its intermission, I'm alone in the theater, the other moviegoers having abandoned it at some earlier point.

After the intermission, the film becomes, relatively speaking, more narratively compelling, in that things happen, yet the characters display the same narcotized, somnambulistic tone, now completely at odds with the dire circumstances in which they find themselves. (Anyone familiar with psychoanalysis will recognize the mute, vaguely conspiratorial affect of the analyst.) By the time the spaceship reaches its destination, Jupiter, only a single crew member has survived. He proceeds to launch himself down to the planet's surface in pursuit of the origin of the enigmatic black monolith uncovered on the moon's surface earlier. From this point onward, the film ceases to be narrative in any conventional Hollywood sense. Whereas the preceding parts of the film are characterized by various lacks—lack of color, lack of action, lack of apparent emotional consequence (save HAL's mournful end)—and whereas before we were stuck in a universe of arrested causality, an addict's nod, the film's finale, the descent and its aftermath, seems to dispense with causality altogether, except in the most primal sense, cinema's persistence of vision. The descent is a headlong rush composed of an extended, and unprecedented, barrage of chromatically oversaturated, spacially distorted, and elliptically sequenced imagery, all interspersed with shots of the astronaut's increasingly hysterical and emotionally overwrought grimaces (a bad trip, the result of some nightmarishly potent, and unexpected, combination of LSD and speed). This is all abruptly terminated by a shift to a very European, very white hotel room in which Bowman, still in spacesuit, observes himself aging progressively 'til the point of death (attended only by the black monolith), and his rebirth as the luminously white starchild, at which point the film ends.

There's of course an inescapably troubling, particularly for a young black kid in the early seventies, racial dimension of the film. First, there is the absolute whiteness of the context (both figuratively and literally). All of the characters are Caucasian and they are, in their demeanor, both archetypically and atavistically white. This is a whiteness that's sterile, creepy, and ultimately seductive (I'd guess Kubrick's background, a Bronx Jew, is relevant here). The interiors they occupy seem devoid of any artifacts that might be read as anything other than the products of an extremely Eurocentric worldview. And second, there is the absence of both black people and/or any apparent sign of blackness. This absence is misleading. Ultimately, I came to recognize the film's highly repressed and anxiety-ridden preoccupation with blackness. And given the times, how could it have been otherwise?

2001's obsession with/suppression of blackness is atypical of the genre only with respect to the elegance of its construction. And who could possibly fully disentangle the clusterfuck of racism (and sexism) that's typical of classic science fiction and its retarded offspring, science fiction films? 2001 is about fear of genetic annihilation, fear of blackness. (Black rage, Black Power, Black Panthers, black planet, black dick, etc.) White phallic objects (starships) move through all-encompassing blackness (space) from one white point (stars) to another. This fear of space, this horror vacui, is a fear of contamination, a contamination of white being by black being which, by the very nature of the self-imposed fragile ontological construction of white being, equals the annihilation of white being.

2001 begins in Africa. The black monolith functions as a catalytic artifact in that it provokes man's evolutionary leap forward from its earlier, primitive (apelike) state. (The initial design of the monolith was in the form of a black pyramid, a clear sign of black civilization.) There's the implication that the monolith generates man's increased capacity rather than simply stimulates some latent ability. This evolutionary leap sets in motion developments which culminate with man's discovery of a second black monolith on the moon's surface. *2001*'s astronauts travel through space in pursuit of (in fact at the directive of) a signal which issues forth from this advanced and clearly more evolved black sentient entity.

(Have you noticed that *2001*'s monolith, Darth Vader's uniform/flesh, and H. R. Giger's alien are all composed of the same black substance?)

2001's white/star child is engendered by a black sentient body, subliminally, and desperately, positing the possibility of pure white being issuing forth from all-encompassing dark matter. A manifestation of white fear of genetic annihilation by the (black) other. This anxiety is played out over and over in numerous science fiction films. For example, in *Alien* all the characters (excepting the white-blooded science officer), male and female alike, are sexually assaulted by the alien and impregnated with black beings. The alien is in fact a six-foot-eight Sudanese, "Bolaji" (never, to my knowledge, given a last name), wearing H. R. Giger's Esu-Elegba–derived jet-black monster suit with penis-tipped head. Yaphet Kotto (ur-Negro signifier if there ever were one) plays the only black member of the doomed crew. And during the initial confrontation, coming face-to-face with the alien, he recognizes it as the bad nigger it clearly is. His pragmatism suggests that he stands the best chance of surviving this encounter, but predictably, he meets his end attempting to prevent the alien from ravaging the helpless white woman. Coming to her rescue, he tells her to move away, but she's frozen (by the alien's magnificence), so, his pragmatism (one could say his sanity) having abandoned him, he moves to get between them. The alien swats him away with his big black tail, grabs him (bringing him face-to-face), and pokes a hole in his head with his chops (teeth). Casting him aside, the alien shifts its attention back to his victim of choice. She stands, breathing heavily, transfixed as the alien slides its tail between her legs. We cut away (but continue to hear her suspiciously ecstatic moans).

In *Star Wars*, Darth Vader/Dark Invader (black body/black voice, in fact the voice of Jack Johnson, James Earl Jones, clearly a blood despite subsequent revisions) is transformed by the Force's "Darkside" (black body engenders a white child, a skywalker no less). And the film's finale, a rush down the Death Star's corridors, to destroy the engendering black womb, Vader's crib, is a diminished and more overtly nihilistic replay of Bowman's Jupiter fall down the corridors of light, a rush to Death. Star. Child.

Why had I been so attracted to *2001*? Apollo generation, the first moon landing had just gone down a few years prior, and I was fairly obsessed with spaceships. I'd followed the progress of the film in magazines like *Popular Mechanics*. *2001* was the first novel I'd ever bought, though I confess not to having read it until after seeing the film. That got me in the theater.

The film's slow, glacial pageantry impressed the altarboy in me, exposing me to what I'd identify now as a minimalist sensibility, a sensibility to which, I believe, I was predisposed by the flatness and austerity of the Delta, by the landscape's beauty and trance dimensions. This exposure dovetailed with a number of other things.

There was my then nascent melancholy and the beginning recognition of a certain sort of categorical constraint, dictated by my blackness, and yet completely at odds with (1) the boundless possibility conveyed to those of my generation by television, and (2) the emancipatory fallout of the Black Power movement. My family's move from the moderately progressive Tupelo to the essentially segregated Clarksdale, situated at the Delta's epicenter, had a cathartic impact, as did a continual and enmeshing confrontation with the extreme deprivations of the region and its abject pleasures. An exposure to the transfixing, and for me unprecedented, blackness of its inhabitants, their arresting beauty and dense corporeal being, the inescapable duality of absence and presence, the inevitable embrace, as a nascent black man, of a certain temperamental cool (a flattened affect), simply put, the dark matter of black being. These all begged certain questions, at the time inarticulate and unformed, to which years later my introduction to Miles Davis provided an answer. Where do I/we enter into these discourses on beauty and being (the answer of course being wherever and however we choose to).

The film ends, I get up in a daze and walk out into the lobby. And even now, thirty years later, I remember exactly, in crystalline detail, what the lobby looked like, the angle the sun shafted through the space, the lint hovering overhead, the drag of the carpet. I looked over and saw the manager, white and older, quietly reading his paper in the otherwise empty lobby. And the thing is, at this point in my life I didn't have unchaperoned interactions with white people, young or old. He was sitting in the ticket booth with the door open so I walked over to him and said, "Excuse me, sir, I've just come out of the movie, could you tell me what it was about?" He looked down at me over his paper, paused a moment, and said, "Son, I've been looking at it all week and haven't got a clue." And that's the last thing I remember. I don't remember how I got home, what other conversations I might have had, nothing. But that brief interaction I've never forgotten. The film had completely leveled our differences, race, class, age. So that for that moment, in the presence of this monumental work, we were equal.

a black hagakure.

a dream of death and the continual dissipation of dense black being (power and consciousness) osiris dismembered (diafra) and a part can't come together (can't remember) though the parts no longer fit, and this not fitting, this growth after dismemberment, keeps us (men and women) harder coming strong (anti entropic beasts) falling together even as we fall apart

would limit the number of blacks that can gather, a boon for Christ, one a bitch two a threat three an insurrection, no getting together coming together no drums rising up so churches, funerals, simple gatherings and places become reunions become rememberance be luciferian (fire, light) be revolution.

to the central conundrum of black being (the double bind of our ontological existence) lie in the fact that common misery both defines and limits who we are. such that our efforts to eliminate those forces which constrain also functions to dissipate much of which gives us our specificity, our uniqueness, our flavor and that by destroying the binds that define we will cease to be, but this is the good death (cachoeira) and to be embraced.

GREG TATE is a longtime staff writer at the *Village Voice*. His books include the 1992 essay collection *Flyboy in the Buttermilk* as well as *Midnight Lightning: Race, Sex, Technology and Jimi Hendrix*. He is also musical director for the fifteen-member-conducted–improvisation ensemble Burnt Sugar.

CARL HANCOCK RUX is a writer, performing artist, and x-foster child whose published and recorded work includes a collection of poetry and prose, *Pagan Operetta* (Fly by Night Press), the novel *Asphalt* (Atria), the albums *Rux Revue* (Sony) and *Apothecaryipx* (Giant Step), and the play *Talk* (TCG Press), which ran at the Public Theater—to great acclaim—in the spring of 2002.

EISA DAVIS is a writer-performer whose recent work includes the plays *Umkovu* and *Paper Armor*. She stars in the upcoming films *Brass Tacks* and *Robot Stories*, and music from her album *Tinctures* has been featured on the Showtime series *Soul Food*. Eisa was born and raised in Berkeley, California.

ROBIN D. G. KELLEY After discovering Marx in his teens, Robin D. G. Kelley spent his 20s drifting between Communist movements until he landed a job as history professor. Currently Professor of History and Africana Studies at New York University, his most recent books are *Yo Mama's Disfunktional!: Fighting the Culture Wars in Urban America* (Beacon, 1997) and *Freedom Dreams: The Black RadicalImagination* (Beacon, 2002).

BETH COLEMAN is a guest lecturer on new media and technology theory at the University of California, Santa Cruz, and a Ph.D. candidate in comparative literature at New York University. When night descends, she becomes DJ M. Singe, cofounder of SoundLab Cultural Alchemy, a freewheeling electronica media artists crew devoted to experiments in the "electrotectural now."

MELVIN GIBBS is a renowned musician and producer and widely considered the best electric bass player in the world. His résumé of collaborations includes work with Rollins Band, dead prez, Arto Lindsay, Sonny Sharrock, Anti-Pop Consortium, Pete Cosey, and DJ Logic. His band Liberation Theology performs regularly in New York and Europe, and he is a member of the co-op band Harriet Tubman.

JONATHAN LETHEM is the author of *Motherless Brooklyn* and four other novels. His stories and essays have appeared in *The New Yorker*, the *Paris Review*, the *Village Voice, Crank, Gas, Brick, Exquisite Corpse*, and a variety of other periodicals and anthologies. He lives in New York City.

MICHAEL C. LADD is an associate professor of English at Long Island University and a much-revered poet and hip-hop producer whose recent work includes the multi-album-length operetta *Majeststicons vs the Infesticons*.

VERNON REID is a musician, producer, and writer who has been published in the *Village Voice, Vibe*, and *Bomb*. His thrice-Grammy-awarded band, Living Colour, reunited last year to reconquer the world. His recent work includes a collaborative project with DJ Logic entitled *The Yohimbe Brothers* and Living Colour's fourth record, scheduled for release this spring.

HILTON ALS is on staff at *The New Yorker* and the author of *The Women* (Farrar, Straus & Giroux, 1997).

MICHAELA ANGELA DAVIS is an urban-culture fashion specialist. She has been a fashion editor at *Vibe* and *Essence*, and is currently fashion director at *Honey* magazine. She has written about the culture of black style for *Scene* and *Code* magazine. Davis has been a creative director on several magazine and book projects and holds a most illustrious and eclectic artist client list. Among her most adored are Diana Ross, Jeffrey Wright, Abbey Lincoln, Prince, Me'shell N'Degeocello, and Herbie Hancock. Her work as a stylist has been seen in *Vogue, Vanity Fair*, and *Mirabella* in addition to countless CD covers and music videos. She is the mother of Elenni Davis-Knight, the inspiration for *Beloved Baby* (Pocket Books), a scrapbook and journal for modern "colored" parents.

CASSANDRA LANE, a journalist for nine years, is an M.F.A. candidate in creative writing at Antioch University, Los Angeles.

TONY GREEN is a widely published music writer who lives in Largo, Florida, with his wife, Dena. He is the leader of the Tampa Bay–based jazz-funk band Jes' Grew, and hosts the weekly *Grooves* show on WMNF 88.5 Tampa.

MANTHIA DIAWARA is an author and filmmaker. He teaches at New York University. His most recent book is *In Search of Africa* (Harvard University Press). His most recent film is *Bamako; Sigi-Kanl.*

LATASHA N. DIGGS, writer and vocalist, is a shape-shifter trainee from the snake people who long ago slithered up from the Pee Dee River to Harlem. She is a 2002 Artist-in-Residence at Harvest Works Digital Media Arts Center. She aspires to one day marry a man named Rolando Juan Carlos Suzuki and live happily ever after causing a ruckus in Barcelona.

MERI NANA-AMA DANQUAH is the author of *Willow Weep for Me: A Black Woman's Journey Through Depression* (Norton) and the editor of *Becoming American: Personal Essays by First Generation Immigrant Women* (Hyperion). Danquah earned an M.F.A. in creative writing and literature from Bennington College.

RENÉE GREEN is an artist, filmmaker, writer, and professor in the Department of Fine Arts at the University of California, Santa Barbara. Her work is presented at Documenta 11, an international art show, and her recent books include *Shadows and Signals/Sombras y Senales* and *Between and Including.*

ARTHUR JAFA is an artist who lives and works in New York. anamibia@yahoo.com

ACKNOWLEDGMENTS

At this time we would like to thank the animating spirit of the universe, members of the academy, and our ancestors, elders, and especially Mom Tate. Also deserving of kudos: our editors MC Becky Cole and OG Gerry Howard for dropping this Big Idea in our lap, our agent at Sterling Lord Literistic, Jim Rutman, and our ever-indispensable daughter/research assistant Chinara Tate, who dug up the Elder Pliny.

—Greg Tate